RACE AND IMMIGRATION IN THE
NEW IRELAND

EDITED BY

Julieann Veronica Ulin, Heather Edwards, and Sean O'Brien

UNIVERSITY OF NOTRE DAME PRESS
NOTRE DAME, INDIANA

Manufactured in the United States of America

Library of Congress Cataloging-in-Publication Data

Race and immigration in the new Ireland /
edited by Julieann Veronica Ulin, Heather Edwards, and Sean O'Brien.
    pages   cm
  Includes bibliographical references and index.
  ISBN-13: 978-0-268-02777-3 (paper : alkaline paper)
  ISBN-10: 0-268-02777-3 (paper : alkaline paper)
    1. Ireland—Race relations.   2. Ireland—Emigration and immigration—
Social aspects.   3. Minorities—Ireland—Social conditions.
4. Immigrants—Ireland—Social conditions.   5. Racism—Ireland.
6. Social change—Ireland.   7. Ireland—Social conditions—1973–
I. Ulin, Julieann Veronica.   II. Edwards, Heather, 1976 December 22–
III. O'Brien, Sean T.
  DA927.R325   2013
  305.9'0691209417—dc23

∞ *The paper in this book meets the guidelines for permanence and durability of the Committee
on Production Guidelines for Book Longevity of the Council on Library Resources.*

CONTENTS

CHRONOLOGY

1922   The Irish Free State extends the right to birthright citizen-
        ship for all children born in the island of Ireland.

1937   Constitution of the Republic of Ireland "renders concrete
        the boundaries of the imagined Irish nation," declaring in Ar-
        ticle 2 that "it is the entitlement and birthright of every per-
        son born in the island of Ireland, which includes its islands
        and seas, to be part of the Irish Nation."

1973   The Republic of Ireland joins the European Economic
        Community.

1989   Highest level of net outward migration from the Republic
        on record (44,000)

1990   The 1990s see the height of EU Structural Funds receipts by
        Ireland, covering the two programming periods of 1989–93
        and 1994–99.

1991   Combat Poverty Association publishes a report stating that
        the rate of poverty in Ireland is one of the worst in Europe.

1992   Ireland's Office of the Refugee Applications Commissioner
        reports 39 applications for asylum.

1993   The European Commission against Racism and Intolerance
       (ECRI) is established by the first Summit of Heads of State
       and Government of the member states of the Council of
       Europe.
       91 asylum applications

1994   Ireland dubbed the "Celtic Tiger"
       Northern Ireland Council for Ethnic Minorities (NICEM)
       is established.
       362 asylum applications

1995   424 asylum applications

1996   Refugee Act 1996
       1,179 asylum applications

1997   SARI (Sport Against Racism Ireland) is formed as a direct re-
       sponse to the growth of racist attacks from a small but vocal
       group of people in Ireland.
       Race Relations Order (NI) outlaws discrimination on grounds
       of color, race, nationality, or ethnic or national origin in North-
       ern Ireland.
       3,883 asylum applications

1998   Good Friday Agreement amends Article 2 of Ireland's con-
       stitution to recognize "the birthright of all the people of
       Northern Ireland to identify themselves and be accepted as
       Irish or British, or both, as they may so choose."
       The National Consultative Committee on Racism and Inter-
       culturalism (NCCRI) is founded in the Republic of Ireland.
       4,626 asylum applications

1999   In the decade between 1989 and 1999, Ireland's GDP as per-
       cent of the EU average grows from 72 percent to 111 percent.
       7,724 asylum applications

2000   Direct provision commences for asylum seekers in Ireland.
       Start of new period of EU Structural Funds (2000–2006).
       Given Ireland's changed status from being one of the poorest

countries of the original fifteen members in 1994 to being one of the wealthier member states in 2000, Structural Funds are significantly reduced for this period.

A University of Ulster report shows that many ethnic minority groups experience racism in the workplace and schools as a way of life. The study, based on more than one hundred interviews with Chinese, African, Indian, and Traveller communities, finds that two-thirds of schoolchildren in the province from a minority ethnic background have been taunted by other pupils about their race, and 14 percent have been assaulted.

Ireland's Illegal Immigrants (Trafficking) Act levels fines or imprisonment upon a person who organizes or knowingly facilitates the entry into the state of a person whom he or she knows to be or has reasonable cause to believe is an illegal immigrant or a person who intends to seek asylum.

10,938 asylum applications. There is widespread homelessness among asylum seekers.

2001   A Reception and Integration Agency (RIA) is set up within Ireland's Department of Justice, Equality and Law Reform to coordinate services for refugees and asylum seekers and to implement integration policy for refugees. Its priorities are the protection of rights, the creation of opportunities to participate in economic, social, and cultural aspects of Irish society, and the development of a tolerant and inclusive society.

NCCRI begins logging reports of racist incidents in May: forty-one incidents are reported for the initial six-month period on record.

53.9 percent of Irish voters reject the Treaty of Nice in a referendum on June 7. The treaty would put in place institutional and other reforms to facilitate expansion of the European Union by up to twenty-seven members. In a joint statement on June 8, the Swedish prime minister, Göran Persson, representing the Swedish EU presidency, and Romano Prodi, the Commission's president, state that the European Union will

"pursue enlargement negotiations with undiminished vigour and determination" and that the "objective of an enlarged Europe must be realized."
10,325 asylum applications

2002   A second referendum on the Treaty of Nice is held October 18 and passes with 62.89 percent of the vote in favor.
For the first time, Census of the Population includes a question on nationality. 5.8 percent of the population usually resident in Ireland is non-Irish nationals.
11,634 asylum applications marks the high point of applications.

2003   January Supreme Court ruling (*Lobe v. Minister for Justice, Equality and Law Reform*) finds that non-EU parents to Irish children do not automatically gain residency rights.
In July 2003 the Irish government announces that immigrants can no longer seek residency based on their child's Irish citizenship. Processing of 11,000 residency claims is suspended. Deportation orders are served to families who will be obliged to take their Irish-citizen child with them when they leave.
Immigration Act Amendments to the 1996 Refugee Act introduced in the 2003 Immigration Act make provision for the minister to designate a list of "safe" countries of origin in relation to which asylum applicants must rebut the presumption that they are not refugees. The list of countries will be kept under review but from September 2003 include Bulgaria, Cyprus, Czech Republic, Estonia, Hungary, Latvia, Lithuania, Malta, Poland, Romania, Slovakia, and Slovenia.
7,900 asylum applications

2004   Treaty of Accession brings the Czech Republic, Estonia, Cyprus, Latvia, Lithuania, Hungary, Malta, Poland, Slovenia, and Slovakia into the European Union.
In *Chen v. Secretary of State for the Home Department,* the European Court of Justice rules that, as a citizen of the European Union, Catherine Chen had a right under Article 18 of the

EC Treaty to reside anywhere in the EU, and that denying residency to her parent(s) at a time when she is unable to look after herself would conflict with this basic right.

Twenty-Seventh Amendment of the Constitution Act is approved by referendum with 79.17 percent of vote: "Notwithstanding any other provision of this Constitution, a person born in the island of Ireland, which includes its islands and seas, who does not have, at the time of the birth of that person, at least one parent who is an Irish citizen or entitled to be an Irish citizen, is not entitled to Irish citizenship or nationality, unless provided for by law."

In November, some seventy racist incidents are reported to NCCRI between May and October, the highest number on record.

Planning for Diversity: National Action Plan Against Racism defines integration as the "range of targeted strategies for the inclusion of groups such as Travellers, refugees, and migrants as part of the overall aim of developing a more inclusive and intercultural society."

The NGO Alliance Shadow Report finds that government policies "have led to increased racism." The report criticizes the government's lack of leadership and action in challenging racism in Ireland and claims its failure to gather adequate data on racist incidents has led to a significant underestimate of their impact on victims and society in general. The report specifically argues that the government's policy of segregating asylum seekers and refusing them the right to work has isolated them from the rest of society and helped to foster resentment against them as "spongers."

Ireland has the second-highest export/GDP ratio among the twenty-five EU member states.

Asylum applications drop below 5,000 (to 4,766).

2005   With guidance from NCCRI, a National Action Plan Against Racism (NPAR) for Ireland is launched with a focus on "reasonable and common sense measures to accommodate

cultural diversity," including the emergence of an "intercultural workplace."
Irish Born Child Administrative Scheme for Immigrant Residency allows immigrant parents to apply for a renewable form
of residency based upon the parentage of an Irish-born child.
4,323 asylum applications

2006   Census finds a population of 4,239,848, with 14.68 percent
        foreign-born from 188 different countries; 10.1 percent of the
        population usually resident in Ireland are non-Irish nation-
        als. In Dublin, over 15 percent of the residents are non-Irish
        nationals.
        For the period 2002–2006, net inward migration peaks
        at 191,000, or 48,000 per year. Population growth peaks at
        81,0000 per year.
        4,309 asylum applications

2007   Bulgaria and Romania join the European Union.
        Nigerian-born asylum-seeker Rotimi Adebari is elected mayor
        of Portlaoise.
        Ireland's Office of the Minister for Integration is founded.
        3,985 asylum applications

2008   In June, Irish voters reject the Lisbon Treaty 53.4 percent
        to 46.6 percent. Ireland becomes the first member state to
        vote twice against an EU proposal. Research identifies loss
        of a commissioner, neutrality, workers' rights, abortion, and
        corporation tax as subjects of importance, particularly to
        "no" voters.
        Ireland becomes the first euro-zone country to enter the
        recession.
        In the midst of the world financial crisis, Ireland's govern-
        ment issues an unlimited guarantee to six main banks (Allied
        Irish Bank, Bank of Ireland, Anglo Irish Bank, Irish Life &
        Permanent, Irish Nationwide Building Society, and the Edu-
        cational Building Society). Ireland's population of 4.5 mil-
        lion is shouldered with an enormous debt of €400 billion

($515 billion), proportionately the highest per capita commitment in the world.

NCCRI is ended.

NICEM successfully establishes the All Party Assembly Group on Ethnic Minority Communities.

NPAR concludes.

3,866 asylum applications

2009   In January, Ireland's government debts become the riskiest in the euro zone.

In April, the Economic and Social Research Institute (ESRI) estimates that unemployment in Ireland will rise to almost 17 percent over the next year. ESRI forecasts that Ireland will experience the sharpest fall in economic growth of any industrialized country since the Great Depression.

In April, Ireland's Central Statistics Office (CSO) reports net outward migration of 7,800.

In June, attacks result in 115 Roma seeking refuge in a city-center Belfast church that is subsequently vandalized. In the weeks following, 100 Roma return to Romania.

In October, sixteen months after the initial "no" vote, Ireland ratifies Lisbon Treaty with 67.13 percent of voters saying yes.

10 percent of Irish primary-school students (approximately 44,000 children) are non-Irish nationals.

NICEM successfully lobbies for a review of Race Relations legislation to bring Northern Ireland up to the same level of protection as given to the rest of the United Kingdom.

2,689 asylum applications

2010   In April, CSO reports net outward migration of 34,500, the highest level on record since 1989. Emigration among Irish nationals increases significantly from 18,400 in April 2009 to 27,700 in April 2010.

Taoiseach Brian Cowen acknowledges that Ireland formally requested support from the International Monetary Fund on November 21.

The European Union, International Monetary Fund, and the Irish government agree to a bailout package of €85 billion. Ireland is the most indebted country in the world. Under the bailout terms, Ireland must cut over €12 billion from the budget each year. Social welfare, education, and health care face astronomical cuts.

In December, Northern Ireland's first Migrant Rights Centre opens in Belfast. At the launch, NICEM executive director Patrick Yu explains that hate crimes against people from ethnic minority communities are increasing because of the impact of the recession. "The economic downturn is causing some to go back home, but there are still 35,000 migrants living in Northern Ireland. However, levels of unemployment among the migrant community in Northern Ireland are three times higher than in the local community."

Immigration, Residence and Protection Bill 2010

Number of asylum seekers drops below 2,000 for the first time since 1996 (to 1,939).

2011   In January, ESRI predicts that as many as 100,000 people will abandon Ireland by April 2012.

Preliminary Census 2011 data shows an increase of 341,421 from Census 2006, representing an increase of 8.1 percent over the past five years, or an annual average of 1.6 percent. The preliminary data suggests that unlike the 2002–2006 period, which showed a clear pattern of net inward migration, the period 2006–2011 shows a strong net inward migration for the first half of the intercensal period, followed by a return to a net outward migration.

The High Court rules that the provision of the Immigration Act forcing non-Irish nationals to produce identification on demand to a garda is unconstitutional.

In March, NICEM reports racial incidents and racial hate crimes have increased on average by 10 to 15 percent over the last ten years. Most migrant workers are not protected under the existing employment law, particularly agency workers or people working for employers who will not renew their work permit despite good performance. Eastern Europe migrants are three times more likely to be unemployed compared with the local average, but only 5 percent are eligible to claim benefits. Ethnic minorities have less legal protection compared to the rest of the United Kingdom.

The Single Equality Bill for Northern Ireland is stalled.

Fine Gael/Labour Coalition plans to press ahead with a proposal drawn up by the previous government to reduce the number of language-support teachers by five hundred on a phased basis by 2014.

As of December 2011 the RIA has thirty-nine accommodation centers spread across eighteen counties in Ireland with a concentrated capacity of 5,980. These include thirty-five accommodation centers, two self-catering centers, one reception center, and one center to assist destitute nationals from EU nations and EU accession states. Under the system of direct provision, these asylum seekers receive room and board and an allowance of €19.10 per week per adult and €9.60 per child but are not allowed to seek employment.

The Immigrant Council of Ireland reports racism in Ireland is on the increase in part because of the recession.

1,290 asylum applications

INTRODUCTION

Ireland's New Strangers

JULIEANN VERONICA ULIN

Ireland has had a long and complex relationship with the stranger. The trope of the stranger in the house has functioned as shorthand for the colonial presence in Ireland, regularly surfacing in literary and political discourse to invoke hostility toward and to demand the expulsion of an outsider inside. Writing in response to the Penal Laws, one Irish author states, "Our inheritance is turned to aliens and our houses to strangers."[1] In poems such as "Óm sceol ar ardmhágh Fáil" (At the news from Fál's high plain), Geoffrey Keating mourns Ireland as contaminated by "a hoard" that should have "no place" there. Host to "hostile trash" and "the litter of every alien sow," Ireland must expel the stranger "without delay."[2] Alternately, the stranger has long been viewed as the recipient of Ireland's legendary hospitality. In his preface to *Foras Feasa ar Éirinn* (circa 1634), Keating himself rejects as "a notorious falsehood" Cambrensis's twelfth-century identification of the Irish as "an inhospitable people."[3] Keating instead quotes Richard Stanihurst's claim in *De Rebus in Hibernia Gestus* (1584) that "the Irish are the most hospitable men, nor can you oblige them more than by visiting them frequently at their own houses of your own accord and without invitation."[4] The history of Ireland's relationship with the stranger is marked by the tension between these opposing frameworks.

In perhaps the most famous modern representation of the former attitude, the title character in William Butler Yeats and Lady Augusta Gregory's *Cathleen ni Houlihan* (1902) attributes her grief to "Too many strangers in the house."[5] Nearly a century later, in a Christmas address to Dáil Éireann on December 16, 1999, President Mary McAleese epitomized the latter attitude as Ireland faced the arrival of a new set of strangers: "We are the first generation to be seriously tested on the bona fides of our legendary hospitality, our 'Céad Míle Fáilte.'"[6] In invoking Ireland's "legendary hospitality" to the stranger, McAleese turned to a vision of Ireland as open and welcoming to the stranger as its identity shifted from a emigrant's point of departure to a destination for immigrants, asylum seekers, and Ireland's own returnees. Newspaper columns such as "Hospitality to the Stranger Should Be a Virtue," "Archbishop Wants Immigration to 'Welcome the Stranger,'" and "Our World Without Strangers" made similar appeals. Yet Kate Holmquist titled her 2006 *Irish Times* feature on migrant experiences in Dublin "Céad Míle Fáilte: The Greatest Irish Myth" in order to identify the conflict between the idealized notion of Irish hospitality to the stranger and the speed of its transformation after over a decade of net immigration.[7]

In response to this historic shift, Gerry Stembridge's satirical television drama *Black Day at Blackrock* (2001) reinterpreted Cathleen ni Houlihan's anticolonial "hope of putting the strangers out of my house" as a call to expel a very different population from the one Cathleen ni Houlihan intended to banish.[8] In the film, the European Union decides to place thirty African asylum seekers in a Blackrock hostel, and the local citizens are divided over what the impending arrival of the outsiders means for their community. In one scene, local schoolteacher Brian confronts shopkeeper Eugene over his claim that "if Kate would only close the doors of this hostel of hers [to the asylum seekers], then we could avoid a lot of conflict in this town."[9] Brian argues against closing the doors and instead for recognition of historical parallels between the experience of the Irish emigrant and the asylum seekers. In the heat of their exchange, the camera pans across the school's stage, where the painted backdrop resembles the iconic setting of *Cathleen ni Houlihan*. An old woman stands looking out of the half door of a cottage in rural Ireland as Cathleen ni Houlihan appears to preside over the argument between Eugene's "simple solution" of expelling the strangers and Brian's search for threads of imaginative connection. The shot positions Brian and Eugene in the foreground of the stage set, signifying the continued power of the designation of Ireland as a house invaded by strangers.

In a later scene in the film, a town-hall meeting is held in the same schoolroom, though now a black curtain conceals the stage's backdrop. Throughout the meeting, members of the community express their deep anxieties that these strangers will destroy the local economy, threaten Christianity, endanger the English language, "assault us in our beds," slaughter the dogs and sheep "for some weird ritual," and expose the town to AIDS and a "plague of foreign diseases." Curtain or not, *Black Day at Blackrock* suggests, Cathleen ni Houlihan's vision of Ireland as a house purged of the stranger casts a long shadow.

In the foreword to his collection of short fiction, *The Deportees and Other Stories* (2008), Irish author Roddy Doyle signals Ireland's rapid transformation, declaring that sometime in the 1990s, "I went to bed in one country and woke up in a different one."[10] Since 1991, each intercensal period in Ireland showed net inward migration, which peaked at 48,000 per annum during 2002–2006,[11] facilitated by a system of "Social Partnership"[12] and the economic boom years of the Celtic Tiger. Ireland offered "Irish hospitality" as well as "a clean slate" and "a new start" to migrants whose "welcome has run out elsewhere."[13] The 2002 Census of Population in Ireland was the first to include a question on nationality, and results indicated that that 224,000 of the total population usually resident in Ireland were non-Irish nationals (5.8 percent). Following the accession of ten new member states to the European Union in May 2004, the Irish government elected not to impose any restrictions on labor mobility, thus opening a labor market of two million to one of seventy-two million.[14] Ireland became a destination for immigrants, those seeking asylum

and a number of its own returnees, drawn back to Ireland by the prosperity. As the 2006 Census of Population reported, a decade after reporting net immigration in 1996, 10.1 percent of those participating
in the census were non-Irish nationals, and 14.68 percent of those participating were born outside of Ireland (Republic).[15]

In Northern Ireland, net emigration in the troubled decades of the
1970s and '80s was followed by a period of balanced migration in the
1990s. In the decade to 2004, Northern Ireland Statistics and Research
Agency (NISRA) reported that the annual average population increase
was around 7,000 persons, primarily as a result of natural causes. In
the period following 2004, a shift occurred in which increase is due to
net immigration more than to natural causes. NISRA reports that the
2005–06, 2006–07, and 2007–08 increases in population were significantly larger at 17,000 people (1.0 percent), 17,500 people (1.0 percent), and 15,900 people (0.9 percent) respectively. In 2001, the agency
reported that 3 percent of births were to mothers born outside the
United Kingdom and Ireland (700 out of 22,000); by 2009, just under
1 in 10 births in Northern Ireland were to mothers born outside the
United Kingdom and Ireland (2,300 out of 24,900).[16]

The arrival of so many newcomers to Ireland in the years after
1996 made the country almost unrecognizable to those who returned
in response to its economic prosperity. As Ireland became home to
increasing numbers of European Union migrants, refugees, and asylum seekers, many of its former emigrants returned as well, seeking
to escape the rising costs of health care and education abroad. Piaras
Mac Éinrí of the Department of Geography in University College
Cork estimates that about half of the 500,000 people who emigrated in
the 1980s and early 1990s returned to Ireland during the boom years.[17]
As the *Irish Times* reported in 1999, these returnees found themselves
"strangers in their own land": "Returning emigrants, lured back by
the booming economy here, are finding that, increasingly, they do not
feel at home in their own homeland. Like Oisín returning from the
delights of Tír na nÓg only to discover that 300 years have passed in
his absence, many returned emigrants have found that the country of
their birth has become unrecognisable, and that the people have become alien in their attitudes."[18]

Nina Bernstein's 2004 *New York Times* article "Back Home in Ireland, Greener Pastures; Immigrants Reverse Their Trek as American Dreams Fade" echoes the same sentiment: "Counselors in immigrant advice bureaus on both sides of the Atlantic say that many returnees will have a rude awakening in Ireland — especially those who were stuck in the underground economy in the United States, unable to travel abroad for fear of not getting back in. The Irish government now puts out brochures warning that they will find not the Ireland of memory, but rather a fast-paced multiracial society where their dollars are weak against the euro and affordable housing scarce."[19] Anthony Finn, a counselor with the Emigrant Advice Centre in Dublin, concurred that the returnees might be shocked at this New Ireland. "They are not returning," he said of the Irish from America. "They're remigrating to a different country." Even The Safe-Home Programme Ireland is cautious. Its mission statement reads: "In recognition of the unique role played by our emigrants, economic refugees, who left these shores, many unwillingly, and whose remittances sustained the Irish economy and were our original 'Celtic Tiger,' the Safe-Home Programme seeks, with support of the booming Irish economy, to repay the just debt owed to those who, in their twilight years want to come home." Yet the group's website, titled "Coming Home? Are You Sure?," warns: "The most important message is that the Ireland of today is a very different country to the one you left."[20]

With these transformations and their attendant challenges and opportunities in mind, the University of Notre Dame hosted an interdisciplinary conference on October 14–17, 2007, addressing the theme "Race and Immigration in the New Ireland." The conference brought together dozens of public policy makers, politicians, religious leaders, intellectuals, and activists. It featured panels like "The Demographics of the New Ireland," "Work and Labor," "Legality and Rights," "Race," "The Experience of Women," "The Linguistic Challenge of Multi-Cultural Ireland," "Social Integration: Fact and Fiction," and "North and South," as well as panels offering comparative international frameworks for immigration policies. The dynamic exchanges over the course of the conference came from the range of perspectives at hand. In not limiting its focus to a single aspect of

immigration's impact on Irish society, the conference provided a plat-
form for dialogue among a broad cross-section of politicians, academics, cultural historians, and activists.

Toward the end of his address at the conference, General Secretary of the Irish Congress of Trade Unions David Begg noted that
there were "darkening economic clouds on the horizon."[21] Begg's
talk focused on the widespread discrimination in wages and conditions of employment and the controversy surrounding the 2005 Irish
Ferries case, interpreting the *Toward 2016 Partnership Agreement,* which
emerged in its wake, as "the single biggest leap forward in social policy
initiated in Ireland."[22] Yet economic growth, he cautioned, was projected to decline to 4.4 percent in 2007 and 2.9 percent in 2008 and
unemployment forecast to rise from 4.4 percent to 5.6 percent in
2008.[23] Begg predicted that this economic instability would greatly
affect Irish attitudes toward the very issues of immigration at the center of the conference. Ireland must realize, he stated, that migration
would not be a transient phenomenon but one that requires substantial planning and ongoing investment in integration. He concluded
his talk with the warning, "This is uncharted territory for Ireland.
Managing immigration up to now has been in a positive economic
context. Even so there have been difficulties. . . . One looks towards
these changing circumstances with some trepidation." Within a year
of the conference, Ireland's economy had collapsed.

The millennial promise of the Celtic Tiger enticed many with its
powerful narcotic of amnesia, a new alternative for a nation better
known for obsessively remembering. Critics asked if the Celtic Tiger
meant "the end of Irish history," as economic prosperity appeared to
offer a chance to wipe the slate clean on everything from language debates, a legacy of economic poverty, traditional dance, and the Rose of
Tralee to the Dublin Docklands.[24] The opportunity to shed a "third
world"[25] identity for another, this one a new, cosmopolitan member of
the global economic elite, made the prospect of "wiping out the past
and creating a cultural blank slate"[26] a seductive one.

Nearly four years after the collapse of the Celtic Tiger, with its
abandoned homes dotting the landscape, the current trends toward
mass unemployment (an eighteen-year high of 14.9 percent in the

Republic of Ireland in June 2012, 7.1 percent in Northern Ireland in June 2012), emigration, protested evictions, and the rise of sectarian violence, the New Ireland is beginning to look familiar. Preliminary Census 2011 reports indicate that the total number of vacant dwellings has risen to 294,202.[27] Data suggest that the pattern over the 2006–2011 period shows a shift from strong net inward migration in the first half of the period to net outward migration in the second half of the period.[28] As of December 2011, Central Statistics Office figures estimate that 252,100 people emigrated from Ireland over the previous four years; 99,700 of them were Irish citizens.[29] In March 2012, the *Guardian* reported that up to 75,000 Irish citizens are predicted to emigrate in 2012—higher than the levels of the late 1980s.[30] The *Irish Times* currently features a blog, *Generation Emigration,* whose banner is designed to look like a boarding gate display at an airport terminal.

As several of the chapters in this volume attest, the recession affected policies and financial resources for integration, pushing talk of an intercultural Ireland to the background as funding evaporated and dialogue shifted to bank guarantees, bailouts, and austerity measures. The more recent columns in *Metro Éireann* have confirmed Begg's warnings about the relationship between downward economic shifts and dialogue about race and immigration in Ireland. As Ronit Lentin notes in her column "Who Speaks for Whom?," "Since the onset of the recession and the [2008] demise of the NCCRI [National Consultative Committee on Racism and Interculturalism], not to mention the budget cuts affecting the Equality Authority (EA) and the Irish Commission on Human Rights, no one has been speaking much about racism. Most Irish people feel they have other priorities as they try to make ends meet, get a bank loan, or secure their pensions."[31] In March 2011, Catherine Lynch, author of the European Network Against Racism report on Ireland, stated that "findings from the report on Ireland indicate that racism has fallen off the political agenda. This is of significant concern, given the risks at the moment including the recession and the rise of extremism in EU member states. . . . If we continue to ignore the problem, racism will be a fallout of the current recession."[32]

Mary Canning, chair of the Irish committee of the European Cultural Foundation, warned that the recession could escalate tensions between immigrants and Irish citizens: "And there is a danger that if the unemployment situation in Ireland worsens, that there would be some element of blame, that people would see new Irish occupying jobs. This could be quite dangerous, and could lead to social unrest and tensions."[33] Dr. Fidèle Mutwarasibo, integration manager with the Immigrant Council of Ireland and an Irish citizen originally from Rwanda, expressed deep concern that many measures included in the National Action Plan Against Racism from 2005 to 2008 had never been implemented. "Worryingly," he noted, "there is also a growing perception—both politically and publicly—that migrant issues are no longer relevant because the rate of immigration to Ireland is falling."[34]

Though the period of mass inward migration has ended, and financial resources for and public attention to integration have dwindled, Ireland will continue to feel the long-term impact of the immigrants, asylum seekers, and returnees who have chosen to make Ireland their home. *Addressing the Current and Future Reality of Ireland's Multi-Cultural Status* (2010), a report emerging from a three-year research project of the Trinity Immigration Initiative, draws on long-term surveys of immigrants, schools, and migrant network projects and finds that despite the economic and social challenges faced by migrants and the need for reform in terms of migrant services, many continue to find the Irish lifestyle and workplaces attractive: "Public expectations, then and now, that migrants return to their country of origin in times of economic recession have largely proven incorrect and diversity is set to remain an important factor in the demography of the country."[35] While recent numbers indicate declining international migration to Northern Ireland, the 2009 School Census report points to the long-term impact in Northern Ireland of students who speak English as a second language. The data from 2009 (the last year for which information from the NISRA is available at the time of this writing) show the steady increase in students with English as an additional language: 4,800 primary students and 2,400 postprimary students reported a language other than English as a "first" language.[36] As Pablo Coppari of the Migrant Rights Centre Ireland states in the interview in this volume (see chapter 2), to view migration as an issue that will disappear with economic prosperity is to ignore the presence in Ireland of a second generation of migrants, as well as immigrants who have completed all of their schooling in Ireland and have no citizenship other than Irish. Coppari argues that there is a grave danger in allowing preoccupation with the economy to facilitate the neglect of human rights and integration issues within Ireland. The attacks on Roma in Belfast in 2009 offered one illustration of how migrants may be scapegoats in a recession.

Recent reports have cited serious and continuing challenges faced by Ireland with respect to integration. Despite "boom time projects," the 2011 *Migration Policy Index* rated Ireland sixteenth out of thirty-one countries in terms of educational success and integration of migrant students, behind many of its EU counterparts.[37] The report praised the political participation of immigrants but was highly critical of family reunion policies for migrants, ranking Ireland last among the thirty-one countries included in this category and stating, "Ireland's family reunion and long-term residence procedures set the least favourable conditions for integration in Europe and North America." The report concluded with its assessment of the negative impact of the economic crisis on integration efforts: "Public bodies and initiatives that further the integration of migrants are severely affected by the crisis through closures and funding cuts." The report specifically cited the reduction in language training and the December 2008 closure of the National Consultative Committee on Racism and Interculturalism (NCCRI), a state body set up to tackle racism.[38] At a time when attention to issues surrounding diversity and integration in Ireland has declined, it must be remembered that the Ireland that moves toward economic recovery will be a diverse and multiethnic Ireland.

Race and Immigration in the New Ireland reflects the reevaluations that followed the original conference in light of the economic collapse and its impact on the discourse surrounding integration in Ireland. Collectively, the essays in *Race and Immigration in the New Ireland* take as their starting point the idea that the New Ireland was never the clean slate that some dreamed but rather refracted many long-standing debates in Ireland. In the conclusion to his chapter in this volume, Robbie McVeigh calls for a broader conceptualization of Irish studies, one that captures the structural complexity of Irishness through an acknowledgment of the dynamic relationship between the two parts of Ireland and the Irish diaspora. Following from this model, the authors address the impact of immigration on sports, education systems, language debates, migrant women's issues, human rights policies, and culture in chapters that consider how Ireland's sectarian violence, its dependence on particularly gendered constructions of the nation, its relationship with the Irish language, its cultural history, its attitude toward its own indigenous population of Travellers, and its historical memory of being undocumented emigrants abroad inform discourse about the New Irish.

In former president Mary Robinson's keynote, which serves as the opening to this collection, she draws a connection between the Ireland that so many emigrants left and the New Ireland that has facilitated its reinvention in a European context rather than in primary relation to its colonial relationship with England. Robinson uses county, Republic of Ireland, and EU reports to discuss Ireland's relationship with its migrant community. She notes that the West of Ireland in her youth was "steeped in the inevitability of emigration" and illustrates the dramatic shift away from this emigrant Ireland with the story of Rotimi Adebari, a Nigerian who came to Ireland as an asylum seeker, settled in the Portlaoise area, and was elected a councillor in 2004 and mayor in June 2007. Robinson notes: "When he settled in Portlaoise with his wife and family, his two children were the only foreign pupils in the local school. Now there are more than thirty nationalities at the school. This, in essence, is the face of modern Ireland."

In the interview that follows, Pablo Coppari of the Migrant Rights Centre Ireland outlines the history of the MRCI and its transformation from an information service for migrants to a dynamic advocacy organization that empowers migrants to lobby the state and educate the community about the issues that face them in Ireland today. Coppari addresses the plight of the undocumented in Ireland, particularly those in domestic work subject to exploitation, the rise of human trafficking for forced labor, and the historical and current role of the Irish experience of emigration in shaping discourse and policy surrounding the undocumented.

In her chapter, "(M)other Ireland: Migrant Women Subverting the Racial State?," Ronit Lentin argues that the Irish state epitomizes a "state of exception" in which state racism combines with biopolitics to control women. Childbearing (Irish) women in the Republic of Ireland have always been central to articulations of nation, and the feminist struggle for gender equality that privileged reproductive rights only met with partial success. In June 2004, 80 percent of the Irish Republic's electorate voted in favor of rescinding birthright citizenship for all children born in the island of Ireland, in existence since the establishment of the Free State. In the Referendum debates the argument shifted from "Irish" women to "nonnational" women as subverting certainties of nation, state, and citizenship. The government's case focused on migrant women allegedly arriving in Ireland to have children who would automatically be citizens; the mothers would then gain residency rights for themselves and their partners. The Referendum came in the wake of the "Irish-born child" ruling, which, based on a 2003 Supreme Court case (later rescinded), no longer allowed migrant parents to remain in Ireland to give "care and company" to their citizen children. Against this backdrop, Lentin questions whether migrant women's contemporary networking activities in post-Referendum Ireland work to resist and extend the boundaries of intercultural Ireland's narrow articulations of race, gender, citizenship, and nation or to affirm these very boundaries. Her conclusion addresses the gender implications of Ireland's integration policies in the period following the onset of the recession.

Robbie McVeigh's "Racism in the Six Counties" challenges the framework for understanding racism in Irish studies. His chapter begins with the question of whether the end to sectarian violence has led to increased racial violence, but it ends by critiquing the superimposition of the sectarian framework to discuss racial tensions in the North.

He argues for the necessity of seeing racism in Ireland as triangular—relating not only to the Republic, but to the North as well as the diaspora. In his focus on media coverage and the "moral panic around racism," he traces a shift from "no problems" to "race hate capital" in the identification of the North. McVeigh argues that a focus on the individual as a locus for racism conceals institutional forms of racism, relegating it to what Mary White, the then minister of state with responsibility for equality, integration, and human rights, defined as "pockets of racism."[39] He maintains that Northern Ireland is not "at peace" and that the post–Good Friday Agreement state has caused minority ethnic people in the North to "live the peace process in reverse." McVeigh challenges popular (and narrow) discussions of Irish race relations and offers a new framework for international and interdisciplinary Irish studies.

In "The Linguistic Challenge of Multicultural Ireland: Managing Language Diversity in Irish Schools," Pádraig Ó Riagáin identifies the significance of language support for migrant children as a means to avoid economic and social disadvantages. He begins by noting the dearth of language-related statistics, including research and data on languages spoken at home by immigrant children. Nonetheless, Ó Riagáin discusses the demographic, social, and linguistic characteristics of migrant children and employs Irish policy statements, EU directives, and correspondence with the minister of education to marshal an argument for alternative models for the linguistic education of migrant students. Taking into account 2011 educational reports and dwindling financial support for educational language instruction, Ó Riagáin examines the challenges to linguistic achievement for Ireland's immigrants.

Verona Ní Dhrisceoil's chapter, "The Irish Language in Twenty-First-Century Ireland: Exploring Legislative and Policy Protections North and South," explores the relationship among law, the Irish language, and identity in the New Ireland. She outlines the debates surrounding the relevance of the Irish language in an increasingly multicultural and multilingual society. Her chapter takes an in-depth look at the impact that the New Ireland of immigration, globalization, and multiculturalism has had on the Irish language. The focus here is primarily legal, taking stock of language legislation and other measures put in place to protect Irish. While the Irish language question has long been a source of debate, Ní Dhrisceoil suggests that the debate has evolved; language discourses have changed focus from decolonization to culture and rights. Ní Dhrisceoil argues for a particular understanding of the place of the Irish language in the New Ireland and the justifications for protection of Irish over and above other minority languages in Ireland. She concludes her chapter with an analysis of the impact of the recession and the proposed policy changes by the 2011 elected Irish coalition government of Fine Gael/Labour on the future of the Irish language.

Mike Cronin's chapter, "Integration Through Sport: The Gaelic Athletic Association and the New Irish," offers a case study of Irish sport and the challenges posed by the New Irish. Cronin examines how the largest sporting organization in Ireland, the Gaelic Athletic Association, is managing its relationship with the New Irish through its strategic vision action plan. Cronin looks at other sporting bodies directed toward integration, such as Sport Against Racism Ireland. While acknowledging the desirability of positive policies in this area, Cronin's chapter questions whether these approaches are workable, given the unique culture and heritage of the association and the tradition of divided sports on the island of Ireland.

Steve Garner's essay serves to question the New Ireland of our title, arguing that the racialized discourse that has seemed more visible since the demographic tilt post-1996 long predates the Celtic Tiger. In "Reflections on Race in Contemporary Ireland," Garner offers a history of the creation of racial discourse in Ireland. Garner discusses the problems of theorizing racism in the Irish context and offers a succinct overview of the "racialization" of social relations from the twelfth century through the sixteenth century. The ideas of cultural difference used to distinguish Gaels from foreigners and strangers in the sixteenth and seventeenth centuries still circulate in different versions and are available for deployment against Travellers and migrants. Garner posits that the Irish learned about "race" at home and away, in the colonial setting and as immigrants to North America, where they internalized notions of domination and racial superiority. In the aftermath

of an economic boom, he argues, "race" in Ireland can only be properly understood by simultaneous reference to the national experiences
of emigration, empire and colonization, multiple layers of governance,
and the neoliberal ideology framing its immigration regime.

President Mary Robinson's two closing questions—"How [do]
we live up to our history, that history of a people that had to leave
our country and find a future elsewhere? How do we treat those who
are in the same position now?"—run throughout these chapters. Con-
cluding this volume, Luke Gibbons expands on these questions in
"'They've Seen It from the Other Side': Ireland, Immigration, and the
Ethics of Memory." Gibbons argues that the treatment of immigrants
should be informed by the cultural memory of the Irish experience
and that this engagement with Ireland's past not only will benefit the
host culture but promises dynamic cultural exchanges and energies
contributed by newcomers to a society in transition. Certainly Irish
culture has begun to register the place and voice of many new communities, as theatre productions reenvision the hardships experienced
by the Irish emigrants abroad as similar to those experienced by asylum seekers in Dublin today. Daniel O'Hara's short film *Yu Ming Is
Ainm Dom* (2003) and the Oscar-winning film *Once* (2006) are just a
few reflections of both the new cultural territory and the reimagin-
ing of some of Ireland's oldest and most identifiable themes—exile,
homelessness, estrangement. Yet as he concludes his chapter, Gib-
bon's concedes that the Irish memory of mass emigration and unemployment has not remained in the distant past, nor has artistic collaboration created any utopias.[40]

If the stranger within has been reconstituted in this New Ireland,
so too has the house. In April 2011, census forms were distributed
to 1.8 million households across the state. The forms were available
in twenty-one languages, reflecting the demographic and linguistic
diversity of the New Ireland. In the epilogue to *Ireland After History*,
David Lloyd suggests that the changes occurring in Ireland present a
chance not merely to extrapolate from the Irish legacy of emigration
and to seek lessons from beyond Ireland's borders but also to imagine new and more liberating conceptions of Irishness. Encapsulating
both the argument for imaginative identification, what Luke Gib-

bons calls "seeing it from the other side," and Ireland's opportunity to make choices distinct from those of other states, Lloyd writes:

> More than ever, this is a moment in which it is possible for Irish immigrants both to identify with and learn from the issues of the Third World and minority people and to direct some of the lessons learnt homewards. As the Irish elites rush towards integration into the new, racialized "Fortress Europe," and the incidence of racist violence against our own immigrant and minority communities climbs, we emigrants need to re-invoke our colonized past. We must be active, not only in America which continues to play out the gambits of colonialism internally and externally, but also in Ireland, bringing back home the knowledge that integration within the dominant order has never been the only or the most liberating possibility.[41]

In a lecture over a century ago, James Joyce described Irish civilization as "a vast fabric, in which the most diverse elements are mingled" and in which "it is useless to look for a thread that may have remained pure and virgin without having undergone the influence of a neighboring thread."[42] The ability to reconcile such "diverse elements" depends upon an Irish identity not delineated by language or blood: "Nationality (if it really is not a convenient fiction like so many others to which the scalpels of present-day scientists have given the *coup de grâce*) must find its reason for being rooted in something that surpasses and transcends and informs changing things like blood and the human word." In bringing together a range of critical voices and approaches, this book seeks to offer a broad and accessible introduction to the possibilities of this New Ireland to surpass, transcend, and inform limited definitions of Irish identity.

NOTES

1. Quoted in Breandán Ó Buachalla, *Aisling Ghéar: Na Stíobhartaigh Agus an Taos Léinn 1603–1788* (Baile Átha Cliath: An Clóchomhar Tta, 1996), 198.

2. Translated by Thomas Kinsella in *An Duanaire, 1600–1900: Poems of the Dispossessed* (Mountrath, Portlaoise, Ireland: Dolmen, 1981), 85–86.

3. Geoffrey Keating, *The General History of Ireland,* translated by Dermod O'Connor (London: Printed by J. Bettenham, for B. Creake, at the Bible, 1723), v.

4. Ibid., vi. Cf. Richard Stanyhurst, *De Rebus in Hibernia Gestus,* vol. 4 (Antwerp: Christopher Plantin, 1584), 33.

5. William Butler Yeats and Lady Augusta Gregory, *Cathleen ni Houlihan,* in *The Collected Works of W. B. Yeats,* vol. 2: *The Plays,* ed. David R. Clark and Rosalind E. Clark (1919; rept., New York: Scribner, 2001), 88.

6. Mary McAleese, "Ireland's Lifting Shadows," Address to the Houses of the Oireachtas, December 16, 1999.

7. Cf. Kate Holmquist, "Céad Míle Fáilte: The Greatest Irish Myth," *Irish Times,* November 3, 2006. See also Breda O'Brien, "Hospitality to the Stranger Should Be a Virtue," *Irish Times,* May 5, 2004; Alison Healy and Liam Horan, "Archbishop Wants Immigration Policy to 'Welcome the Stranger,'" *Irish Times,* March 3, 2005; Declan Kiberd, "Our World Without Strangers," *Irish Times,* December 12, 2006.

8. Yeats and Gregory, *Cathleen ni Houlihan,* 90.

9. *Black Day at Blackrock,* directed by Gerard Stembridge, Venus Productions, 2001.

10. Roddy Doyle, *The Deportees and Other Stories* (New York: Viking Penguin, 2008), xi.

11. *Census 2011 Preliminary Report,* 10, www.cso.ie/en/census/census2011 preliminaryreport.

12. Tim Hastings, Brian Sheehan, and Pádraig Yeates, *Saving the Future: How Social Partnership Shaped Ireland's Economic Success* (Dublin: Blackhall Publishing, 2007).

13. "Hostages to Fortune," *Irish Times,* August 8, 1998.

14. David Begg, General Secretary, Irish Congress of Trade Unions, "Managing the Labour Market: Implications of EU Expansion and Ireland's Experience," address to Race & Immigration in the New Ireland Conference, University of Notre Dame, October 14–17, 2007. The ten new member states admitted in 2004 were Cyprus, Czech Republic, Estonia, Hungary, Latvia, Lithuania, Malta, Poland, Slovakia, and Slovenia.

15. According to "Persons Usually Resident and Present in the State on Census Night Classified by Nationality and Age Group," 2006, 419,733 of the 4,172,013 declaring non-Irish as nationality (10.1 percent); see www.cso.ie/en/statistics/population/personsusuallyresidentandpresentinthestateoncensus nightclassifiedbynationalityandagegroup. According to "Persons Usually Resident and Present in the State on Census Night, Classified by Place of Birth

and Age Group," 2006, 612,629 of the 4,172,013 participants indicating a birth outside Ireland (Republic), or 14.68 percent; see www.cso.ie/en/statistics/population/personsusuallyresidentandpresentinthestateoncensusnightclassifiedbyplaceofbirthandagegroup.

16. Migration Statistics Northern Ireland, press release, 2009, www.nisra .gov.uk/demography/default.asp18.htm; Population and Migration Estimates Northern Ireland, NISRA, 2009, www.nisra.gov.uk/archive/demography/population/midyear/mye_report_2009.pdf.

17. "Difficulties on Horizon for Those Planning to Leave," *Irish Times,* December 29, 2011.

18. "Strangers in Their Own Land," *Irish Times,* August 8, 1999.

19. Nina Bernstein, "Back Home in Ireland, Greener Pastures: Immigrants Reverse Their Trek as American Dreams Fade," *New York Times,* November 10, 2004.

20. "The Safe-Home Programme Ireland: Coming Home? Are You Sure?" March 1, 2012, www.safehomeireland.com/ireland.htm.

21. Begg, "Managing the Labour Market."

22. *Towards 2016 Partnership Agreement,* www.taoiseach.gov.ie/attached _files/Pdf%20files/Towards2016PartnershipAgreement.pdf.

23. Alan Barrett, Ide Kearney, and Martin O'Brien, *Quarterly Economic Commentary* (Dublin: Economic and Social Research Institute, Autumn 2007), verso.

24. "Let Us Opt Out of Irish," *Irish Times,* September 9, 2005; "No Dancing," *Irish Times,* August 8, 1998; "A Thorny Year," *Irish Times,* August 8, 2004; "Goodbye to the Docks," *Irish Times,* December 12, 2006. In 1996, the economy of the Republic outperformed that of the United Kingdom for the first time (Colin Coulter and Steve Coleman, eds., *The End of Irish History? Critical Reflections on the Celtic Tiger* [Manchester, UK: Manchester University Press, 2003], 3).

25. Cf. Thérèse Caherty, *Is Ireland a Third World Country?,* report of a conference held in the Teachers' Club, Dublin, April 20, 1991, Organized by the Centre for Research and Documentation, Belfast (Belfast: Beyond the Pale Publications, 1992). See also Terry Eagleton, Fredric Jameson, and Edward W. Said, *Nationalism, Colonialism, and Literature* (Minneapolis; University of Minnesota Press, 1990), 60.

26. "Wiping Out the Past and Creating a Cultural Black Slate," *Irish Times,* May 5, 2003.

27. "120,000 Homes on Ghost Estates," RTÉ News Ireland, October 21, 2010; "Ireland's Unemployment Rises to 18-Year High of 14.9% Despite Tide of Emigration," *Washington Post,* July 4, 2012; "Northern Ireland Unemployment Rises Again," *BBC News,* June 20, 2012; Michael White, "An

Irish Election in a Time of Staggering Debt and Quiet Rage," *Guardian* (London), February 14, 2011; Patrick Counihan, "Activists and Politician Stop the Sheriff in Irish Eviction Attempt," *Irish Central,* February 22, 2012; Gerry Moriarty, "Why the Dissident Danger Is Growing," *Irish Times,* April 30, 2011; Dan Keenan, "Dissidents Vow to Kill More Police Officers," *Irish Times,* April 26, 2011. The 2006 census was the first to include data on vacant dwellings, indicating 266,322 vacancies. Preliminary results from the 2011 census suggest a 10.5 percent increase in vacant dwellings; see *Census 2011 Preliminary Report,* 18.

28. The Central Statistics Office notes that these preliminary results should be treated with caution. A profile of migration and diversity is scheduled to be published based on in-depth analysis of the results in October 2012. *Census 2011 Preliminary Report,* 12.

29. Stephen Carroll, "Difficulties on the Horizon for Those Planning to Leave," *Irish Times,* December 29, 2011.

30. Helen Carter, "Celtic Tiger at Bay: A New Generation of Migrants Crosses Irish Sea," *Guardian* (London), March 8, 2012.

31. Ronit Lentin, "Reawakening Anti-Racism," *Metro Éireann,* April 29, 2010.

32. Jamie Smyth, "Call for Government Action on Racism," *Irish Times,* March 22, 2011.

33. Alison Healy, "Warning Recession May Raise Racist Tensions," *Irish Times,* June 24, 2010.

34. Elaine Edwards, "Call for Election Focus on Immigrants," *Irish Times,* February 17, 2011.

35. Trinity Immigration Initiative, *Addressing the Current and Future Reality of Ireland's Multi-Cultural Status,* www.tcd.ie/immigration/css/downloads/TIIReport01.07.10.pdf.

36. *Long-Term International Migration Statistics for Northern Ireland, 2008–2009,* NISRA, November 2010, pp. 18–19, www.nisra.gov.uk/demography/default.asp18.htm.

37. Cf. *Migration Integration Policy Index,* www.mipex.eu/ireland.

38. "Language Support Teachers Cut," *Irish Times,* December 3, 2010: "English Language Support Teachers' Association (ELSTA) is astounded at the proposed cut of 1,200 teachers in the area of English as an Additional Language (EAL) for students for whom English is not their mother tongue. As the recently published Intercultural Education Strategy 2010–2015 clearly shows, while some immigrants are leaving Ireland, 'there is still a significant inward flow of migrants and the recent profile of migrants is changing, with an increasing proportion in the 0–15 year old age category.'"

39. Catherine Reilly, "There's No Black or White Ireland," *Metro Éireann,* May 27, 2010.

40. An example of artistic collaboration can be seen in the African Arambe Theatre Company's 2006 production of Jimmy Murphy's play *The Kings of the Kilburn High Road,* which was directed by Bisi Adigun and starred Dublin-based African actors in the roles of Irish laborers in London. The 2008 Dublin Theatre Festival also featured a rewriting of J. M. Synge's *The Playboy of the Western World* by Nigerian director and playwright Bisi Adigun and Roddy Doyle, in which the playboy is recast as a Nigerian refugee in contemporary Dublin. The collaboration between Adigum and Doyle has since collapsed into a series of court battles as of this writing.

41. David Lloyd, *Ireland After History,* vol. 9, ed. Seamus Deane, Critical Conditions (Notre Dame, IN: University of Notre Dame Press in association with Field Day, 1999), 106.

42. James Joyce, *The Critical Writings,* ed. Ellsworth Mason and Richard Ellmann (New York: Viking, 1959), 166.

CHAPTER ONE

IMMIGRATION IN IRELAND

*A Keynote Address by the UN High Commissioner
for Human Rights*

MARY ROBINSON

I would like to begin with the issue of Irish identity.[1] Let me share with you a lesson I learned when I said, in an emotional evening on the night I was elected as president of Ireland, that I would place a light in the window of Áras an Uachtaráin for all of those who had had to emigrate from Ireland over the years, over the decades. I learned about the power of symbols. The light was not in fact a candle as we had originally intended, but a specially built lamp with no off-switch. It has shown its light 24/7 for seven years, and indeed my successor, President McAleese, continues the idea of a light. But what I had not really understood was the power of that light. The way that it touched millions of people of Irish descent around the world and reengaged them in connecting with a modern Ireland of the 1990s.

I remember when I addressed both houses of the Oireachtas on the subject of the Irish diaspora. I said that that kind of larger sense of an Irish family spread around the world would help us on the island of Ireland to have a broader, more diverse, more inclusive sense of our own identity. This broader identity would help us to build links of friendship and of social and business contacts in a very holistic way between North and South on the island of Ireland.

And I had not foreseen or understood at that time how another opening up of Irish society in the dramatic increase in migrants coming into Ireland and the slowing of emigration out of Ireland would pose new and complex challenges to Irish identity. In the Ireland that I grew up in—the West of Ireland in County Mayo—the next parish was in fact considered to be Boston. We were steeped in the inevitability of emigration, the sad loss of young vitality, which was captured by the journalist John Healy in his book, *No One Shouted Stop: Death of an Irish Town.*[2] It was captured in the toast *bás in Éirinn,* "May he be lucky enough to die in Ireland."

Some population and migration estimates of the year up to April 2006 are very interesting, very striking, very challenging, and, I think, very encouraging. The number of immigrants into Ireland in the twelve months up to April 2006 is estimated to have been 86,900—the highest figure recorded since the present series of annual migration estimates began in 1987.

The estimated number of emigrants in the same period out of Ireland was 17,000, which gave a net migration figure of 69,900. The natural increase in the population—the difference between the births and deaths for the year ending April 2006—was 34,200. So births had exceeded deaths by 34,200. The combined effect of the natural increase and migration resulted in a population increase of 104,100, that is 2.5 percent of the population, bringing the estimated population of Ireland to 4.235 million at that time. The breakdown of those figures is also interesting. Nearly half, 43 percent, of immigrants were nationals of the ten new EU accession states, which joined the European Union on the first of May 2004. Almost 26 percent (23,000) of the immigrants were from Poland, while 7 percent (over 6,000) were from Lithuania. More than half (54 percent) of the immigrants were ages twenty-three to forty-four, while a further 28 percent were ages fifteen to twenty-four. One in ten of the migrants were children under the age of fifteen. We have a Europe worried about an aging population, but our migrants are keeping our demographic profile much younger than many other European countries.

This new reality is both a huge challenge and a great opportunity for modern Ireland. There is a good practice in developing what I would call a bottom-up, county-specific approach to migration in Ireland. Last December, on my way back for Christmas as a now migrant of a temporary nature, I was invited to launch a report on immigration, integration, and social provision in Castlebar in my native county, Mayo. The report is entitled *Building a Diverse Mayo.*[3] The invitation came from a small, nongovernmental organization called Mayo Intercultural Action (MIA). The chairperson of MIA is a Kenyan woman who lives in a hostel in County Mayo. I cannot tell you how empowered she was to be chairperson of this very active group and to be an agent for change about her future—not just a passive, silent migrant in a remote county in Ireland where she was not understood. I could see in her face and in the faces of the other members of the MIA how much being together in this Mayo Intercultural Action meant to those participating.

The report received financial support from the Mayo County Council and also at the national level from the Department of Social and Family Affairs. It was compiled by two skilled consultants, two women who knew how to address the various issues. As I came to Castlebar for the meeting, I picked up a copy of the *Mayo News,* a weekly newspaper in the county. I was really amazed, but also pleasantly surprised, to see that it carries a page every week now in Polish because there is that demand. I was also very pleased in the composition of the Mayo Intercultural Association to see that women were to the fore and that women's issues were to the fore in the report; the feminization of migration also applies to the situation in the modern Ireland.

The aim of *Building a Diverse Mayo* is first to provide a profile of immigrants and identify their specific needs. Secondly, to examine to what extent service providers and other agencies are addressing these needs. Thirdly, and very importantly, to identify the needs of service providers in their responses to the needs of new communities. And fourthly, to inform and direct future actions and initiatives by both statutory and voluntary agencies in the county.

I want to refer to two comments in the report. The first is on health care. In my work in leading Realizing Rights, I focus on global health and access to health care.[4] So I had a particular interest in what the MIA would say about the access of these new migrants to health care. This is what the comment stated:

> Migrant workers have considerable difficulties in finding their way around the healthcare system and personal difficulties when there is no adequate language in common between the health practitioner and the patient. It is unclear what entitlements migrant workers with work permits or who do not yet have long-term residency have to health services. While undocumented migrant workers were not interviewed in this research, it is widely understood that they have no entitlement to basic healthcare in Ireland and issues can arise in emergencies. Asylum seekers have particular and unacceptable difficulties. It is not possible for visiting healthcare workers, including doctors, to examine patients in privacy. Mothers have no privacy in breastfeeding.

The second comment I want to refer to is about the broader integration: "Integration is a complex and lengthy two-way process for the host county and for immigrants. Creating the conditions for integration requires an understanding of the very real barriers that exist for immigrants attempting to participate in Irish society." The Habitual Residence Condition, introduced in 2004, involves a qualification of being resident for two years in order to be eligible for social assistance payments and child benefits. This also involves proving that the migrant's center of interest lies in Ireland.

The Habitual Residence Condition has proven to be a major obstacle in the way of integration as well as a cause of hardship. There can be neither integration nor equality without the full enjoyment of health, education, housing, and social protection. Direct provision undermines the quality of life for asylum seekers, prevents them from contributing to society, and serves to create the conditions for segregation rather than integration. This relates to the prohibition on asylum seekers from being able to seek employment pending a resolution of their asylum status.

The findings of this detailed study of one county are echoed in the feedback I received when I consulted a friend of mine who works with the homeless in Dublin. Here are some of her concerns:

> Immigrants who may have been working in Ireland for less than two years, if they lose their jobs or get into difficulties, do not qualify for social welfare under the Habitual Residence Condition. Indeed, initially those in this category who ended up homeless were only allowed one night in sheltered or hostel accommodation. However, while that rule has been relaxed, the shortage of that type of accommodation continues to cause serious problems. Most of the people are extremely neglected, very much like the Irish of a generation ago, who went to the United States and the United Kingdom. One recent week we [at Realizing Rights] had people from twelve different countries. In running services for people who are homeless, we must confront another issue, which does not receive much attention, namely the amount of racism and ethnic intolerance, which sometimes expresses itself in violence. Indeed, when addressing racism, we need to be very conscious now, as well, that there are many different ethnic groups living in Ireland and there can be very serious tensions between many of these different groups. On a regular basis we witness this tension between people from different ethnic groups that come to us for help. Perhaps the biggest problem that the rise in immigration has created is that services like ours are being overwhelmed. Recently and for the first time in thirty years, we had to close our doors one morning, as the numbers seeking help swelled to such an extent that it would have been unsafe to allow any more people in.

All of us, including the embassies of the countries where immigrants come from, must work together to ensure everyone who needs help receives it. But it remains a continuing problem that people on the frontline are not consulted by those running national services. This failure means that when initiatives are taken in the homeless area to help address racism, they may make the situation worse. The failure to plan properly for the primary education needs of the population means that we now have primary schools, such as the recently established one in Balbriggan, attended only by children of immigrant parents.

This situation is partly due to the Catholic Church's control of education: Catholic children are given priority, a device that has created an unwitting ethnic or racial bar, as most immigrant children are non-Catholics. This school in Balbriggan was featured in a recent article in the *Guardian*:

> Under a dark sky and with a statue of Christ, arms outstretched and welcome, it seemed just another opening day in the life of an ordinary Irish primary school. But the school in Balbriggan, County Dublin, which finally opened its doors yesterday morning, has been the centre of a national controversy, which has highlighted how Ireland is failing to cope with the influx of tens of thousands of immigrants. Ireland's newest primary school is overwhelmingly black, the majority of its pupils with parents from Nigeria and some, judging by the number of mothers in headscarves, from the Islamic faith. The school was created out of incompetence rather than design. A huge population increase, partly due to immigration from Africa, China, and Eastern Europe, has put enormous pressure on the school system. The result, according to one local councillor, has been the creation of a mini apartheid in the seaside town. With the new emergency school, almost exclusively filled with children of immigrants, dozens of children from non-Irish ethnic backgrounds had been turned down by local Catholic schools, principally because they didn't hold Catholic baptismal certificates. More than 90 percent of schools in the Republic are run by the Catholic Church. Up to 100 children were facing the new term with no place at primary school in the north county Dublin region.[5]

This story points to the crucial need for finding constructive ways to address these problems.

Lest I seem to only point to the negative and the problem areas, let me also note that in June 2007, Ireland elected its first black mayor, Rotimi Adebari, a Christian from Nigeria, who arrived seven years ago in Ireland as an asylum seeker. He went to the Portlaoise area and was elected a councillor in 2004 and is now the mayor of Portlaoise. When he settled in Portlaoise with his wife and family, his two children were the only foreign pupils in the local school. Now there are more than thirty nationalities at the school. This, in essence, is the face of modern Ireland.

One of my toughest tasks as the UN high commissioner for human rights was to serve as secretary general of the World Conference Against Racism in Durban held August 31–September 7, 2001. I did not choose that task. It was thrust upon me. Two earlier world conferences against racism had collapsed, and the question was, Could we have a successful outcome? I am very proud of the fact that we did have a successful outcome in Durban. I still get incredible and wild criticism from some sources about not controlling the anti-Semitism that was a huge problem in the run-up to the proprietary regional conferences, especially the one that was held in Tehran.

I have been not only vilified but castigated as a war criminal. It meant a lot to me that only a week ago at an event on the west coast, quite unexpectedly a relatively young Jewish woman came up to me and said, "I was in Durban for the world conference." I expected she would raise something difficult. She said, "I remember the anti-Semitism. And I remember you coming into a room one evening where we were all gathered, and holding up these cartoons and saying, 'This is not acceptable.'" These were horrible cartoons, vilifying the Jewish people. She reminded me that I had said, "I am a Jew. Everyone at this conference should sense themselves to be a Jew. That is what this conference is about. It is a conference against racism, discrimination, xenophobia, anti-Semitism."

I was really heartened that she said that from her perspective, because I have heard so much of the other side. On the other hand, in so many places that I visit, I get praised for the fact that we had a successful conclusion to the World Conference Against Racism. The black Brazilian population found that it changed their situation. For many of the indigenous population of Latin America, it made a huge difference. For the Daoists in India, even though they did not get their claims and situation on the agenda, they highlighted their sense of being discriminated against in India, and they developed networks with nongovernmental organizations.

The impact of the Conference Against Racism on individual countries is also very significant, and I am glad to note especially the impact on modern Ireland. In May 2001, the National Consultative Committee on Racism and Interculturalism established a system of reporting every six months on recorded incidents relating to racism in Ireland. Up-to-date reports are available through December 2008, and you can look at those reports and see what migrants say about what was said about them, racist slurs, how newspapers (inadvertently, perhaps, but certainly in a very racist way) cover events. These are recorded, and attention is drawn to them.

Meanwhile, the National Action Plan Against Racism 2005–2008 was launched by the Irish government in 2005, fulfilling the commitment made at Durban to have a national plan of action in every country.[6] There are five objectives to that plan of action, which is overseen by a strategic monitoring group.

The first is effective protection and redress against racism including a focus on combating discrimination, assaults, and threatening behavior and incitement to hatred.

The second is to ensure economic inclusion and equality of opportunity, including a focus on employment, the workplace, and poverty.

The third is to accommodate diversity in service provision.

The fourth is to ensure recognition and awareness of diversity.

And the fifth is full participation in Irish society. The fifth objective is concerned with enhancing the participation of cultural and ethnic minorities in Irish society, including a focus on the political level, the policy level, and the community level. The importance of that plan of action is that the government set out its five objectives and can be held to account on what it seeks to achieve. It is up to civil society to hold it to account.

There are also other bodies that play a significant role. The Human Rights Commission has as part of its remit the responsibility of looking at discrimination and monitoring these effects. The European Commission Against Racism and Intolerance (ECRI) provides a considerable outside oversight of Irish approaches to tackling racism. In 2006, the European Commission Against Racism and Intolerance published its third report on Ireland, which gave credit for progress.[7] In particular, the European Convention on Human Rights Act of 2003 enabled Irish people for the first time to invoke the convention before the Irish courts. Also, we honored the adoption of both the Equality Act of 2004 and the National Action Plan Against Racism.

However, the report on Ireland did point out that its recommendations from earlier reports had not been implemented. In the interest of "keeping them honest" I will just refer to that part of the report of the European body:

Ireland has not yet ratified protocol Number 12 of the European Convention on Human Rights which contains a general prohibition on discrimination. Although it is currently under review, the criminal legislation has not been amended to include sufficiently strong provisions for combating racist acts, which affect in particular visible minorities and Travellers. Further measures are necessary to raise members of minority group's awareness of existing mechanisms for seeking redress against racism and racial discrimination. There is also still a need for the establishment of policies aimed at integrating asylum seekers and refugees into Irish society. Furthermore, the increase in demand for non-denominational or multi-faith schools must be met. The Employment Permits Act 2006 requires close monitoring in order to ensure that its implementation addresses some of the problems faced by non-Irish workers in the workplace such as racism and discrimination. Measures for integrating Travellers into society need to be reinforced, in particular in the area of employment. National Traveller organizations should be further involved and included in these initiatives.

The report spells out in more length some of the ways in which Ireland in the European Union context could further implement the recommendations in the two earlier reports.

So it seems to me that we know that much has changed in the modern Ireland. There are certain structures that have been put in place. There is stocktaking within Ireland and also the European Union. I hope by now I have convinced you of why this is an important conference, gathering the experts that I have seen on the agenda for the next few days. From a certain distance, it confers a certain opportunity not to score political points, but to look constructively at the situation. We may be able to address the complex and equally vital challenges and opportunities for the modern Ireland.

I have decided that although I do not have any specific role, and indeed in many ways it is wiser not to be involved directly in policy issues affecting modern Ireland as a former president, I have decided to stick with this issue. I mentioned at the beginning the memorable launch of the report *Building a Diverse Mayo* last December. I was very proud of Mayo on that occasion. If every county in Ireland were to carry out the same approach and we had *Building a Diverse Cork,* a *Diverse Kerry,* a *Diverse Donegal,* a *Diverse Meath,* this would be really significant. It would mean joint involvement of national and county funding and resourcing and support, but very strong participation by community groups and civil society groups.

This coming December, when I am back in Ireland again at Christmastime, I have been asked to help launch a report on irregular migration and the experience of undocumented migrants in Ireland for the Migrant Rights Centre in Ireland.[8] I learned quite a lot from working on that report, and it is one of these key issues about who we are, how we define ourselves, how inclusive we are, how we live up to our history, how we live up to those Famine years, when so many hundreds of thousands left on the coffin ships and came here, came to Grosse Île that I visited in Canada, came to Argentina, to various parts of the world and had to make a new future.

And so I would like to end with the words of somebody from outside Ireland reflecting on the challenges that we face. Thomas O'Grady, who grew up on Prince Edward Island and is currently director of Irish studies at the University of Massachusetts in Boston, writes in his poem "The Miracle":

> What if, against all reason, rhymes
> could thwart that fickle thief
> and move us to contend
> with our age's falling light? Sometimes
> hearing is believing. Belief
> is still what saves us in the end.[9]

His words reflect on where we came from, that Ireland of *No One Shouted Stop,* of *bás in Éirinn,* of so many stories of emigration and so many writers who had to leave Ireland to feel they could breathe and write about the country.

And now we have this vibrant so-called Celtic Tiger—but it is not a Celtic Tiger for quite a number of people, particularly some of these new migrants. Yet it is very diverse, and it is admired by many people around the world. That is what I also hear—"Isn't it wonderful, what's happening in Ireland?"—and I am pondering myself. We need to dig deeply and find some good guidance on how we move forward and how we live up to our history, that history of a people who had to leave our country and find a future elsewhere. How do we treat those who are in the same position now?

Q: As an Irish American with a strong identity in the Irish American diaspora and as someone who is intending on going back to Ireland, I am wondering what the attitude seems to be among Irish people toward Irish Americans who may be moving back to Ireland or people from the Irish diaspora who have an Irish identity who are now becoming immigrants within Ireland?

A: It is an interesting question, and I will give you a subjective answer. Others may have other answers. I have a sense that there was more of a welcome in the 1990s. We really loved the idea of talented, high-achieving Americans or Irish who had spent a lot of time in America and had skills coming back. I think now it is a little more competitive—"jobs are scarce, and you are coming in and taking our jobs." I see you nodding—it seems to be your experience. So that is

another way in which we should realize how lucky we are. Most of
the people who left Ireland in the dark days of the Famine and pre-
Famine and post-Famine left with no help from the Irish state. Eavan
Boland wrote a poem, "The Emigrant Irish": "Like oil lamps we put
them out the back, of our houses, of our minds." We put them out
of our hearts and minds; we did not pay any attention. And yet there
is that incredibly strong bond, and the light somehow touched that
chord. So we should realize in the modern Ireland how lucky we are
that people like you want to do exactly what you want to do, and we
should be open, and we should make it possible and find the policies
instead of making it, "Is this taking jobs?" and about work permits,
and undocumented Americans in Ireland. Really we should be welcoming because we are a small island. It is a competitive world, and
our human resource is our greatest asset. The idea that talented young
people of Irish heritage that are part of this wider Irish family would
want to come back is a golden asset to modern Ireland. So do come.

Q: One of the main differences between Ireland and the United
States and how we face our mutual immigration challenges is that
Ireland is firmly embedded in the European system of human rights
as well as the wider international system of human rights. Can you
share with us how being part of a wider human rights system, a robust system, is helping the Irish people understand what their obligations are to the new people among them, that they cannot just turn
inward and parochial but must actually look to see what the international consensus is on these questions?

A: Ireland has benefited from the pressure of the wider participation in two streams, the European Union and the Strasbourg Convention on Human Rights and Fundamental Freedoms. This is true
in equality in work, in equality in social welfare, in lots of areas. And
now it is true in the scrutiny of how Ireland is implementing its commitments. I mentioned the commitment at the UN level, following
the Durban conference, to having a plan of action. But it is the European oversight that will really be quite telling, much more so than the
UN oversight, which exists but will be more general and happen less
often. The year 2008 is the European year of intercultural dialogue.
So that will also have an impact.

I have been quite shocked, being based in New York for the last five years, at the increasingly harsh language in the discourse on migration in this country. When I was studying in the Harvard Law School and when I was following US politics and general policy over the years, the United States was so much better than Europe in its policies toward migrants. We admired the way in which the United States was giving leadership and was having this great policy of integrating those who came into the country. And many went from green card to becoming US citizens if they wanted to, and it was an admirable system. But since I have landed, I just cannot believe how it is getting worse and worse. I find the labeling of human beings, hardworking decent people who come because they desperately want to help to improve their families and get out of deep poverty—to call them "illegal aliens" is to me quite shocking, frankly. First of all, I have this image of people with antennae sticking out of their heads. We fought a battle in Ireland over how children should never be described as illegitimate, and we won that battle in the 1970s. You just do not call human beings "illegitimate" or "illegal," because they are human beings. The Universal Declaration of Human Rights says we are all born free and equal in dignity and rights. So yes, irregular. Yes, undocumented. Yes, people broke the law. That is all legitimate to say. But I really feel that there needs to be more concern about the implicit racism of language such as "illegal aliens." It is doubly negative.

Q: When you were talking about the EU's report, I noticed there was some linkage of the situation of immigrants to Ireland with the situation of the Travellers. I thought that was a topic that might call for more commentary in the sense that the question of human rights and bigotry with respect to the Travellers is one that obviously predates the Celtic Tiger and the situation of the immigrants to Ireland in the last fifteen years. I have two questions. How would you say that the new immigration questions have affected the attitudes toward and issues about the Travellers? Secondly, and maybe more controversially, how has the Traveller community complicated the questions with respect to the immigrants to Ireland?

A: When we're talking about race and migration, I do think that we have to—from an Irish perspective—know that there is the indigenous, very big issue of the way in which we treat the Travelling community. It is something that I have always been aware of, and I took cases when I was practicing as a barrister, and I tried as President of Ireland to reach out particularly to the Travelling community, because they needed it very much. A focus on migrants that does not also encompass the Travelling community has two dangers. It can tend to diminish focus on the Travelling community and their need to be more fully addressed in a way that is supportive of their core identity and not trying to integrate them in a way that undermines their sense of their identity and their past as the Travelling community. At the same time, it must ensure that their children have access to education, to health care, to job opportunities, to participation in public life. They are quite a sizeable population—at least 23,000 members of the Travelling community who are both self-identified as such and want to be regarded as a sizeable and visible minority—and they still face discrimination in all kinds of ways.

The Travelling community have their place and space in the Irish mind, and it is not an entirely friendly space and place. Migrants from outside are a newer challenge. What I would see as being more of a distinction is between those from the ten new EU member states—the Poles, the Lithuanians, the Latvians, who can be assimilated more easily—and those from North Africa, from Nigeria, who are much more likely to suffer racism. I remember, and it is still quite a memory, being asked by a small group of women of African background living in Ireland if they could come and see me in Áras an Uachtaráin when I was president. There was a group of about thirteen women. One of them was a teenager. They came, and they sat around the dining room table with me for about three hours, and we talked. It was the first time that I realized that on almost a daily basis they were suffering different kinds of racism, either explicit or people slowing their speech to talk to them as if they were only half intelligent. The teenager who was among them was born in Ireland and said, "I cannot tell you the number of times I have been told, 'Why don't you go back to your own country?'" It was not understood that somebody who was black could be Irish in the Irish-born sense. Now, I think attitudes have changed quite a bit since then. There is still racism, and it is still reflected in these reports that I mentioned, the six monthly reports. They do spell out the slurs and the threats and the hate crimes that occur. And it is good that the reports do, because otherwise people might underestimate. I do think that there is a broad recognition in Ireland that migrants have been good for the Irish economy, good for this Celtic Tiger. They are seen as a new challenge, whereas the Travelling community is the familiar, the known, and often the sidelined. This sizeable minority within Ireland also must be given a better space and place in the context of Ireland having a more thoughtful and considerate approach to the issues of how we treat new migrants into the country.

Q: I want to challenge you and ask you about something you omitted. In your reconceptualization of our Irishness as including the diaspora, which was powerful and very empowering, I feel that some unintended consequence ensued. Suddenly the Irish felt reenabled to reconceive Irishness in blood terms, leading—unintended on your behalf—to the Citizenship Referendum of 2004. Automatic citizenship is no longer being given to people born on the island of Ireland, as had been the case since 1922, yet it is available to people who are not born in Ireland but who might have had an Irish grandparent. That created a racist divide between those people who are entitled to citizenship and those who are not. Citizenship is an issue you did not treat. For instance, Rotimi, the mayor of Portlaoise, does not have Irish citizenship. The woman who headed your Mayo project still resides in an asylum hostel and does not have citizenship, and probably will not get it. Neither her children nor Rotimi's children are Irish citizens. This is a real issue where human rights actually stop at the threshold of citizenship.

A: It is an absolutely fair point. I was very saddened and disappointed with the Citizenship Referendum of 2004. I thought it was rushed into, not properly thought through. There was no white paper consultation, and there was a panic about maternity hospitals and a hundred or so pregnant women coming to Ireland to have their children. Is that so bad? Is that so terrible? We changed, very fundamentally, a point. At the same time, on the local authority side, I have always been proud of the fact that people could vote and stand for local elections in Ireland after a six-month residency. That was a good move, and that is what has helped the mayor of Portlaoise and my Kenyan woman friend who is now chairperson of the Mayo Intercultural Association.

Q: What is your opinion on how much we should try to preserve a culture and how far we should go to appreciate the fluctuation that the culture will undergo as it is influenced by others?

A: Again, a very thoughtful question. You make me think about the year 1972, when Ireland was deciding by referendum whether we would join the European Economic Community as it was in those days. Many friends of mine were on the other side of that debate and said, "Look, we fought for centuries and now we have achieved fairly recently Irish independence, Irish national sovereignty. Are we going to lose this in a homogeneous Europe?" I respected that viewpoint, and it was passionately argued, but I felt at the time that Ireland would benefit from a membership of a wider number of European countries that had decided to limit some parts of their sovereignty in a shared way, while still retaining a lot of independence, as the countries of the European Union have. This would allow Ireland to come out from under this terrible colonial umbrella that we were fixated about. Irish policy was always seeing ourselves somehow in the shadow of our relationship with Britain. The referendum was positive and we became a member on the first of January, 1973. I really felt that it gave a new vitality to Irish culture because now we were part of a union, then of nine countries; then it became fifteen; now it is twenty-five. Those countries admire Irish culture. They admire the fact that we have the two languages, that we have a long historical experience. They see us in a way that is validating our sense of the importance of our culture. And it is not that colonial relationship. So I would say the same now about this vibrant Ireland.

I know that there are people who are questioning, "Are we going to lose our essential values?" My reference point is County Mayo. That is where our home is, that is where I go when I go back to Ireland most of the time. It is just so much better than when I was growing up, when schools were closing, district courts were closing, because there was not the population to support them. Now schools are having to accommodate children from very different backgrounds, and teachers are challenged, and health providers are challenged. One of the things about this report is we have to actually resource and train our teachers, our police, our nurses, to understand the kind of vitality of this. But it does not make us less Irish. It makes us more excitingly vibrant in being the people who used to go and who now receive other people and who have this sense of an Irish destiny. I think it is wonderful—that sense of multicultural vibrancy, being one of the youngest countries in a Europe that is aging, having all of this talent that is coming in. Migrants who have the courage and the resourcefulness to move from a country are generally those that are the most skilled, that are the ones that are entrepreneurial, achieving, and who want to get places. We are lucky to have them. I think we need to trade our destiny; we're not a narrow, homogeneous people anymore. Thankfully we are a people who spread to many, many countries of the world. We gathered in that Irish diaspora, and now within the island of Ireland we are seeing that diversity. It is one of the best things that could have happened. But it is also a challenge.

NOTES

1. This chapter includes an excerpt from the keynote address given at the conference "Race and Immigration in the New Ireland," University of Notre Dame, October 14–17, 2007, by Mary Robinson, former president of Ireland and then UN high commissioner for human rights, and excerpts from the question-and-answer session that followed.

2. John Healy, *No One Shouted Stop: Death of an Irish Town* (Cork: Mercier, 1968).

3. Mayo Intercultural Action, *Building a Diverse Mayo*, A Report on Immigration, Integration & Service Provision, December 2006, www.integrating ireland.ie/userfiles/File/Database/BuildingaDiverseMayo.pdf.

4. Realizing Rights (www.realizingrights.org) was founded in 2002 by Mary Robinson.

5. Henry McDonald, "Ireland Forced to Open Immigrant School," *Guardian* (London), September 25, 2007.

6. Department of Justice, Equality and Law Reform, *Planning for Diversity: The National Action Plan Against Racism*, www.nccri.ie/pdf/ActionPlan.pdf.

7. European Commission Against Racism and Intolerance, *Third Report on Ireland,* December 2006, www.coe.int/t/dghl/monitoring/ecri/library/publications_en.asp.

8. *Life in the Shadows: An Exploration of Irregular Migration in Ireland,* Migrant Rights Centre Ireland, 2007, www.mrci.ie/Reports-&-Leaflets.

9. Thomas O'Grady, "The Miracle," in *What Really Matters,* The Hugh MacLennan Poetry Series (Montreal: McGill-Queen's University Press, 2000), 59.

CHAPTER TWO

AN INTERVIEW WITH PABLO ROJAS COPPARI OF THE MIGRANT RIGHTS CENTRE IRELAND

JULIEANN VERONICA ULIN

The Migrant Rights Centre Ireland (MRCI) celebrated its tenth anniversary in 2011. The organization focuses on participation and empowerment of migrants through action groups; training migrants in leadership, media relations, and lobbying the state; and educational outreach to the community through creative projects that convey issues facing migrants. To date, the MRCI has achieved a "bridging" visa for the undocumented, €2.5 million in legal judgments and awards, protections for domestic workers, and reforms in the work permit system.

Pablo Rojas Coppari is a strategic advocacy officer at MRCI, with emphasis on irregular migration and trafficking for forced labor. He has a BA in applied languages and an MA in international development and intercultural studies from the University of Lille III, France. Prior to joining the MRCI, Pablo undertook research and casework for former unaccompanied minors seeking asylum with the Dutch Refugee Council, and worked on research projects on language and cultural issues of ethnic minorities across Europe in the European Centre for Minority Issues in Flensburg, Germany. This interview was conducted on March 22, 2012.

Julieann Ulin: Can you give us a little background about yourself and about how you came to work with Migrant Rights Centre Ireland?

Pablo Coppari: I was a master's student in international development and intercultural studies at the University of Lille III, France. As part of my master's, I applied to do an internship with the MRCI here in Dublin. I came four years ago to do a six-month internship with them and have been working here since, first as a caseworker and then as a project worker, always in the area of undocumented migrants and human trafficking for forced labor.

JU: In 2011, you celebrated the MRCI's tenth anniversary. How has it evolved over the last ten years?

PC: The MRCI was set up in 2001 by the Missionary Society of St. Columban as a voluntary service concerned mainly with providing information for migrant workers in Ireland. It started with a focus on Filipino migrant workers, since there is a strong connection and historical tie between the Columban missionaries and the Philippines. At that time, it was a voluntary organization focused on providing information to communities that were arriving in Ireland. This was at the beginning of the Celtic Tiger, and there was a big arrival of migrant workers but little to no service at all to migrant communities. There was a need for the provision of consistent and good information to migrant workers who didn't know about their rights and entitlements or where to get the right information.

Then as time progressed, we saw there was a need for more than simple information provision. There was a need for casework to be done and for someone to advocate on behalf of those finding themselves within the system. We managed to get our first funding in 2003 to conduct our first strategic planning. That is when we employed our current director, Siobhán O'Donoghue. From there, the MRCI went on to become a more professional organization, and we evolved from a voluntary organization to a nongovernmental organization with a paid, professional staff. We are now on our third strategic plan.

JU: You provide services annually to over five thousand migrant workers. Can you speak about the concerns of those workers and the challenges they face in Ireland today?

PC: At the core of the MRCI is the resource center. It is a drop-in clinic open from Monday to Wednesday, ten AM to four PM. That's the time when people can just walk in and get information and get answers to their questions about immigration, employment laws, social welfare, and just talk about their problems.

From that resource center, queries and concerns can be routed internally to our different projects or referred externally to other agencies. We do a lot of casework for undocumented migrants, and we also refer them to a legal panel when it comes to employment law and entitlements. We currently have a forced labor project; whenever we identify people who have been exploited or are suffering in forced labor, we refer them internally and assist them in reporting the crime or exiting the situation.

We also have two support groups: the Domestic Workers Action Group and the Restaurant Workers Action Group. We bring together domestic workers or restaurant workers, and we have weekend or evening meetings in which they can talk about their problems and share the issues affecting them. Those discussions will influence the campaigning plan of those action groups.

JU: In particular, can you speak of the different challenges faced by non-EU migrants?

PC: The MRCI has always had a focus on working with the most vulnerable population of migrants in society, and by definition that means we emphasize working with the undocumented migrants and those in the work permit system, which by definition are outside the EU. We do provide information and some assistance to EU migrants, particularly around employment law. But by virtue of their legal immigration status EU migrants don't face the same problems; they can move freely and can take up employment without the need of employment permits. There is exploitation of EU migrants, but it is easier for them to exit the situation because that will not affect their legal immigration status.

The next category of vulnerability would be migrants who are in the work permit system and have a temporary immigration status that is tied up with their work permit. They do not have the right to change employers; they can only work for that particular employer designated on the work permit. If they lose that job or they are exploited and they want to exit the exploitive situation, they take a big risk of losing their immigration status and not being able to obtain a new work permit because of the ever more restrictive conditions.

Then, on the third level, are people who are undocumented and by default cannot access any form of social welfare entitlement and are continuously at risk of prosecution or arrest and receiving a deportation order.

JU: One of your stated priorities is to increase public awareness of issues involving migrant workers. How have you seen the public attitude toward migrants shift as a result of the economic collapse of the Celtic Tiger?

PC: Overall, the public attitude toward migration has changed because of the economic recession. That change in attitude would include all of the three categories above. Migrants in general would be accused of taking local jobs, taking jobs from Irish people.

At the moment, we are still in the situation where irregular migration, undocumented migrants, is not a big issue. When the media talks about migrants, it is not usually irregular migration that is discussed. When people talk about undocumented migrants, they say, "We cannot afford to regularize them—there are not enough jobs for everyone, there are not even enough jobs for Irish people; so how can we regularize undocumented migrants?" And it's actually the discourse around jobs and employment that is the main driver to exclude people. So it becomes more difficult now to advocate on behalf of undocumented migrants since we know they are in competition with other migrants from the European Union or with non-EU migrants and also with Irish citizens. That is the new problem that has arisen with the economic downturn.

JU: Can you talk about the Centre's focus on domestic workers, who often comprise a kind of invisible and unregulated labor force particularly subject to physical and economic exploitation?

PC: At the core of the work of the MRCI has been the Domestic Workers Action Group; it has been up and running for almost eight years now. That work and that group came together at first to recognize domestic work as a particularly vulnerable category of employees. At first the group was about creating a space for domestic workers, who were often confined to their place of employment, to just come out on their time off and meet other domestic workers and talk and socialize and realize that the problems they are facing in their employment and in their lives are not unique to them but are common problems in the sector. If the issues are long hours and unregulated labor, then we need to lobby the government to try to acknowledge domestic work as a sector of employment that needs more regulation. These strategies evolve over time and through different methodologies.

The Domestic Workers Action Group is very creative in bringing awareness to issues facing their work sector. They created a quilt that traveled around the world and put domestic work issues in context.[1] They have a drama group. They are now involved in creating a musical piece. They have photography and film projects. It is always about exploring different and creative ways of conveying issues that affect domestic workers. In the beginning it was exploitation and confinement. Now those issues are still there, but we are also seeing other problems that are more prominent, such as workers being exploited in the houses of diplomats[2] or au pairs not being paid minimum wage.[3] There is also trafficking for forced labor, which is very common in the domestic work sector.

JU: In Irish airports there are now signs that offer information on recognizing human trafficking and that provide information on reporting it. Your organization has brought a great deal of attention to the practice of human trafficking, forced labor, and modern slavery. You also advocated for criminalizing forced labor and have helped 169 victims of forced labor. Can you give a sense of the scale of these problems in Ireland and the challenges faced by victims and observers reporting it?

PC: It has to be said that MRCI's knowledge of human trafficking and forced labor has grown and developed as we have had to face this issue. So we are sure that there have been cases that slipped through the cracks or cases preceding the criminalization of human trafficking in June 2008. The problem is that since we have had legislation criminalizing trafficking for forced labor, there's been really strict criteria applied to identify victims. What we are finding is that the bar is too high and there are things that have to be proven, like cross-border movement. But sometimes the recruitment and movement happen within Ireland, and people are still put in the situation of forced labor. The way the legislation is now interpreted puts too much of a burden of proof on the victim. It overemphasizes certain aspects, such as movement, and this is not responding to the scale of the problem. So what we have said is that either the government needs to change the interpretation or tweak the legislation now, or it needs to come up with new legislation to assist victims of forced labor who might not meet the criteria for trafficking.

If we have helped over 160 people, it is just the tip of the iceberg. Victims of forced labor live in such high isolation, they live in such fear. For these 169 people to approach us is a big thing, but we have to imagine how many more there are living in fear and confinement, unable to get the proper information. We have to find a way to help them to exit an exploitative situation.

JU: Can you talk about the impact of fluctuating minimum wage on migrant workers in the service industries?

PC: Just before this new government took over in March 2011, the old government made a cut on the minimum wage from €8.65 to €7.65. At that time, MRCI, together with trade unions and other community organizations, came out against that cut because of how it disproportionally affected those in lower socioeconomic classes and migrant workers. Well, the good outcome was that the minimum wage cut was reversed last year, because we got the agreement by our current coalition partners in government that they would reverse the minimum wage cut when they got into power. That did happen.

But what also happened alongside the minimum wage cut was the dismantling of the Employment Regulation Orders, which had allowed certain sections such as restaurant workers, construction sectors, and the security sector to set their own minimum wage. So where the minimum wage was €8.65, then maybe the minimum wage for the restaurant industry might be €10. And all those different service minimum wages were developed through a complex system of trade union and collective bargaining and employee and employer participation. The government dismantled all those Employment Regulation Orders, so now the national minimum wage is €8.65 for everyone regardless of sector of employment. That did have a big impact on migrant workers, because they are concentrated in retail, construction, restaurant, and cleaning sectors. Some in those sectors have seen their pay cut from €12 an hour to €8.65. Even though government says it would be illegal to take a worker who was earning €12 an hour and reduce their salary to €8.65, the employers found ways of making people redundant and hiring new people at the new, lower salaries. Employers would find ways around the legislation to lower their costs.

This is part of a problem in which government is sending the wrong message by tackling the salaries of those earning the least in our society rather than protecting them. We need to find ways of promoting recovery based on higher contributions from those earning more; we should not focus on targeting those who earn less in our society. Or at least we need to share proportionately in the recovery of the economy.

JU: Your organization estimates that there are thirty thousand undocumented migrants living in Ireland. How has the Irish historical experience of being undocumented migrants shaped this conversation? I'm thinking particularly of the Irish memory of being part of that undocumented labor and domestic work sector.

PC: It definitely does. The experience of migration is very much alive in Ireland, both from the former experience of people going to the United Kingdom or the United States as laborers and domestic workers and from the new wave of Irish emigration now, as young people who are finishing school are leaving for Australia and New Zealand and Canada. So in the Irish psyche and the Irish public sphere people talk about emigration all the time. Our government goes every year to Washington, DC, to lobby the American government to introduce a solution for undocumented Irish in the United States. But at the same time, there is a level of hypocrisy from our government. They use the word "undocumented" for the Irish in America but use the world "illegal" for those migrants living here in Ireland.

It is a positive and a negative thing because there are politicians who are arguing that we cannot ask for benefits for Irish living abroad if we are not going to look at our own problem. But there are other people in politics, in the media, and just in layperson's terms who say that the American Irish have a different connection to Ireland than, let's say, a Chinese Irish or a Nigerian Irish has to China or Nigeria. So it's actually something that we use a lot—the Irish psyche of migration—in our work because the experience of every immigrant is the experience of being an emigrant. Every immigrant is an emigrant first.

JU: The MRCI has recently conducted research suggesting that ethnic profiling is being facilitated by the Irish state. Can you speak about that research and its reception?

PC: Ireland shares a common travel area with the United Kingdom, so there are no borders between Northern Ireland and the Republic as part of the Good Friday Agreement. So there is a need for easy movement. But what we have seen for the past five years is an increase in checks around the border area and in border counties, and this has also moved to the big cities like Dublin, where people randomly were being asked for identity documents. But the problem is that EU citizens are not obliged to carry the identity documents, so by definition those controls are illegal, as it gives the Garda the right to ethnically profile people. By the way they look, the Garda can say, "They are not Irish citizens; they are not EU citizens." An Irish citizen or an EU citizen can always say, "I don't have my identity document," and they will be fine—they cannot be prosecuted. But non-EU migrants always have to prove the fact that they are because of the way they look.

Before our report, there was a big case last year about a naturalized Irish citizen who was stopped in Dublin and was asked to provide documentation.[4] He said "I am an Irish citizen, and I don't have my

Irish passport here, but you can come with me to my house to get it, or I can have my wife bring it." He was not believed and was treated as if he was an undocumented migrant; he was arrested and detained for a number of hours. As a consequence of that particular case, there was a High Court challenge, and the High Court actually said that the current legislation that requires that non-EU migrants must carry legislation at all times is anticonstitutional. So now it is under review.

What we did in our report is that we researched the experience of going across borders by traveling across or going on trains to see whether certain migrant workers were being singled out. We are not saying that the state does not have a right to check identity, but these checks have to be systematic. It can't just be people of color, people with a certain look. The state has acknowledged the fact that there is a problem, but it still hasn't delivered a proper, structured solution to it. What is very sad is that nowadays we are no longer a country where people are arriving for three or five years and then leaving; we are now in the second generation of migrants—we have people who have done all of their schooling in Ireland, people who do not have another citizenship other than Irish citizenship—and they are still being treated as foreigners and made to go through the embarrassment of being singled out.

We need the government to give a proper response that acknowledges that Ireland is now a diverse country and that you can no longer define someone as Irish just because they are white or have freckles or they have a particular accent. Ireland is now a multiethnic and diverse country.

JU: You note that the number of migrants coming to Ireland has slowed. How do you see migrant workers in Ireland today in relation to the economic recovery?

PC: The numbers of migrants coming to Ireland has slowed. Even still, there are a number of people coming in relation to family reunification. The research has proven that migration is crucial for economic recovery; in order to promote recovery, jobs need to be created, and there is always a certain level of jobs that are filled by migrant workers, not by EU citizens or Irish workers.

But we are also saying that a way of helping the recovery is by regularizing the undocumented migrants. We estimate thirty thousand undocumented migrants. We could bring them into the taxation system by giving them documents and allowing them to pay taxes from their employment and contribute to the economy. According to a survey, over 60 percent of the undocumented workers have some form of employment either part-time or full-time. So this is a big loss for the government in that they are not collecting that tax. So we say that not only would a regularization program be self-sufficient, but it would also actually raise revenues for the state. Undocumented migrants have a big part to play in the recovery of Ireland.

JU: How do you see the role of the Migrant Rights Centre evolving in the future?

PC: The MRCI is now an organization that puts emphasis on campaigning for issues of social justice that affect certain sectors of migrant workers in Ireland.

The main difficulty for the MRCI at the moment is that funding for NGOs working in the area of migration and integration has been drastically reduced both from the state and from philanthropic organizations. One of our main challenges is fundraising to a level that allows us to sustain our work, because the issues are still there and in fact they evolve over time, so we cannot simply leave the sector.

As we look to the future, we are moving toward becoming more of a membership-led organization, one that operates more in conjunction with the people we help. We want to get the second generation of migrant workers more involved in the structure and in the decision-making portion of our work. This will partly solve the problem of resources. We are looking into becoming more of a membership-led organization within the next three years.

JU: How can people best help the Centre accomplish its goals?

PC: It's about talking about the issues and understanding the issues and about promoting a positive message about migration in Ireland and outside of Ireland. Try to know the facts and not victimize or stereotype the migrants or stigmatize them. Raise the positive perception of immigration to this country.

In addition, MRCI is in need of donations and funding to continue its work to promote justice, empowerment, and equality for migrant workers and their families. This support can be from large organizations interested in our work to solve root causes of problems facing migrants or individual donors assisting individual migrants. We would like people to acknowledge the positive impact of the work of the MRCI and stay engaged with what we are doing through our website, www.mrci.ie.

Migration doesn't only affect migrants because a migrant worker is also a child, an older person, a mother, a father. We want to make migrant issues an issue not just for migrants but for our society as a whole.

NOTES

1. See "Domestic Workers Speak Through Art," Migrant Rights Centre Ireland, www.mrci.ie/opening_doors, for more information about the "Blurred Boundaries" quilt project, along with other artistic projects including drama by Acting Out for Hope and Change, photographic exhibitions, and film projects.

2. See "Anger Over 'Diplomatic Immunity' in Embassy Employment Dispute," *Metro Éireann,* December 3, 2009; "Hidden Abuse of Diplomats' Domestics," *Irish Times,* November 27, 2010; "Filipino Diplomat Accused of Hiring Maid for Just €25," *Irish Independent,* February 5, 2011.

3. "Au Pairs 'Treated Like Slaves' as Job Market Dries Up," *Evening Herald* (Dublin), November 19, 2010.

4. See Jamie Smyth, "I Told Him I Was an Irish Citizen and Left My Passport at Home. He Didn't Believe Me," *Irish Times,* March 26, 2011.

CHAPTER THREE

(M)OTHER IRELAND

Migrant Women Subverting the Racial State?

RONIT LENTIN

PROLOGUE

Let me begin with two, seemingly unrelated stories. On July 23, 2004, a badly decomposed body, described by the media as that of "a black non-national woman," was discovered in a black plastic bag on a river bank in Kilkenny. Because she arrived as an asylum seeker in 2000 and, like all asylum seekers, had been fingerprinted, gardaí identified the body (by cross-checking her fingerprints through databases at the Garda National Immigration Bureau) as that of twenty-five-year-old Paiche Onyemaechi, a married mother of two.[1] She turned out to be the daughter of the Malawian chief justice, Leonard Unyolo, and a lap dancer and prostitute. She had gone missing two weeks before her headless body was found by a local woman walking her dog. According to media reports, Onyemaechi, exploited by the pimp she was working for, had seemingly decided to go it alone. After her brutal murder, other African prostitutes working in Ireland became frightened and were reportedly leaving Ireland for the relative safety of the United Kingdom. Within days of her murder, media representations of Onyemaechi shifted from "black body" to "headless hooker."[2]

Paiche Onyemaechi's is a typical gendered story of twenty-first-century global Ireland, standing at a crossroads between what was, during the economic boom of the late 1990s and early years of the new century, Ireland's globalized economy and contemporary migratory movements. Her story intersects with several elements of Ireland's migratory reality. First, as the daughter of an elite Malawian family, she left a state whose president built a three-hundred-room palace worth $100 million, even though Malawi is one of the world's poorest states, most of whose eleven million people survive on less than $1 a day, to seek asylum in Ireland.[3] Second, as the mother of two children born in Ireland, Onyemaechi had most probably exited the asylum process and applied for residency as the mother of Irish-citizen children. Third, finding herself working in Ireland's thriving sex industry, Onyemaechi, judging by media reports, most certainly found herself in a twilight zone of exploitation and danger. Finally, nothing much has been reported in the media about Paiche Onyemaechi's murder since 2004, in comparison to the wide media coverage of the trial of the husband of Irishwoman Rachel O'Reilly, whom he is accused of murdering in October 2004. Paiche Onyemaechi and her life, former *Irish Times* editor Conor Brady wrote in the *Village,* "were far removed from the experiences that are typical of modern Irish life. . . . She was an immigrant, an African . . . who was living in that darkened world that touches on illegality. . . . Whatever happened to her . . . has nothing to do with us."[4] To the contrary, her story says something profound about Irish identity in post–Celtic Tiger Ireland.

The second story may seem unrelated at first: On January 31, 2005, I appeared on the RTÉ 1 program *Questions and Answers,* together with Micheál Martin, then minister for enterprise and trade and now the leader of Fianna Fáil who was defeated in the 2011 elections. One of the topics discussed was the supposedly high number of pregnant migrant women having babies in Ireland in order to gain citizenship for their children and residency rights for themselves. The minister argued that "many" migrant women were presenting at the last stages of pregnancy, putting pressure on the maternity hospitals. I challenged him to say how many was "many"—to which he had no answer.

During the commercial break, the minister told me off air that he "knew" of a Nigerian woman who gave birth to quintuplets and who "had the first one in Nigeria and hopped on a plane to have the other four in Ireland." When I challenged Martin, a former minister for health and children, about this utterly illogical scenario, he said that he believed that indeed "airlines should not let these women on the plane."

The story related to me by Martin was only one of many urban legends circulating in Ireland in relation to asylum seekers who, according to rumors, were receiving money for drink, large cars, and luxury apartments. Taken together, these two stories illustrate not only the extent of spin engaged in by state actors anxious to justify holding, and winning, the 2004 Citizenship Referendum, but also the profoundly gendered nature of the Irish debates about immigration.

INTRODUCTION

In June 2004 the Irish government held a referendum on citizenship, in which nearly 80 percent of the electorate voted in favor of rescinding the right to birthright citizenship for all children born in the island of Ireland, a right that had been in existence since the establishment of the Free State in 1922, and limiting citizenship only to children born in Ireland who have one parent who is a citizen or is entitled to citizenship. The government of the Republic based its argument in favor of the Citizenship Referendum on the claim that migrant women were allegedly coming to Ireland to give birth to Irish citizens and thereby gain residency rights for themselves and their partners. The referendum came after the 2003 "Irish-born child" Supreme Court ruling, which withdrew the process by which migrant parents had the right to apply to remain in Ireland to give "care and company" to their citizen children.

This chapter has two parts. In the first theoretical part, I argue that the Irish state has created what Giorgio Agamben calls a "state of exception,"[5] in which state racism combines with what Michel Foucault calls "biopolitics,"[6] in a contemporary move from institutional to constitutional racism.[7] My main argument is that state racism assumes gendered forms and that women migrants are specifically targeted by the state through their mothering role. Putting this in a wider context, while childbearing (Irish) women have always been central to articulations of nation, the 2004 Citizenship Referendum shifted the argument from "Irish" (m)others to "nonnational" (m)others as subverting certainties of nation, state, and citizenship. Mothering always has a component of othering, hence my use of parentheses when discussing migrant (m)others.

The second, more empirical part is based on my research with migrant women's networks, which, within a short time, have become beacons of civil participation and migrants' active agency. Here I question whether migrant women's nascent networking activities in post-Referendum Ireland work to resist and extend the boundaries of intercultural Ireland's narrow articulations of race, gender, citizenship, and nation, and offer both a new dimension of gender equality struggles and a new challenge for Irish feminism, which has thus far failed to stand up to the racial state in support of migrant women. In their effort to integrate their members into Irish society in conjuncture with the state's integrationist policies, do such networks in fact reaffirm those very boundaries? Indeed, since the onset of the recession, despite their avowed success in providing migrant women with a public forum to address their issues, migrant women's and other migrant-led associations are finding that the space available to them is increasingly shrinking.[8]

THE REPUBLIC OF IRELAND:
RACIAL STATE OF EXCEPTION?

The Italian political philosopher Giorgio Agamben draws on the Foucauldian concepts of biopower and biopolitics to develop an argument about the tendency of modern nation-states to withdraw legal rights and protection from citizens and noncitizens alike. Foucault's argument in *Society Must Be Defended* (1975–76) is that whereas the premodern sovereign addressed his power to killing unwanted people, the modern state's biopower is addressed to living beings and, more specifically, to their mass as population. According to Foucault, there is a difference between the sovereign power of the old territorial state ("to make die and let live") and modern biopower ("to make live and let die"). If the old order exerted the right to kill, the new biopower aims to make the care of *life* the concern of state power, exercised by governmental technologies such as the hospital, the psychiatric clinic, the prison, and—I would add—the refugee camp, refugee hostel, and direct provision center. The duty to defend society from itself (often articulated as the need to defend the *body* of the nation, as well as the state, from its immigrant and indigenous others) means that the modern nation-state can scarcely function without racism. Rather than serving one group against another, race, Foucault argues, becomes a tool of state conservatism, a racism that society practices against itself.

Developing Foucault's ideas, Agamben insists that while biopower may be more marked in modern nation-states, theorized, each in its own way, by David Theo Goldberg's "racial states," it has always existed as part of sovereignty.[9] Although like Foucault, he sees biopower peak in Nazism's concentration and extermination camps, Agamben updates the concept to the twenty-first century in relation to refugees in detention camps and reception centers and "unlawful" combatants in places such as Guantanamo Bay, Cuba. In each of these spaces, "zones of exception" are formed where, like in the Nazi camps, inmates exist in a zone of indistinction, both at the mercy of sovereign power and outside the protection of the law. This circular logic means, according to Agamben, that in our age "the state of exception comes more and more to the foreground as the fundamental political structure and ultimately begins to become the rule."[10] Increasingly in states of exception, the application of the law is suspended, and different categories of people are reduced to what Agamben calls "bare life"— the Roman legal category of *homo sacer* (sacred man—he who can be killed at the sovereign's whim yet cannot be sacrificed). While the concepts of "biopower" and "biopolitics" and "state of exception" are still evolving and remain contested, they meet the core theoretical challenges of understanding contemporary racism and its relationship to globalization and the state, as they posit a fundamental connection between racism and nation-state biopolitics.

In the wake of the Citizenship Referendum, like all modern nation-states, though in a specific form, the Republic of Ireland must be theorized as a racial state. According to Goldberg, racial states, each in their own way, exclude in order to construct homogeneity (which is always "heterogeneity in denial"), while appropriating difference through celebrations of the multicultural.[11] The racial state is a *state of power,* asserting its control over those within the state and excluding others from entering its borders or from access to citizenship. Through seemingly innocuous mechanisms such as constitutions, the law, border controls, policy making, bureaucracy, and census categorizations, but also invented histories and traditions, modern nation-states are defined in terms of their power to exclude and include in racially ordered terms.

Goldberg outlines two traditions of thinking about racial states. The first, which he calls naturalism, fixes racially conceived "natives" as premodern and naturally incapable of progress. The second, which he calls historicism, elevates Europeans over primitive or underdeveloped others as a victory of Western progress.[12] Understood as the space of white men of property, the racial state's historicist progressivism aims to assist, through amalgamation and assimilation, its racial others to undo their uncivilized conditions. But beneath its liberalism, historicism camouflages racism and is ultimately about the ordering zeal of modernity. Goldberg makes a specific reference to the law. As a technology of racial rule, it is central to modern nation-state formation, promoting ethno-racial categorization and identification, charting national identities through legislating on immigration controls and citizenship rights, shaping race in legal terms, and threading it into the fabric of the social.[13]

However, as Robbie McVeigh and I argue, theorizing the Republic of Ireland as a racial state must be firmly embedded in a global context.[14] New formations of transnational capital, new patterns of migrant labor, a whole new variant of European racism focused on asylum seekers and migrants, as well as the new, supposedly benign imperialism of the War on Terror have immediate implications for how we make sense of racism in Ireland. The Republic of Ireland's exponential economic growth at the turn of the twenty-first century has led to its restructuring as an exclusive racist state where, despite the recent downturn in the economy, labor migrants were articulated as crucial to ensuring "our" continuing economic growth, while asylum seekers are increasingly prevented from landing to present their applications,[15] and where citizenship parameters are being redefined to suit the state's purpose.

In 2004, having (temporarily) closed the route to residency of migrant parents of Irish-citizen children, the Irish government held the referendum aimed at making *jus sanguinis* (blood-based citizenship) the principle on which children born in Ireland are entitled to automatic citizenship (overturning eighty-three years of *jus soli* or soil-based citizenship entitlement, in place since the establishment of the Free State in 1922). The Referendum's main rationale—couched in the persuasive discourse of defending the integrity of Irish citizenship— was that Ireland's citizenship laws were being exploited, since they were superior to the other twenty-four EU member states. The government also employed the case of Mrs. Chen, a Chinese national residing in the UK who gave birth to her child in Northern Ireland and who won a European Court recommendation to be allowed to reside in Britain having had an Irish-citizen child, as further justification for the need to defend Irish citizenship from abuse.[16] The Referendum provides a starting, or turning, point for analyzing the Republic of Ireland as a racial state, moving the analysis from institutional racism to constitutional racism, and to racism without major racist organizations. The situation in which the state declares itself antiracist while enacting increasingly draconian immigration legislation leads to "racism without racism."[17] Rather than being generated by individual or institutional prejudice, racism in post–Celtic Tiger Ireland is absorbed into the very structure of the liberal state.

(IRISH) WOMAN AND NATION

Compelling as Agamben's theorization of the state of exception is, it is surprising that he does not gender his theorization of either the state of exception or "bare life." My work on women Holocaust survivors extended Agamben's concept of *homo sacer* to theorize the female *femina sacra*—she whose life, sexuality, and productivity stand at the mercy of the sovereign power of the racial state.[18] The key point is that these categories remain not only racialized but also inescapably gendered.

Hannah Arendt argued that in the system of nation-states, the so-called sacred and inalienable rights of man (*sic*) ultimately lack protection at the moment in which they no longer take the form of rights of citizens.[19] The term "nation," Agamben also reminds us, derives from *nascere* (to be born).[20] Therefore the passage from divinely authorized royal sovereignty to national sovereignty means that in the transformation of "subject" into "citizen," birth—or bare, natural life as such—becomes for the first time the immediate bearer of sovereignty. This also entails the passage from *jus soli* (birth in a certain territory) to *jus sanguinis* (blood-based birth to citizen parents), hence the centrality, but also the ambiguity, of the notion of citizenship in modern political thought.[21] This very passage from *jus soli* to *jus sanguinis* citizenship was the main consequence of the 2004 Citizenship Referendum, bringing Ireland firmly into the family of racial states where full rights are reserved only for blood-based citizens.

My argument is that these transformations have deep, gendered meanings. As the producers of future generations, and the symbolic tropes of nations,[22] women are marked and controlled differently from men, despite universal claims to gender equality. As the nation-state makes nativity the foundation of its sovereignty, when women step outside ethno-national or moral boundaries (and because they are the producers of "racially undesirable" others), they are often banned as impure and transgressive.[23] This was clearly illustrated by the positioning of childbearing migrant women in the lead up to the Citizenship Referendum in what became known as the "Irish-born child" controversy.

While the Irish debates on immigrants' citizenship and residency rights occasioned by increased immigration obscured the fact that *jus soli* citizenship right was not merely a consequence of the 1998 constitutional amendment of Article 2 as part of the Good Friday Agreement (GFA), the GFA amendment also meant, as was ruled in the 1990 Fajujonu Supreme Court case, that migrant parents of children born in Ireland, who were thus Irish citizens, had a claim to residency in Ireland to provide "care and company" to their citizen children. This ruling, which resulted in several thousands of migrant parents gaining residency rights, was overturned in 2003, when the Supreme Court ruled in the Lobe and Osayande appeal that nonnational parents no longer had a strong case to be allowed to remain in Ireland to bring up their children.[24] The Lobe and Osayande case involved two families of Czech Roma and Nigerian origin respectively, against whom deportation orders had been made. While the parents claimed that their decision to remain residents was in their children's best interest, the Supreme Court ruling privileged the state's right to deport and the "integrity of the asylum process" over these citizen children's rights.[25] The ruling illustrated Agamben's argument that refugees (or in this instance, migrant parents of Irish-citizen children) form an unstable category between "man" and "citizen." In this sense, the refugee (or the migrant parent) "is truly the 'man of rights' . . . the first and only real appearance of rights outside the fiction of the citizen that always covers them over. Yet this is precisely what makes the figure of the refugee so hard to define politically."[26]

The Irish media debates following the 2003 Supreme Court ruling exposed a contradiction between nationality and citizenship. The *jus sanguinis*–based rights to Irish citizenship allows up to third-generation Irish emigrants to claim Irish citizenship, while at the same time, the state was contesting the *jus soli* citizenship rights accorded to children of migrants and consolidated by the GFA insertion of Article 2 into the constitution.

"Nonnational" women (a euphemism for migrants from countries outside the European Economic Area[27]) became central to the public debates surrounding both the Irish-citizen children crisis and the Citizenship Referendum, and thus signified new gendered racial configurations of global Ireland. These debates illustrate not only orchestrated moral panics about "floods of refugees," but also the positioning of sexually active migrant women as a danger to the state and the nation, a long-standing claim made in relation to sexually active

Irish (m)others having children out of wedlock. As Zygmunt Bau-man[28] reminds us, birth is usually the only natural, no-questions-asked entry into the nation; yet by securing a victory in a referendum aimed at outlawing birthright citizenship for the children of migrant (m)oth-ers, the Irish state has broken this link between birth and nation. At the same time, representations of "woman" and "nation" in Ireland have been historically intertwined, with Ireland represented as Dark Rosaleen and Cathleen ni Houlihan, and with (Irish) women seen as securing the common good through their maternal roles and their "life within the home," as articulated in Article 41.1 of the Constitution.[29]

By contrast, in the Citizenship Referendum debates, nonnational (m)others were othered and posited by the state as subverting the na-tion and the common good by (m)othering the next generations of Irish citizens. Thus political and media debates regarding migrant parents of Irish children and the Citizenship Referendum were not only racialized but also profoundly gendered (as the stories recounted in the prologue demonstrate). Media accounts describing migrant (m)others as being pregnant on arrival, and arriving in Ireland with-out booking a maternity hospital place, positioned them as central to the racial configuration of the Irish state.[30] Furthermore, the govern-ment accused migrant (m)others of "flooding" Dublin's maternity hospitals, an accusation that demonstrates clearly what Etienne Bali-bar calls "crisis racism."[31] In the context of the Citizenship Referen-dum, this assumed gendered meanings, putting the blame for the Re-public of Ireland's overburdened and understaffed maternity services on migrant (m)others, allegedly all arriving at the last moment to have children-citizens in Ireland (even though the actual figures do not sup-port such accusation). Indeed, according to Dervla King, despite gov-ernment claims, no comprehensive figures were produced by Dublin maternity hospitals on the residency status of the women who pre-sented for delivery.[32] King stressed that women giving birth in Dublin's maternity hospitals were not all migrants, and even when they were, she noted the heterogeneity of immigrants into Ireland having babies in Ireland, including returning Irish emigrants, EU nationals, labor migrants, asylum seekers, refugees with status, students, and spouses of non-EU nationals.

The racial state initially used the maternity discourse to tighten Irish citizenship laws, even though the directors of Dublin's maternity hospitals firmly denied claims by former minister for justice Michael McDowell that they had "pleaded with him to change the law on the citizenship issue."[33] However, the argument later shifted as the minister admitted the maternity crisis was a "side issue" and that the real issue was "the integrity of the Irish citizenship law."[34] Thus migrant (m)others were scapegoated by the racial state as subverting the integrity of Ireland's citizenship laws, even though the minister admitted that the increasing numbers of nonnational births were a symptom rather than the root cause.

Foucault argues that biopower's control of populations means that the nation is conceived as a "body" and that state power becomes essential to the "life" of the nation (this explains the utility of genocide in getting rid of "lives unworthy of living" in order to protect the *body* of the *volk*). This resonates with Nira Yuval-Davis's argument that as the nation is invested in women carrying the burden of its representation, women's bodies demarcate the symbolic and material boundaries of national, ethnic, and religious collectivities, while also being the sites for contesting these boundaries.[35]

Developing this argument, Eithne Luibhéid argues that discourses and practices that target childbearing, asylum-seeking women have provided the Irish government with a way of reconstituting the Republic as a sovereign space while also generating new modes of racialization and racial hierarchies.[36] Not only do migrant (m)others, as Luibhéid argues, "re-nationalize the nation," they also reconstruct Irish heterosexuality, precisely when it has been deconstructed following the decriminalization of homosexuality and in relation to the current debates on partnership rights of nonheterosexual partners.[37]

At this point it is worth remembering that positioning nonnational (m)others as *intentionally* mothering the next generation of Irish citizens continues the insidious positioning of sexually active Irish women as a danger to themselves, to men, and to the nation and as subverting traditional constructions of Irishness. As the *Irish Times* columnist Fintan O'Toole argues,[38] stigmatizing nonnational mothers continues a two-hundred-year old tradition of policing unwed Irish (m)others by incarcerating them in Magdalene Laundries, where they were silenced and enslaved by church and state powers that "had long been the focus of suppressed Irish national identity," and whose moral authority in relation to everything to do with morality, sex, and the family had been tacitly accepted by successive Irish governments.[39]

Moreover, focusing state attention on female reproduction is even more insidious, having long been part of the history of the Irish state. Ailbhe Smyth, writing about the constitutional prohibition on abortion in relation to the 1992 X Case, called Ireland "a police state," where women with unwanted pregnancies were forced to seek abortions in another jurisdiction.[40] Nonnational (m)others, whose bodies destabilize the nation's boundaries through giving birth to future Irish generations, are specifically targeted by the racial state when the boundaries of who is entitled to reside in its territory are at issue.

The debates relating to Irish-citizen children and the Citizenship Referendum featured both deep gendering and a disavowal of racial harassment, assuming Irish whiteness as unproblematic. Fintan O'Toole was the only media commentator to insist that the 2003 Supreme Court ruling was underpinned by racism, arguing that while Irish citizenship can pass from one generation to another if the person is white, even if not residing in Ireland, it does not apply "in those foreign countries that we see as somehow not part of 'us.'"[41]

Having laid the theoretical foundations, I now move the discussion forward in time, describing how women migrants' own activities both respond to their post-Referendum racialization and provide new opportunities for gendered struggles. I also ask whether migrant women's networking activities subvert or reaffirm intercultural Ireland.

FROM "IRISH-BORN CHILDREN"
TO MIGRANT WOMEN'S NETWORKS

In July 2003, when African migrant (m)others of Irish-citizen children started receiving deportation letters, Salome Mbugua, national coordinator of AkiDwA—the African Women's Network—contacted me.

Together we founded the Coalition Against Deportations of Irish Children (CADIC). CADIC campaigned for nearly two years, during which the minister for justice, equality, and law reform consistently refused to consider any en masse regularization of the residency rights of migrant parents of Irish-citizen children. The state categorized these Irish-citizen children of migrant parents as "Irish-born children," thus racially differentiating them from all other children born in Ireland.[42] The 2003 ruling had made 11,500 migrant parents candidates for deportation. Among the 341 people actually deported, there were 20 Irish-citizen children who were made to leave Ireland with their deported parents.

However, on January 15, 2005, six months after the Citizenship Referendum was passed with a substantial majority, the minister reversed the ruling according to which migrant parents of citizen children were not allowed to apply for residency, and announced details of new administrative arrangements for parents of Irish citizens born before January 2005 to apply for residency. By June 15, 2005, 17,877 applications were received, the majority of which were granted. The Department of Justice, however, ruled against family reunification rights for these migrant parents, and CADIC continued to campaign, contending that "the right to family life of Irish citizen children is a right protected by the Irish Constitution and the European Convention on Human Rights and Fundamental Freedoms" and insisting that "that there cannot be a blanket refusal of family reunification and that the circumstances of each individual case must be taken into account when a decision on family reunification is made."[43]

AkiDwA's initiative, activated through networking with several Irish and migrant nongovernmental organizations (NGOs), brought about the subversion of the racial state's intent to redefine the boundaries of Irish citizenship and residency rights.[44] However, AkiDwA's central role in CADIC's success has been largely written out of the history of this particular campaign, seen as led by Irish-led NGOs such as the Children's Rights Alliance and the Irish Council of Civil Liberties. Reminiscent of the writing out of history of the participation of women in the Irish national struggle until the advent of feminist historiography, this chapter redresses this omission.[45]

As more women migrate, increasing numbers are establishing their own gendered migrant associations and networks, transferring skills and resources and transforming notions of appropriate gender behavior.[46] Migrant networks can consolidate ties and nodes, and while networks are often fluid forms of social association,[47] some migrant women's networks become structured organizations that support migrant women globally. The contradiction between the relative invisibility of women in migration studies and their hypervisibility on city streets and in relation to state policies owes its existence to the household remaining a central unit of analysis, even though it is only one piece in a complex jigsaw puzzle. Saskia Sassen posits the "feminization of survival," which means that women increasingly migrate as independent agents.[48] Furthermore, with the increasing entry of Western women into the labor market, the "care deficit" in relation to domestic and care work tends to be bridged by economically active migrant women from developing countries across continental divides. The burden of caring for the household and family members is thus transferred from Western women to migrant women.[49] While the feminization of migration sustains the flows of migrant women, migration also facilitates migrant women's connection with loved ones and compensates for the absence of family support networks by creating alternative networks in their countries of settlement.[50] Because women often send home a greater proportion of their income as remittances,[51] and because they are often more inclined to invest in alternative networks, migrant women's networking is much more than an attractive metaphor in describing transnational migrant associations. Indeed— perhaps due to their premigration activities with development organizations in their countries of origin—the term "network" is often retained by women migrants' diasporic associations.

AkiDwA was founded in 2001 by a group of seven African women. AkiDwA's activities have included support and information for African and other migrant women, awareness raising, education and training, combating gender-based violence; influencing state and local authority policy, organizing cultural events, and extensive networking with other migrant women's networks in Ireland and abroad and with officials from the state and NGOs. In the Irish context Aki-DwA defines itself as a network of networks, linking with regional and local networks of African women throughout Ireland. AkiDwA also published *Herstory,* ten stories of women migrating, and commissioned research on the experience of African women in the Irish labor market and on gender-based violence.[52] Throughout its short history, AkiDwA has built alliances with diverse groups of women, both migrant and native, to mobilize on particular issues. The intersection of gender and race underpins the group's rationale for coming together: members do not want to be spoken for by either white women or African men (as expressed by AkiDwA's mission statement).

AkiDwA's national director, Salome Mbugua, describes her vision (emphasis added): "My vision for AkiDwA . . . as we are working on the networking, we are letting people know about AkiDwA, and we are saying that it's mainly about *women speaking out about issues that are affecting them.* . . . My vision is to see AkiDwA having a women's centre. . . . My hope is also that *the issue of migrant women will be more visible in the Irish system.* Because at the moment, it's still very invisible."[53] In many ways, Mbugua's vision has been realized, as both she and AkiDwA have raised the visibility of migrant women considerably. Mbugua herself serves or has served on the boards of several state bodies, including the Equality Authority and the Task Force on Integration. AkiDwA's membership list has 2,250 individual members from over thirty-five countries and thirty-two affiliate organizations. AkiDwA is also working with migrant and Irish NGOs on issues of asylum, migration, health, gender-based violence, female genital mutilation, employment and housing rights, education, and advocacy.

Some migrant women engage in transnational family and community networking with kith and kin in their home countries. For instance, many Filipino domestic workers leave their children in the care of family members and send money home to maintain their families.[54] The networking activities in Ireland of migrant women like these are often based on older gendered practices of face-to-face interaction, creating bottom-up "webs of dialogue" aimed at alleviating the pain of migration.[55] Face-to-face networking as practiced by migrant women's networks in Ireland, such as AkiDwA, is not so different from older forms of women's networking through narratives and practices of mutual assistance, evident in Jewish women organizing in community-oriented networks or Italian migrant women, who play a major role in keeping alive family relations in the diaspora.[56] As Carla De Tona documents, migrant women are often better informed than men about what's going on in their families; for example, Italian migrant women's informal connectivity spreads from Ireland to Italy and to other countries where relatives and friends have migrated, creating informal, gendered transnational networks.

New transnational networks of migrant women operating in twenty-first-century Ireland signal networking processes beyond and across the home country / new country trajectory, as new transnational spaces of cross-national boundary alliances, some based on occupational status (i.e., the network of women domestic workers, or international nurses' associations) and others based on a joint origin (i.e., AkiDwA, which privileges Africa as its members' common origin above their national and ethnic identities). Although new forms of migration—labor, asylum, and other—have been shaping the reracialization of Irishness in new ways, another factor, until the onset of the recession, was a racial state determined to construct an integration policy and declare its intercultural intentions while at the same time restricting immigration.

Although most migrant-led networks were and still are seriously underfunded and underrepresented, they have taken part in conversations on needs, discrimination, rights, and entitlements through involvement in a variety of state and NGO fora. Thus, on the one hand, old, informal networking processes, like those engaged in by older groups of migrants in Ireland, did not become part of the integration and intercultural conversations. On the other hand, newer, perforce more formal networking processes, like networks of domestic women migrants (facilitated through the Migrants Rights Centre Ireland) and of African women migrants, were supported by the "intercultural industry" through state, church, and NGO integrationism. These newer groups were brought into conversations about citizenship status, labor entitlements, and more "female" concerns, such as gender-based violence, female genital mutilation, sex discrimination, sex trafficking, and the connections among migration, marriage, and family reunification (as campaigned for by CADIC).

The question I pose here is whether these networks succeeded in subverting the racial state—like in AkiDwA's initiative in relation to migrant parents of Irish-citizen children, which brought about the establishment of CADIC and eventually, once the Citizenship Referendum was passed, the overturning of the Supreme Court ruling. Do these networks, in their emphasis on *integrating* members into Ireland's ever-changing ethnoracial migratory reality, in fact reaffirm the racial state's biopower, assisting it in claiming its commitment to racelessness? As Goldberg argues, this commitment grows out of the modern state's self-promotion in the name of rationality and the recognition of ethnoracially heterogeneous states.[57] Through their involvement with actual networking processes as well as their integration into coalitions, alliances, and organizations in Ireland and beyond, key network organizers, such as AkiDwA's Salome Mbugua, helped their networks mature and also facilitated their co-option into the new spaces of integration and diversity as determined by the racial state.

CONCLUSION: LISBON AND BEYOND?

The 2004 Citizenship Referendum enabled a new racialization of Irishness through, among other things, targeting migrant (m)others. While immigration remains a feature of post–Celtic Tiger Ireland, its components are changing to adapt to the Republic's evolving economic circumstances. Although the 2006 census identified 419,733 people, or 10 percent of the population, who defined themselves as non-Irish, the economic downturn meant fewer work permits being granted, a drop in the number of migrants from Eastern Europe registering for work, and a rise in the number of immigrants signing up for unemployment benefits.[58]

Since the mid-1990s the Irish state has referred to refugees, asylum seekers, and migrants as a "problem," using terms such as "bogus refugees" and "illegal immigrants," and claiming that asylum seekers were falsifying their claims. But while immigrants are often blamed for Ireland's social and economic problems, from overcrowded maternity hospitals to the current downturn in the economy, foreign nationals continue to be most affected by job losses since the recession. Of the 64,500 people who lost employment between the final quarters of 2010 and 2009, 35,000 were foreign nationals.[59] Despite this, and given that in 2010–11 some 9,000 migrants were refused welfare benefits even though many live in dire poverty,[60] some Irish people continue to blame migrants for the failings of Irish state and society.

I want to conclude by teasing out some gender implications of Ireland's immigration and integration policies. One development with serious gender implications was the prohibition on EU citizens married to non-EEA citizens from residing in Ireland. In 2007 the European Commission investigated the decision by the Department of Justice, Equality and Law Reform (DJELR) to deport thousands of non-EU spouses of EEA citizens, insisting that these couples reside first in the EEA spouse's own country—this despite an EU directive that states that non-EU family members of EU citizens should automatically be permitted to work and live in the European Union.[61] This decision—which, according to the DJELR, aimed to rule out child marriages and marriages of convenience—epitomized the post–Citizenship Referendum era in Ireland, when intercultural Ireland disavowed racism and promoted integration, and at the same time restricted in-migration to include only those migrants it needed in order to maintain a certain way of life, spoke the language of racelessness, denied racism, and reproduced "racism without racism."

In 2008, the European Court of Justice upheld the rights of EU citizens and their non-EU spouses who wish to live together in Ireland by forcing the Irish government to reverse this measure and ruling that Irish legislation must implement the relevant EU directive on the rights of EU citizens and their family members to move and reside freely within the EU. The result of this reversal of fortunes means that the 1,500 people who have sought information and support from the Immigrant Council of Ireland will now be able to live together in Ireland, without having to move first to another EU-member state.[62] This EU ruling, however, did not fully rule out "marriages of convenience," with interesting gender implications. In 2010 the fact that some 15 percent of all civil marriages are sham marriages was exposed. Most of the suspected sham marriages are between Eastern European women—mainly from Latvia and Lithuania—and men from Pakistan, Bangladesh, and India. The men seek residency rights through marriage to EU citizens, and they are willing to pay the women several thousand euros.[63] Thus poor migrant women from Eastern Europe, whom the state cannot protect, are exploited by men who desire European residency rights.

Post-Referendum measures, and in particular developments since the onset of the recession, have serious implications for migrant women. In 2008, AkiDwA spearheaded a submission to the Dáil Joint Committee on Justice, Equality, Defence and Women's Rights on the gender implications of the proposed Immigration, Residency and Protection Bill. The submission notes the absence of gender considerations in relation to asylum and protection and highlights the need to establish clear gender-related guidelines for all the processes relating to the adjudication of female asylum and protection claims, with particular reference to female genital mutilation and gender-based violence, which are specific sources of trauma for women seeking asylum.[64] In the current recessionary climate, in which immigration is debated (if at all) largely in terms of economics and even the minister in charge of integration expressed a hope that the economic downturn will mean that immigration will become "more manageable," AkiDwA's initiative seems crucial in reminding us that immigrants are not merely economic units but also gendered and raced human beings. In theory, AkiDwA's initiatives had the potential to become a focal point for a campaign around the redefinition of both Irishness and (m)otherhood. However, although the initiative dates back to 2008, the bill was not introduced by the Fianna Fáil–Green coalition, which lost the elections to a Fine Gael–Labour coalition in February 2011, as immigration, interculturalism, and integration have largely been erased from Irish public political culture.

NOTES

1. Conor Lally and Ralth Tenthani, "Murder Victim Is Malawian Judge's Daughter," *Irish Times,* July 30, 2004; "Mourners at Funeral Told Not to Listen to Rumours," *Irish Times,* July 31, 2004.

2. Eamon Dillon, "Hooker Buried with No Head," *Sunday World* (Dublin), August 1, 2004; see also Ronit Lentin, "Black Bodies and 'Headless Hookers': Alternative Global Narratives for 21st Century Ireland," *Irish Review* 33 (2005): 1–12; Ronit Lentin and Robbie McVeigh, *After Optimism? Ireland, Racism and Globalisation* (Dublin: Metro Éireann, 2006), 97.

3. "President of Malawi Moves to $100 Million Palatial Residence," *Irish Times,* December 23, 2004.

4. Conor Brady, "Some Deaths Don't Sell Newspapers," *Village,* November 13–19, 2004, 46.

5. Giorgio Agamben, *State of Exception,* trans. Kevin Attell (Chicago: Chicago University Press, 2005).

6. Michel Foucault, *Society Must Be Defended: Lectures at the Collège de France, 1975–76* (London: Allen Lane, 2003).

7. As argued by Lentin and McVeigh, *After Optimism?*.

8. See Ronit Lentin and Elena Moreo, eds., *Migrant Activism and Integration from Below in Ireland,* Migration, Diasporas and Citizenship (Basingstoke, UK: Palgrave Macmillan, 2012).

9. David Theo Goldberg, *The Racial State* (Malden, MA: Blackwell, 2002).

10. Giorgio Agamben, *Homo Sacer: Sovereign Power and Bare Life* (Stanford, CA: Stanford University Press, 1995), 10.

11. Goldberg, *Racial State,* 16.

12. Ibid., 43. See also Sinéad Ní Shuinéar, "Othering the Irish (Traveller)," in *Racism and Anti-Racism in Ireland,* ed. Ronit Lentin and Robbie McVeigh (Belfast: Beyond the Pale Publications, 2002), and Lentin and McVeigh, *After Optimism?*, 11, for a discussion of racial naturalism and historicism in the Irish context.

13. Goldberg, *Racial State,* 141–47.

14. Lentin and McVeigh, *After Optimism?*; Goldberg, *Racial State,* 92–93. And, as McVeigh argues, Northern Ireland is a "racial statelet" (Lentin and McVeigh, *After Optimism?*, 145–63).

15. Mark Kelly, *Immigration-Related Detention in Ireland: A Research Report for the Irish Refugee Council, Irish Penal Reform Trust and Immigrant Council of Ireland* (Dublin: Human Rights Consultants, 2005).

16. Ivana Bacik, "An Assessment of the Chen Opinion by the Advocate General in the European Court of Justice," in *Challenging the Myths* (Dublin:

The Labour Party, 2004); Lentin and McVeigh, *After Optimism?*, 54. It is worth emphasizing, however, that in Mrs. Chen's case there were no resource implications for the Republic, but rather for the British state, illustrating yet again, Ireland's clientalist obligations toward the integrity of racist immigration and citizenship policies in Britain and the European Union (Lentin and McVeigh, *After Optimism?*, 55).

17. Lentin and McVeigh, *After Optimism?*, 164.

18. Ronit Lentin, "*Femina Sacra*: Gendered Memory and Political Violence," *Women's Studies International Forum* 29, no. 5 (2006): 463–73.

19. Agamben, *Homo Sacer*, 126.

20. Ibid., 128.

21. Ibid., 128–29.

22. Nira Yuval-Davis and Floya Anthias, "Introduction," in *Woman-Nation-State*, ed. Nira Yuval-Davis and Floya Anthias (Hampshire, UK: Macmillan, 1989).

23. Nira Yuval-Davis, *Gender and Nation* (London: Sage, 1997).

24. John Maddock and Charles Mallon, "10,000 Parents of Irish Babies to Be Deported," *Evening Herald* (Dublin), January, 23, 2003.

25. Siobhán Mullally, "Defining the Limits of Citizenship: Children, Family Life and the *Jus Soli* Principle in Irish Law," unpublished paper, distributed by CADIC, 2003; Ronit Lentin, "Illegals in Ireland, Irish Illegals: Diaspora Nation as Racial State," *Irish Political Studies* 22, no. 4 (2007): 433–53.

26. Agamben, *Homo Sacer*, 131.

27. The EEA comprises the twenty-seven members of the European Union plus Iceland, Liechtenstein, and Norway. Defining migrants from outside the EEA zone as "nonnational" extends the remit of the "national" in a rather bizarre way.

28. Zygmunt Bauman, *Liquid Love: On the Frailty of Human Bonds* (Cambridge: Polity, 2003).

29. For further discussion of the link between Irish woman and nation, see Ronit Lentin, "'Irishness': The 1937 Constitution and Women: A Gender and Ethnicity View," *Irish Journal of Sociology* 8 (1998): 5–24, on the gendering of the Irish constitution; Gerardine Meaney, "Sex and Nation: Women in Irish Culture and Politics," in *Irish Women's Studies Reader*, ed. Ailbhe Smyth (Dublin: Attic, 1993), on women in Irish culture; and Helen Robinson, "Becoming Women: Irigaray, Ireland and Visual Representation," in *Art, Nation and Gender: Ethnic Landscapes, Myths, and Mother-Figures*, ed. Tricia Cusack and Síghle Bhreathnach-Lynch (Aldershot, UK: Ashgate, 2003), on Ireland, women, and visual representation.

30. Gemma Doherty, "The Right to Citizenship," *Irish Independent*, January 23, 2003; Ronit Lentin, "Pregnant Silence: (En)gendering Ireland's Asylum

Space," *Patterns of Prejudice* 37, no. 3 (2003): 301–22; Ronit Lentin, "Strangers and Strollers: Feminist Notes on Researching Migrant M/others," *Women's Studies International Forum* 27, no. 4 (2004): 301–14; Lentin, "Black Bodies."

31. Etienne Balibar, "Racism and Crisis," in *Race, Nation, Class: Ambiguous Identities,* ed. Etienne Balibar and Immanuel Wallerstein (London: Verso, 1991), 217–18.

32. Dervla King, *Immigration and Citizenship in Ireland* (Dublin: The Children's Rights Alliance, 2004).

33. Liam Reid, "Masters Deny Seeking Change of Status on Non-nationals," *Irish Times,* March 13, 2004.

34. Mark Brennock, "McDowell Changes Argument on Referendum," *Irish Times,* April 9, 2004.

35. Yuval-Davis, *Gender and Nation,* 45–46.

36. Eithne Luibhéid, "Childbearing Against the State? Asylum Seeker Women in the Irish Republic," *Women's Studies International Forum* 27, no. 4 (2004): 335–50.

37. Lentin and McVeigh, *After Optimism?,* 108.

38. Fintan O'Toole, "The Sisters of No Mercy," *Observer* (London), February 16, 2003.

39. Fintan O'Toole, "Law with a Dangerous Edge of Racism," *Irish Times,* January 24, 2003.

40. Ailbhe Smyth, "The Politics of Abortion in a Police State," in *The Abortion Papers, Ireland,* ed. Ailbhe Smyth (Dublin: Attic, 1992).

41. O'Toole, "Law with a Dangerous Edge."

42. The unit dealing with residency rights for migrant parents of Irish-citizen children was given the acronym IBC.

43. CADIC, *Information for Parents of Irish Citizen Children: Family Reunification* (Dublin: CADIC Coalition, 2007).

44. AkiDwA's networking with NGOs was done circuitously and arguably for reasons that had nothing to do with humanitarian considerations but rather with the state's reluctance to engage in costly legal proceedings.

45. See also Liam Coakley and Claire Healy, *Looking Forward, Looking Back: Experiences of Irish Citizen Child Families* (Dublin: Integration Ireland / CADIC Coalition, 2007).

46. Carla De Tona and Ronit Lentin, "Overlapping Multi-Centred Networking: Migrant Women's Diasporic Networks as Alternative Narratives of Globalization," in *Performing Global Networks,* ed. Karen Fricker and Ronit Lentin (Newcastle, UK: Cambridge Scholars, 2007).

47. Stephen Fuchs, *Against Essentialism: A Theory of Culture and Society* (Cambridge, MA: Harvard University Press, 2001), 252.

48. Saskia Sassen, "Global Cities and Survival Circuits," in *Global Woman: Nannies, Maids and Sex Workers in the New Economy*, ed. Barbara Ehrenreich and Arlie Russel Hochschild (New York: Metropolitan Books, 2003).

49. Pauline Conroy, "Migrant Women: Ireland in the International Division of Care," in *Women's Movement: Migrant Women Transforming Ireland*, ed. Ronit Lentin and Eithne Luibhéid (Dublin: Trinity College Dublin, 2004); Ehrenreich and Hochschild, eds., *Global Woman*.

50. Nadje Al Ali, "Gender Relations, Transnational Ties and the Rituals among Bosnian Refugees," *Global Networks* 2, no. 3 (2004): 249–62.

51. *UNFPA State of World Population 2006: A Passage to Hope: Women and International Migration*, United Nations Population Fund, 2006, 29.

52. AkiDwA, *Herstory: Migration Stories of African Women in Ireland* (Dublin: AkiDwA, 2006); AkiDwA, *Black African Women in the Irish Labour Market* (Dublin: AkiDwA, 2007); AkiDwA, *Understanding Gender-Based Violence: An African Perspective* (Dublin: AkiDwA, 2008). For a complete list, see www .akidwa.ie/publications.

53. Author's interview with Salome Mbugua, 2005.

54. As argued by De Tona and Lentin, "Overlapping Multi-Centred Networking."

55. Robert Holton, "Network, Discourses: Proliferation, Critique and Synthesis," *Global Networks* 5, no. 2 (2005): 209–15.

56. Carla De Tona, "'I Remember When Years Ago in Italy': Nine Italian Women in Dublin Tell the Diaspora," *Women's Studies International Forum* 27, no. 4 (2004): 315–34.

57. Goldberg, *Racial State*, 203.

58. Lorna Siggins, "Immigration 'Will Settle Down to Manageable Level'—Lenihan," *Irish Times*, June 19, 2008.

59. "Unemployment Rises to 14.7%," *Irish Times*, March 16, 2011.

60. Jamie Smyth, "Welfare Payments Denied to Over 9,000 Migrants," *Irish Times*, March 28, 2011.

61. "Thousands of Couples Get Deportation Notice Letters," *Irish Times*, August 30, 2007.

62. "European Court of Justice Finds Ireland in Breach of Spousal Rights," *Irish Times*, July 25, 2008.

63. Jamie Smyth, "Just Three Out of 150 Objections to Marriage Upheld," *Irish Times*, March 21, 2011.

64. Submission to the Dáil Joint Committee on Justice, Equality, Defence and Women's Rights on the Immigration, Residence and Protection Bill, from AkiDwA, Cairde, Immigrant Council of Ireland, Integrate Mallow, Integrating Ireland, Irish Family Planning Association, Mayo Intercultural Action, Migrant Rights Centre Ireland, and Women's Aid, May 20, 2008.

CHAPTER FOUR

RACISM IN THE SIX COUNTIES

ROBBIE MCVEIGH

When in 2006 the *Sunday Tribune* asked, "Has Peace Made Us the Race Hate Capital of the World?,"[1] the question encapsulated a particular moment in the evolution of the dynamic between race and the Northern Ireland state. The "us" was post–Good Friday Agreement (GFA) Northern Ireland. And "we" were firmly and self-consciously on the road to peace. The upsurge in race hatred contrasted starkly with the mood music of "conflict transformation." Moreover, as the question intimated, many assumed a link between these phenomena: "peace" was seen to have some causal role in the rise in race hate. The putative end of sectarian conflict was offered as a possible explanation for the advent of racism.

The situation has further escalated in the interim. Arguably the "riot" in 2009 involving Loyalists and Polish fans at a Poland–Northern Ireland soccer match marked a new juncture in the relationship between minority ethnic groups and the police.[2] This resulted in an immediate "ethnic cleansing" of Eastern Europeans from Loyalist areas.[3] And this was followed in turn by a "pogrom" of Roma families in Belfast later in the year.[4] This episode attracted significant worldwide attention. As the pogrom against the Roma proceeded, Northern Ireland's only minority ethnic member of the Legislative

Assembly—who led opposition to the anti-Roma violence—was being death-threatened by Loyalists. Meanwhile the Ulster Defense Association's youth wing was sending signed bomb threats to minority ethnic organizations across Belfast.[5]

These developments connect with earlier explorations of the dynamics of race in Northern Ireland. The question of racism in contemporary Northern Ireland revisits the theme of Robert Moore's seminal 1972 essay, "Race Relations in the Six Counties."[6] Moore's analysis situated Protestant–Catholic and Unionist–Nationalist relations within a sociology of racism paradigm—at that time even the possibility of other race relations in Northern Ireland was rarely considered. This particular reading of the sociology of conflict and inequality in the Northern Ireland state continues to the present. For many commentators sectarianism is understood and understandable as a specific form of racism.[7]

This question has obviously been compounded by the parallel development of a "new racism" targeted at recent migrants. A generation ago the debate was characterized in relatively simple terms as the question of whether sectarianism was to be understood as racism (or race relations). The contemporary situation must situate a putative continuation of Northern Ireland racism in terms of Protestant–Catholic relations alongside a largely undisputed recognition of the increasing prevalence of "new" antiblack, antirefugee, anti–migrant worker racism. The *Sunday Tribune* headline marked a new high point in the hyperbolization of journalistic accounts of rising racism across Northern Ireland. But the question of whether peace has *caused* a rise in racism captures the subject of this essay very well. It addresses the growing importance of racism as an explanatory and political challenge alongside recognition of the fact that this has not occurred in a vacuum— it is evolving in a place and polity that has been arguably defined by particular notions of race and racism for its entire colonial history.[8]

ETHNICITY IN THE SIX COUNTIES

Just as there is no question that the significance of racism in the Six Counties has changed over recent years, the subjects of this new racism have also changed radically in the context of the arrival of new migrant-worker communities. But these new ethnic boundaries are being established alongside existing ethnic fault lines. The defining ethnic interface in the north of Ireland was created between native Irish and Scots and English planters during the Plantation Period in the late sixteenth century. The demographics of this interface were given definitive shape in the Six Counties by An Gorta Mór—the Famine of 1845–51. The massively disproportionate death and emigration of Catholics in the north of Ireland created for the first time a majority in the six northeastern counties. This demographic transition made possible the creation of a Northern Ireland statelet legitimized by Protestant majoritarianism in 1921. This ethnic balance remained fairly constant throughout the history of the Northern Ireland state—although incremental Catholic growth over recent decades has threatened to undermine the legitimacy of the state, as the Catholic proportion tends toward 50 percent. In the 2001 census this Catholic–Protestant ethnic ratio (coyly identified as "community background") stood at 44 percent / 53 percent (See Table 4.1).

Table 4.1. Ethnicity in the Six Counties[9]

	All persons	Catholic	Persons with community background		
			Protestant and other Christian (including Christian-related)	Other religions and philosophies	None
Percentage of Total Population	1,685,267 100%	737,412 44%	895,377 53%	6,569 —	45,909 3%

Already a majority of schoolchildren in Northern Ireland are Catholics (see Table 4.2).[10] The census of 2011 will generate significant interest as people follow the progress of the Catholic–Protestant ratio, alongside the "Other" category, which now contains a much larger minority ethnic population.

Table 4.2. Ethnicity in All Nursery, Primary, Postprimary, and Special Schools in the Six Counties[11]

Protestant	Roman Catholic	Other Christian	Non-Christian	Other/ no religion/ not recorded	Total
126,172	164,488	7,545	1,364	25,478	325,047
38.8%	50.6%	2.3%	.4%	7.8%	100%

Historically the dominating Irish/British, Catholic/Protestant ethnic boundary in the Six Counties arguably left little space for other ethnic groups. But there were small minority ethnic communities in the Six Counties even before the inception of the Northern Ireland state—notably Jews and Irish Travellers. The 1960s saw the growth of a new people of color population—mostly Chinese and South Asian—as part of a much larger migration to the United Kingdom from colonies and former colonies in the postwar period. This relatively small minority ethnic population—Chinese, South Asian, Traveller, and Jewish—was the subject of the first discussion and activism around racism in the north of Ireland in the 1980s and 1990s.[12] This discourse ultimately led to the recognition of the need for antiracist measures and the passing of the Race Relations Order (Northern Ireland) in 1997. Even as recently as the 2001 census, however, the most striking dimension of ethnicity in Northern Ireland was its whiteness—99.15 percent of the population was identified as white. The entire minority ethnic population was 0.85 percent of the population, and the largest single minority ethnic group, the Chinese, made up only 0.25 percent of the population.[13] This population has, however, been supplemented remarkably in the intervening period by a new generation of migrant workers from Eastern Europe and outside the European Union.[14]

The Good Friday Agreement certainly contributed to a degree of marked economic growth. In this sense peace has made Northern Ireland a much more attractive place to minority ethnic communities. While northern economic growth failed to match the spectacular excesses of the Celtic Tiger in the south of Ireland, it created a demand for new migrant labor. This new migration reconstituted the nature of minority ethnic communities in the north. None of this is straightforward in terms of its effects on the existing dynamics around race, ethnicity, religion, and language in the Six Counties. The longer-established minority ethnic communities (sometimes somewhat confusingly self-defined as "settled") had been mostly Chinese and South Asian people of color communities from the English-speaking Black Commonwealth as well as Jews and Travellers; the new minority ethnic communities are mostly white people (mostly non–English-speaking) from accession states of the European Union, particularly Poland. Therefore, Eastern European migration has the ironic consequence of making the population even whiter and even more Christian; within this it has another impact—since migrants are largely from (Catholic) Poland, it begins to affect the Catholic–Protestant differential.

The work of the Northern Ireland Statistics and Research Agency (NISRA) in this area provides the best current estimate in terms of numbers:[15]

> After decades of emigration exceeding immigration, and a period of balanced migration flows in the 1990s, the recent period from mid 2004 to mid 2007 has seen immigration exceed emigration by 26,000. . . . The expansion of the EU in 2004 is the main source of the increased flows of migrants. . . . In the year to June 2007, some 9,000 people [from EU accession states] registered to work in Northern Ireland, a similar level to the previous year. However, the latest figures from the Home Office suggest that the flow is slowing (8,000 in the year to March 2008). . . . By number, Polish migrants are the largest group of migrants from the new EU states, accounting for about 60% of such migrants. . . . Non-EU residents coming to work in Northern Ireland require

work permits, and there is a continued flow of about 2,000 persons per year, although numbers in the year to June 2007 are slightly down on previous years. Indian and Philippino [*sic*] are the largest nationalities applying for work permits.[16]

Beyond these baseline data, we can identify certain characteristics of this new migrant-worker community. First, the community is far from homogeneous. There are huge differences in terms of national origins, ethnicity, and gender across different sectors. Second, there are significant differences in terms of both residency and work status across different sectors. At present *most* migrant workers in Northern Ireland come from EU accession states—Romania, Bulgaria, Poland, Lithuania, Latvia, Estonia, Czech Republic, Hungary, Slovakia, and Slovenia—with a majority of these coming from Poland.[17] There are also substantial but decreasing numbers of non-EU migrants on work permits whose status is characterized by the absence of full rights to reside. The most vulnerable and "invisible" migrant workers of all are undocumented workers, who may have no right to reside, let alone work, in Northern Ireland. Thus migration into the Six Counties has moved away in the course of the last ten years from a black, majority-world character toward a white, European one.

This profound shift in the nature of migration and minority ethnic demography was no accident. It developed in the context of wider UK state shifts in migration policy as New Labour developed its policy of "managed migration." Crucially, the new UK migration regime aimed at "ending of employment routes to the UK for low-skilled workers from outside the EU except in cases of short-term shortages."[18] A key implication of this policy for Northern Ireland is that the makeup of the migrant worker population has shifted significantly over time. Whatever the intention, the policy has had the consequence of replacing workers of color from outside the EU with white EU workers. Twenty years ago the modal minority ethnic person in Northern Ireland was black, probably English-speaking, and almost certainly from a former British colony; at present the modal person is white, speaks English as a second language (if at all), and comes from a part of Eastern Europe within the EU. The current economic downturn is very likely to affect this migration and significantly reduce the levels of new migrants wanting or able to migrate to Northern Ireland. In this context it would seem likely that these minority ethnic communities become further racialized in the context of economic recession. (This is also likely to further "whiten" migration, since EU citizens have an absolute right to migrate, while non-EU citizens may be denied work permits in an increasingly recessive labor market.) Whatever the future holds, it is clear that recent migrant-worker trends have already transformed the ethnic demography of the Six Counties permanently. A sizeable second-generation minority ethnic community is already in evidence: "In 2007, 1,900 births here (8% of all births) were to mothers born outside the UK and Ireland, compared to 700 such births in 2001. Of these, 800 births in 2007 were to mothers from A8 countries, compared to 10 such births in 2001. Early indications are that births to A8 mothers are increasing further in 2008."[19]

Thus the in-migration that has occurred since the GFA and accelerated since the expansion of the EU has created a new distinct ethnic bloc, often characterized as the "BME community" ("Black and Minority Ethnic"), to which both existing ethnopolitical blocs—Protestant and Catholic, Unionist and Nationalist—will necessarily pay increasing attention.[20]

FROM "NO PROBLEMS ARISING FROM RACISM" TO "RACE HATE CAPITAL OF THE WORLD"

Over the last decade Northern Ireland has become a place in which racism increasingly matters. Crucially it matters no longer solely to small, vulnerable minority ethnic groups outside the political mainstream but also to the whole body politic. Academics, journalists, and politicians have all begun to engage with the question of racism in the Six Counties.[21] While in the past the question of race relations in the Six Counties was arguably a minority interest for a few academics and republicans, it is now part of what defines the landscape of post-GFA Northern Ireland.[22] This transition has been quite remarkable. The media construction of a particular moral panic around racism in

Northern Ireland constitutes a phenomenon itself. As we have seen, Northern Ireland was traditionally characterized as a place defined by the absence of racism. The popular characterization of this was that people were too busy being sectarian to be racist. But this line was also sanctioned by the state. As late as 1992 the definitive British government's Central Community Relation Unit (CCRU) response to demands for antiracist legislation was that the case was "not proven": "Successive Governments believed that there was insufficient evidence of problems arising to warrant legislation equivalent to that in Great Britain."[23] In other words, for the British government there was until recently insufficient evidence of there being any racism *at all*. It did however finally accept the logic of the need for protection, and this was provided by the Race Relations Order 1997—thirty-two years after the first British antiracist legislation had been enacted. Even after this, racism did not seem to matter to anyone but the relatively small resident minority ethnic population. It was still assumed that if Northern Ireland was of interest at all in terms of the sociology of racism, it was because there was so little racism rather than so much. As recently as 1998 the *Belfast Telegraph* could carry the headline "Sectarianism Is Ulster's Racism" without irony—Northern Ireland was still a place where it was implied sectarianism filled the gap occupied by racism in other places.[24]

Within two years, however, rising racism attracted the attention of the media in a new way. First, a government-commissioned research report suggested that racism was "now twice as significant than [*sic*] sectarianism in the initial attitudes of the population in Northern Ireland." Ironically this research found the most negative racist attitudes applied to Irish Travellers.[25] Arguably anti-Traveller racism had been a constant for the entire duration of the Northern Ireland state.[26] Certainly there is little evidence to suggest that it had been markedly intensified by the peace process or the GFA. Despite the fact that this seemed to indicate continuity rather than change in terms of racism in Northern Ireland, the novelty of racism in the Six Counties was seized on by different media. For example, the BBC reported "Racism Is Growing in Northern Ireland": "A report on racial prejudice in Northern Ireland says racism is now twice as common as sectarianism."[27] This media narrative often explicitly or implicitly linked this phenomenon to the peace process. Now that people were no longer too busy being sectarian, they had sufficient time to be racist as well. It implied a replacement theory—sectarianism was being replaced by racism—the significance of racism was increasing as the significance of sectarianism decreased.[28]

Over the next few years the hyperbole truly kicked in. Racism was "Ulster's New Bigotry" in 2003,[29] with a "900% increase in race hate crimes,"[30] and within a year Northern Ireland had been identified as the "race hate capital of Europe." In 2004 the *Guardian* published a defining piece under the banner headline of the "Racist War of the Loyalist Street Gangs":

> Northern Ireland, which is 99% white, is fast becoming the race-hate capital of Europe. It holds the UK's record for the highest rate of racist attacks: spitting and stoning in the street, human excrement on doorsteps, swastikas on walls, pipe bombs, arson, the ransacking of houses with baseball bats and crow bars, and white supremacist leaflets nailed to front doors. Over 200 incidents were reported to police in the past nine months, although many victims don't bother complaining any more.[31]

This investigation made explicit the elective affinity of the new racism and Loyalism—a subject on which the state remained coy for another couple of years. By now this phenomenon was attracting attention outside Britain and Ireland. The *New York Times* offered its analysis:

> Belfast, once the engine of violence between Catholics and Protestants, is being seized by a new kind of hostility—racism, fueled in large part by the recent arrival of Asians, blacks, Indians and Pakistanis in Northern Ireland, which in 2001 was still 99 percent white. During the so-called Troubles, the violent 30-year conflict between Catholics and Protestants here, few immigrants, no matter how desperate, chose to settle in Northern Ireland. That slowly began to change with the 1998 Good Friday Agreement, which ushered in a period of relative peace and prosperity.[32]

This international interest further ratcheted up the hyperbole: Belfast became characterized as the "most racist city in the world" in leading German magazine *Der Spiegel*: "Protestant Ulster militias are criminals and drug dealers, they assault Chinese immigrants, paint swastikas on walls and have managed to turn Belfast into the world's most racist city."[33]

The process reached its apogee in a 2007 article. Racism was by now presented as part of a broader package of bigotry; homophobia and other hate crimes compounded the data presented on race: "Northern Ireland is the hate capital of the western world, according to new research by the University of Ulster. Not only does Northern Ireland have the highest proportion of bigots—just ahead of Greece—but the bigots are on average more bigoted than those in other countries."[34] The issue attracted further world attention in the summer of 2009, when a pogrom against Roma EU citizens from Romania unfolded in Belfast.[35] Once again Belfast was pronounced the race hate capital of Europe, and once again media across the world struggled to make sense of resurgent racism in the Six Counties.[36]

While some of media coverage involved the media reporting on itself, world attention was being drawn to a phenomenon that was both real and significant. The story was reproduced around the world. From *Al Jazeera* to the *New York Times* and from *Le Monde* to *China Daily*, the rise in racism in the Six Counties had become world news. There is an inevitable temptation to dismiss this as hyperbole: some coverage involved sound investigative journalism, but some involved tabloid caricature.[37] The reporting often offered no more than a tenuous connection between research and statistics, and the statistics were themselves sometimes far from robust and certainly open to critique. This caveat does not, however, imply that racism was becoming less significant. The hyperbole itself reflected a new racism emerging in the Six Counties.

THE "NEW RACISM"

While there was undoubtedly an element of moral panic about racism during this period, a new reality was developing for most minority ethnic people. Northern Ireland—after peace, after the GFA—had become a much colder house for minority ethnic people. Here the notion of a "new racism" is useful. This racism has certain defining features. First, it emerged in the wake of the peace process. Second, while it continued to target existing minority communities, it focused on new and expanding communities, particularly asylum seekers and migrant workers. Finally, it involved widespread and routine violence that the state appeared unable to address.

The reality of this new racism was captured in detail in the report *The Next Stephen Lawrence? Racist Violence and Criminal Justice in Northern Ireland*.[38] Drawing on the testimony of hundreds of clients of the Northern Ireland Council for Ethnic Minorities (NICEM), the analysis suggested that the criminal justice system in Northern Ireland was still in a "pre-MacPherson situation."[39] In other words, Northern Ireland had somehow been bypassed by all the reforms of the British criminal justice system that followed the Stephen Lawrence Inquiry and the MacPherson report. MacPherson forced the British state to acknowledge institutional racism for the first time and radically transform its response to racist violence.[40] Certainly the NICEM report provided plenty of evidence of the need for further work in Northern Ireland. Testimony included that of an African Caribbean man who had been called a nigger by an off-duty police officer:

> How did I feel? The whole system was making me confused and angry—it is still making me angry. Because I've got kids, I've a little daughter. What do they expect me to do if someone calls her a nigger? Are they going to say that's all right, it's part of this society and we have to accept it? . . . At the time when this all happened, there was all the publicity about how racism was on the increase and that the PSNI was going to do something about it and clamping down on it and taking it seriously, and there they had it right in front of their faces and they still chose to do nothing.[41]

At its worst this research suggested criminal culpability on behalf of the PSNI (Police Service of Northern Ireland) and the criminal justice system. For example, in one case the PSNI returned a suspect—whom they had heard racially threaten a victim's life, who had been involved in a racially aggravated assault, and whom they believed to be intoxicated—to the area where they knew the victim lived. The PSNI claimed—in a way that was both disturbing and factually correct—that cases like this were rarely prosecuted. Moreover, the person who had made the death threats later systematically attacked the house and eventually forced the family to move.[42] In the context of this kind of evidence, the "race hate capital of the world" depiction began to look less far-fetched than it had at first. A situation in which paramilitary organizations were active in practicing racist violence might be one indicator of a race hate capital. A situation in which the police and criminal justice system appeared incapable of doing anything about such racist violence would be another.

The pervasive nature of racist violence as a defining feature of this new racism provokes a more general critique of Northern Ireland state intervention on race. Elsewhere the British state had made it abundantly clear post-MacPherson that criminal justice was central to racial justice. In Northern Ireland, the criminal justice system was proving either unwilling or unable to address racism in a society that, however hyperbolically, was becoming identified around the world as a hotbed of racism and racist violence. The most remarkable admission of all was the acknowledgment by the Independent Monitoring Commission (IMC) that Loyalist paramilitaries had opened another front and were "targeting ethnic minorities." This bears emphasis: Loyalists were now in a new dynamic of racist violence despite the peace process and the Good Friday Agreement. The IMC's initial silence on racist violence was itself striking, since the body was charged with overseeing normalization—the upsurge in racist violence could hardly be described as a move toward normality.[43] But it was no less striking when the IMC finally decided to comment on the issue:

> One important step would be for loyalist paramilitaries, including the UVF [Ulster Volunteer Force] and RHC [Red Hand Commando], to *stop* targeting nationalists and ethnic minorities. We hope the PUP [Progressive Unionist Party] will give a clear and robust lead on this. . . . Another important step would be for loyalist

paramilitaries, including the UDA [Ulster Defense Association], to stop targeting nationalists and members of ethnic minorities. We hope that the UPRG [Ulster Political Research Group] will give a clear and robust lead on this.[44]

It was odd that the IMC launched into this instruction to stop targeting members of ethnic minorities, given that it had never recognized that the groups had started targeting them. Nevertheless, the analysis was confirmed three months later: "As with the PUP, we said we hoped the UPRG would give a clear and robust lead to the UDA to stop targeting nationalists and ethnic minorities. We still await evidence of progress in this regard. We very much hope that there will be significant progress before our next report."[45] It might have been expected that this revelation would merit media coverage of racism in the Six Counties around the world. Yet it received almost no attention. Just as bizarrely, racist violence disappeared off the radar of the IMC again. None of the subsequent IMC reports indicated that the targeting of minority ethnic people by Loyalist paramilitaries had stopped. Yet the monitoring of such activity by the IMC certainly appears to have ended, despite alleged ongoing Loyalist paramilitary involvement in racist intimidation and violence.

Thus the key body charged with monitoring normalization failed to address racist violence by Loyalist paramilitary groups, then addressed this violence in an arbitrary and piecemeal manner, and finally disregarded the violence again—despite the fact that the racist violence remained constant according to other indicators. In other words, post-GFA Northern Ireland looks far from peaceful from the perspective of people of color. The conclusion that racism does not matter enough in Northern Ireland appears inescapable. Bizarre though it may seem, rising racist violence has become a function of normalization.

This is not to suggest, however, that racism now simply assumes the same forms in Northern Ireland that it does elsewhere in the world. While the threat of racist violence to groups like the Roma is hardly specific to Northern Ireland, the failure of the police to take any responsibility for defending people from racist violence was unusual in the Belfast context. The PSNI only became proactive in helping the families move out and return "home"—in other words, its key intervention was to facilitate the removal of the Roma. There has been organized Loyalist racist violence against people of color and Eastern Europeans in Belfast for over six years, and yet the PSNI has failed to come up with any effective strategy for protecting these communities.

The collusion that denied Loyalist involvement was much more widespread than with the PSNI and has been emblematic of the state response to racist violence in Northern Ireland over recent years. As the pogrom against the Roma proceeded, the UDA's youth wing was sending signed bomb threats to minority ethnic organizations across Belfast. The threat against the Islamic Centre, which was signed by Ulster Young Militants (the youth wing of the UDA) and Combat-18, stated: "Get out of our country before Bonfire Night. If you don't, your building will be blown up. Keep Northern Ireland for white British people. For God and Ulster."[46]

This begs the question of what more a Loyalist paramilitary organization has to do to prove that it is involved in racist violence. It is equally tempting to ask what further evidence would be needed before the state begins to acknowledge that a problematic relationship exists between Loyalist paramilitarism and British fascism and racism. The reality in Northern Ireland thus features these phenomena: racist pogroms are being reported around the world; minority ethnic elected politicians are being death-threatened by Loyalist and fascist organizations; minority ethnic organizations are being bomb-threatened by Loyalist and fascist organizations; and the state is responding with studied unconcern. How is this situation tenable in a polity that both sees itself and remains seen as being at peace?

THE RECONSTITUTION OF ANTIRACISM
AS "GOOD RELATIONS"

Why has the post-GFA state in Northern Ireland proved so incapable of addressing racism, particularly racist violence? The answer lies less in its commitment to tolerate racism than in its inability to address sectarianism. Northern Ireland continues—more than ten years after the GFA—to be a polity defined by sectarianism.[47] Despite all the rhetoric about peace, the Six Counties continues to be a place where sectarianism remains widespread and institutionalized. If we want to know why there is so much racism in a "peaceful" Northern Ireland, we must begin by understanding how the rhetoric of peace has developed both alongside and within the continuing state management of sectarianism.

This persistence of sectarianism in Northern Ireland is far from being simply the last kick of pre-GFA conflict. Rather it represents the emergence of a new, post-GFA Northern Ireland state in which both racism and sectarianism remain deeply embedded, albeit in new forms.[48] The fact that so many different people around the world are desperately keen to present this formation as at peace means that any counter-narrative—particularly any analysis of the racism and sectarianism of the new state—finds little audience. Northern Ireland "at peace" remains a place where sectarian violence is routine.[49] Even more disturbingly it remains a place in which Loyalist paramilitary organizations are involved in this violence and where the criminal justice system often appears incapable of providing justice to its victims and survivors. Recent sectarian killings bore many of the hallmarks of pre-GFA violence: evidence of Loyalist paramilitary involvement, police inaction, incompetence and undue leniency on behalf of the criminal justice system. Like the old Royal Ulster Constabulary, the PSNI was quick to repudiate Loyalist paramilitary involvement, despite powerful evidence to the contrary.[50]

However, one of the most blatant and disturbing recent examples of the ongoing institutionalized nature of sectarianism across the criminal justice system was the response to the murder of Catholic schoolboy Thomas Devlin in 2005.[51] Here a sectarian murder in which the perpetrators had Loyalist paramilitary connections and were known to the police was allowed to go unprosecuted until the victim's family forced the issue. As his mother put it, the Public Prosecution Service was "failing the people of Northern Ireland."[52] This was indeed a criminal justice failure of Stephen Lawrence proportions, but it has so far received very little critical attention.[53] This kind of institutionalized sectarianism is part of the post-GFA settlement. Moreover, the inability of the new state formation to address sectarian violence crucially defines its profound incapacity to do anything much about the new racism. It is no coincidence that the hallmarks of institutionalized sectarianism—failure to police violence appropriately, failure to prosecute known perpetrators, denial of Loyalist paramilitary involvement—resonate with the experiences of racist violence by minority ethnic groups.

The Northern Ireland state position on race has been determined from the first by the commitment to do nothing that might undermine the state management of sectarianism.[54] After the GFA, racism and sectarianism were progressively integrated in a "good relations" project that failed to acknowledge or address the seriousness of either. For example, Section 75 of the Northern Ireland Act 1998 (which, the British government asserted, carried out the GFA) places a statutory duty on public authorities to promote equality of opportunity "between persons of different racial groups" as well as a range of other categories like religious belief, political opinion, sexual orientation, and gender. In addition, without prejudice to this obligation, public authorities are obligated to promote good relations between persons of "different religious belief, political opinion, or racial group." As the post-GFA state settled down, the Office of the First Minister and Deputy First Minister (OFMDFM) took charge of this project. It continued to integrate racism and sectarianism as issues of good relations and to increasingly prioritize these over other equality issues.[55] Gradually, other equality categories have been downgraded—the good relations project is now about racism and sectarianism. When the office's report on good relations was published in 2007, the synthesis was complete and the symbolic hierarchy of relations made very clear: "Priority Outcome 1: Northern Ireland society is free from racism, sectarianism and prejudice."[56] This approach continued with the OFMDFM's much criticized *Programme for Cohesion, Sharing and Integration* document in 2010.[57]

Broadly, therefore, the community relations paradigm has coopted antiracism. This has allowed the Northern Ireland state, which

had so recently denied the existence of racism, to eagerly address its reality. But this process of state antiracism took very specific and problematic forms. This new construction found definitive expression in
the words of Northern Ireland policing and security minister Ian Pearson in 2004: "Racism, like sectarianism, is the product of a destruc-
tive and ugly mindset."[58] This definition is far removed from the Mac-
Pherson report's definition of racism that supposedly informed and
transformed the approach of the British state to racism (as well as the
party and government of Minister Pearson). If racism is defined in this
bland and theoretical manner, it is rendered reformable but in a way
that ensures its most malevolent aspects remain unaddressed. The institutional racism addressed by the MacPherson report is replaced by
Pearson's "ugly mindset" definition. With this finesse, state culpability
is removed almost entirely. The state does not have an ugly mindset,
nor do its civil servants or its statespersons; ipso facto the state is not
part of the problem.

  This redefinition of racism continued apace, as the community
relations paradigm was reconstituted as "good relations." Now racism and sectarianism were the twin evils to be addressed by the new
paradigm. This process involved a deal of audacity. The community
relations industry, comprised of individuals, community groups, and
NGOs working to promote interaction and understanding between
Protestant and Catholic communities, had remained loftily aloof from
the process of demanding protection from racism in Northern Ireland, yet it now placed itself in the forefront of antiracism. Even more
disturbingly, it constructed an intervention that was incomprehen-
sible even to itself, as the Community Relations Council (CRC) made
clear: "An agreed definition for the promotion of good relations does
not currently exist. . . . Words such as sectarianism, racism, equality
and diversity can have different and sometimes, loaded meanings as
people work through issues from individual and community view-
points."[59] While this circuitous language had been part of the community relations industry for years, it was quite a different matter once it
pertained to racism. For, whatever might be said about sectarianism,
Northern Ireland was not in the forefront of analyses of racism or anti-
racism. One might have expected the state to do little than utter a mea

culpa and acknowledge shamefacedly that its refusal for generations to acknowledge any problem with racism or any need for antiracism might have contributed to the rise in racism. One might have expected it to look to the history of the United States or Britain and to the MacPherson report. While racism might conceivably be regarded as "new" in Northern Ireland, it is palpably not new elsewhere. There is a wealth of intellectual analysis, political struggle, and state intervention from around the world to help make sense of the rise of racism in the Six Counties.

The post-GFA state paid almost no attention to any of this, however, since it already knew the answer—its own tried and tested community relations paradigm. Soon the state was reconstituting racism with the same vigor that it had addressed sectarianism—racism was to be an "ugly mindset," and it would be addressed with the same intellectual rigor as sectarianism—lots of agonizing about "agreed definitions" and "loaded meanings" but little evidence of a program to stop people of color being burnt out of their homes, let alone any broader commitment toward racial equality and justice. The appropriation of racism had quite bizarre implications. The community relations industry never committed itself to equality—it has one of those "loaded meanings" that cause so much trouble—so its preferred referent was "equity." But this now became the limit of racial aspiration as well. In other words, a concept with highly questionable references in terms of sectarianism was superimposed on the politics of racism, where it had no justification or context whatsoever.

The Northern Ireland government's long history of resistance to any form of antiracism has been forgotten. In addition, antiracism has been coupled to an existing state paradigm for managing sectarianism. This has resulted in an approach that profoundly distorts efforts to address rising racism. Racism has become a function of unpleasant people—institutional racism and state racism are left unacknowledged alongside institutional sectarianism and state sectarianism. The good relations paradigm has now trumped notions of racial justice and equality and even the most basic protection from racist violence.

The hegemony of "good relations" is emblematic of a profoundly pathological state formation in which *everyone* is in government. Cre-

ationists and climate-change deniers sit in government alongside athe-
ists and environmentalists, British Israelites with socialist revolution-
aries, monarchists with republicans. This might suggest a "rainbow
coalition," but it looks increasingly like a social and political formation
characterized by the most profound moral and political entropy. The
accusation of "sectarian discrimination" by one minister against another is countered by the accused with the suggestion that the charge
itself constitutes "incitement to hatred"—neither resigns, and nothing changes.[60] This governmental entropy has a direct bearing on our
discussion of race and racism. Because if we aggregate the failure to
address the new racism with the long-standing inability to address institutional sectarianism against Catholics, the notion of "race hate
capital of the world" looks not too far off the mark from at least one
perspective. This is less to do with the extent of the problem than
with the remarkable capacity to pretend that there isn't any problem.
For example, the annual Twelfth of July commemoration of the victory of the Protestant William of Orange over Catholic James II has
been reinvented as Orangefest, which presents itself as a major tourist
attraction in the wake of the GFA. However, many associated bonfires
remain adorned with Irish tricolors, as well as racialized dummies
(from Lundy to Gerry Adams) to be immolated. They are routinely
adorned with the genocidal imperative KAI (Kill All Irish) or KAT
(Kill All Taigs) or ATAT (All Taigs Are Targets).[61] And yet everyone—
from the tourist board to the OFMDFM—encourages us to enjoy
Orangefest to the full. A state formation that continues to produce
such expressions in its political culture has a problem with race; one
that insists that such political culture should be *celebrated* has an even
more profound problem.

IRISH STUDIES AND IRISH RACISM

We need to address a broader philosophical and methodological point
here that says as much about Irish studies as it does about Irish racism:
it is clear that racism in the north is connected to racism in the south.[62]
Moreover, the theorization of Irish racism should specifically address

this interconnection.[63] This perspective connects with a broader conceptualization of Irish studies that could be characterized as a trialectic—a dynamic relationship between the two parts of Ireland, north and south, and the Irish diaspora. In other words, most subjects in Irish studies should pay close and particular attention to the way in which these three elements of Irishness structure and interact with each other. This approach is less political than theoretical: it suggests that partitionism in Irish studies is wrong not because it is politically reactionary but because it fails to tell the whole story. Put simply, it fails to capture the structural complexity of Irishness.

If this is true generally in Irish studies, it is true with greater reason with regard to the study of Irish racism. Most recent work on racism in Ireland or Irish racism might be characterized as Republic of Ireland studies. In this sense the work is partitionist by default and rarely addresses the centrality of either the north or the diaspora in the dynamics of Irish racism. For example, it is simply wrong to say that Muslims are the third largest religious group in Ireland—they are the third largest group in the Republic of Ireland. Presbyterians remain the third largest religious group in Ireland once figures for membership of the Presbyterian Church in Ireland are aggregated across the border. Equally it is simply wrong to assert that in 2011 there are 200,000 Poles in Ireland, when we mean the Republic of Ireland; there are around 50,000 in Northern Ireland and 250,000 Poles in the whole of Ireland. In other words, when we address scholarship on racism and ethnicity in Ireland, the Republic of Ireland studies approach is profoundly incomplete. The consequence is usually flawed social science and flawed Irish studies.

The implications of this approach to Irish studies also extend beyond the trivial or the definitional. They cut to the very heart of the nexus of Irishness and racism—the question of why there is racism in Ireland and what might be done about it. Take, for example, the most important moment in the racialization of Irishness over recent years, the Citizenship Referendum of 2004. The trialectic of Irishness was at the core of this process. Notions of Irish nationality and citizenship had been constructed in the context of the diaspora and the relationship of the Irish state to the Six Counties. The racialization of Irishness associated with the Referendum and the dawn of the (southern) Irish racial state occurred because of the specific influence of connections to the diaspora and Northern Ireland on southern Irish politics. For all the rhetoric about pressure on maternity units and concern about pregnant mothers, the Referendum was instituted because of the Chen case.[64] This case crystallized issues arising from GFA-related changes to the Irish constitution. These changes constitutionalized citizenship and nationality for the first time in a way that threatened the integrity of EU member state sovereignty and border control.

It bears emphasis that the Chen case had almost no implications for the Republic of Ireland (since people who acquired Irish citizenship this way were living in the north and aspired to relocation elsewhere in the EU), but it had huge implications for British and EU citizenship through British jurisdictional control of Northern Ireland. Citizenship guaranteed by the GFA to people born in the north of Ireland meant that Britain could not control its sovereignty. Yet this reality provoked a crisis of Irish nationality and citizenship—not a crisis in Britain or the EU. Moreover, the Irish state intervened in ways that undermined the GFA. Both Irish citizenship and the GFA were reconfigured profoundly by a situation (children born in Northern Ireland to non-EU citizen parents acquiring Irish citizenship) that had little immediate effect on the Republic of Ireland. In other words, the racialization of the Republic of Ireland is absolutely *not* understandable with reference only to the internal dynamics in the Republic of Ireland. While this essay addresses the specificity of racism in the Six Counties, it is written from a position that challenges the possibility of doing this hermetically. Racism in the Six Counties is no more capable of internal understanding or solution than racism in the Twenty-six Counties or in the Irish diaspora.

On the other side of this coin, racism in the Six Counties might arguably be better located in terms of British studies. Enoch Powell—arguably the most influential British racist of the last fifty years—found his political home within Ulster Unionism. The most obvious racist political links are between Loyalists and British racist and fascist organizations.[65] Most recent racist violence in the Six Counties

has centered in Protestant, working-class areas that present as deter-
minedly British. Moreover, this racism has often been justified in terms
of the "un-British" character of the migrants. Loyalist antiracism has
also focused on the un-British nature of racism.[66] In other words, the
Irishness of racism within Unionist and Loyalist communities is at
least questionable; it might seem more appropriate to locate it within
pathological expressions of Britishness that characterize both British
racism and Unionism/Loyalism. But this view too misses the point.
While the conscious expression of Unionist/Loyalist racism is often in
terms of Britishness, and this rise takes place within the British state,
there remains an integrity to the notion of Irishness. These pathological expressions of Britishness—both popularly and at the level of
the state—occur precisely because they are located in Ireland. They
assume particular forms because they are in Belfast and Portadown,
not Bradford or Finchley. In this sense, racism in the Six Counties
remains a defining element of Irish studies.

CONCLUSIONS

Irish studies has a key role to play in understanding racism in the Six
Counties. But to play its role effectively, it has to escape two intellectual limitations. First it has to reimagine Irishness (and its relationship to racism) as a trialectic with a complex synergy among Northern Ireland, the Republic of Ireland, and the Irish diaspora (which
includes diasporic communities both from and within Ireland). Second, it has to recognize that neither race, nor racism, nor ethnicity,
nor ethnic boundaries are novel to Ireland. The core subject matter
of Irish studies was established by a native–settler, British–Irish,
Catholic–Protestant conflict that is both embedded in Irish history
and central to the Irish present. In other words, we need to begin by
recognizing that race and racism are not new phenomena to Ireland
but, rather, definitive of Irishness. With this paradigm established, we
can properly address the substance of the question of racism in Ireland in general and racism in the Six Counties in particular.

From this vantage point, has peace made Northern Ireland the race hate capital of the world? None of the hyperbolic soubriquets of recent years seems entirely appropriate. While racist violence has reached new and frightening levels in the Six Counties, it is still not on a par with other polities in which institutional racism is embedded across whole political systems or where racist murder is routine. (For example, the incidence of racist murder remains higher in Britain and the south of Ireland than in the Six Counties.) Thus Northern Ireland is not the "race hate capital of Europe," nor Ulster the "hate capital of the Western World," nor Belfast the "most racist city in the world." Acknowledging this, however, is different from suggesting that there is not a profound problem with racism in the Six Counties. Furthermore, there is substance to the notion that peace has contributed to the ratcheting up of racism in Northern Ireland. This is because rising racism is a function of the post-GFA state—in this sense, peace *has* made Northern Ireland a place in which people receive little protection from an escalating racism. In a profoundly contradictory way, the outworking of the peace process is indeed a cause of the latest manifestations of racist violence. Part of the reason is simply that economic prosperity linked to peace attracted more migrant workers and refugees and therefore more subjects for racism. Moreover, the approach of the post-GFA state to racism is defined by its approach to sectarianism. The post-GFA state cannot address racism appropriately because it is still incapable of addressing sectarianism appropriately. Moreover, not addressing sectarianism is arguably the definitive characteristic of the GFA and the "good relations" state formation it produced.[67]

The Northern Ireland state is presented as reformed, postcolonial, at peace. It is none of these things. The most cursory examination of the experience of migrant workers and people of color confirms a situation that is far distant from any reasonable notion of being at peace. Racism—alongside continuing sectarianism—must be understood as a characteristic of the present rather than a vestige of the past. This reality poses real problems in terms of the mood music of the contemporary north of Ireland—nobody in the north from Sinn Féin to

the Democratic Unionist Party wants to overproblematize the Northern Ireland state. Both Irish and British states have a keen interest in
supporting the thesis that the legitimacy crisis of the Northern Ireland state is over and that there is no longer any significant Northern Ireland problem. Most other actors—including crucially the US
government—want it that way as well.

It remains the case, however, that peace has produced a profoundly dysfunctional state formation. The "Kill All Irish," "Kill All
Taigs," and "Kill All Huns" graffiti plastered across countless gable
walls should confirm that all is not well.[68] Any social formation that
disregards the genocidal imperative is already frighteningly far down
the continuum toward "race hate capital." Moreover, a polity in which
the suggestion of sectarian discrimination by one government minister is identified as incitement to hatred by another seems unlikely to
be able to address these problems with the necessary maturity and urgency. Throw in the rise in racist violence directed toward new migrants and people of color, and there is the suggestion of a gathering
ethnic crisis across Northern Ireland.

In other words, the Six Counties ignores the "race hate capital of
the world" accusation at its peril. Race remains profoundly relevant in
Northern Ireland not because the post-GFA state is run by committed
racists but rather because tackling racism is less important than other
state agendas. As if to prove the point, the notion that Northern Ireland has replaced apartheid South Africa as the race hate capital of the
world has been characterized by a startling unconcern among those
who run the post-GFA state. For many people, ignoring the roots of
racism may well seem a necessary evil in the interests of stability. But
ignoring institutional violence and discrimination in the hope that political tensions will disappear was what led to the conflict in the Six
Counties in the first place. For different reasons, actors inside and outside Northern Ireland have repressed the reality of racism in the hope
that it might just fade away: because addressing it might destabilize
the peace process, because addressing it might raise profound questions about the nature of the post-GFA state. Meanwhile, minority
ethnic people have lived the peace process in reverse: for them post-

GFA Northern Ireland involves more paramilitary violence, more discrimination, and less state protection from racism than ever. Emblematic of this situation, many of the Roma forced out of Belfast in the summer of 2009 have returned,[69] and some of these families have been made homeless again—this time by eviction rather than racist violence.[70] Once again the PSNI were in attendance "because of concerns for the families' safety." The outcome was the same as that which followed the pogrom—Roma men, women, and children homeless on the streets of Belfast. Yet this time there were few voices of sympathy or solidarity. In this regard Belfast was no longer atypical. It was behaving like the rest of Europe, with its studied unconcern for the situation of the European Union's poorest and most marginalized ethnic group.

This episode was in all likelihood an indication of worse to come. As the current world economic crisis unfolds, Northern Ireland is likely to become an ever colder house for all black and minority ethnic communities as they are scapegoated for the downturn in the economy.[71] This situation will be further compounded by the elective affinity between Loyalism and racism and the proven ineffectiveness of the Northern Ireland criminal justice system to address either racism or sectarianism. This problem affects everyone in the Six Counties—not just people of color and migrant workers and refugees. A Northern Ireland state that continues to attract the unwelcome sobriquet of "race hate capital of the world" is definitively not at peace—with either its citizens or itself.

NOTES

1. Suzanne Breen, "Has Peace Made Us the Race Hate Capital of the World?" *Sunday Tribune* (Dublin), July 2, 2006.

2. "Local Poles 'Pick Up the Pieces,'" BBC News, March 30, 2009.

3. "'40 Flee' After World Cup Riots," BBC News, April 9, 2009.

4. See "Unhappy Return: Fear and Loathing Await Fugitives from Belfast Racism," *Guardian* (London), June 26, 2009; "Northern Ireland: Hard Times for Roma Who Fled Belfast," BBC News, July 9, 2009.

5. See S. Jamison, "Islamic Centre Gets Bomb Threat," *South Belfast News,* July 2, 2009.

6. Robert Moore, "Race Relations in the Six Counties: Colonialism, Industrialization and Stratification in Ireland," *Race and Class* 14 (1972): 21–42.

7. See Robbie McVeigh, "Theorising the Racism/Sectarianism Interface," in *Rethinking Northern Ireland: Culture, Ideology and Colonialism,* ed. David Miller (London: Longman, 1998); Robbie McVeigh and Bill Rolston, "From Good Friday to Good Relations: Sectarianism, Racism and the Northern Ireland State," *Race and Class* 48 (2007): 1–23. Sectarianism should be understood as a specific form of racism, along with anti-Semitism and Islamophobia.

8. McVeigh, "Theorising"; McVeigh, "The British/Irish Peace Process and the Colonial Legacy," in *Dis/Agreeing Ireland: Contexts, Obstacles, Hopes,* ed. James Anderson and James Goodman (London: Pluto, 1998).

9. Northern Ireland Statistics and Research Agency (NISRA), *Northern Ireland Census 2001: Key Statistics* (Belfast: Stationery Office, 2002), Table KS07b.

10. Schools statistics also provide one key indicator of the growing minority ethnic communities. In 2007–08 there were 5,665 pupils with English as an additional language at schools in Northern Ireland. This has increased from 1,366 in 2001–02. "Number of Pupils with English as an Additional Language at Schools in Northern Ireland," Department of Education, United Kingdom, 2008, www.deni.gov.uk/eal_time_series_-_suppressed_updated_0708.xls.

11. "Religion of Pupils by School Type and Management Type, 2007/08," Department of Education, United Kingdom, 2008, www.deni .gov.uk/pupil_religion_series-4.xls.

12. Paul Hainsworth, ed., *Divided Society: Ethnic Minorities and Racism in Northern Ireland* (London: Pluto, 1998).

13. NISRA, *Northern Ireland Census 2001,* Table KS06.

14. Robbie McVeigh, *Migrant Workers and Their Families in Northern Ireland: A Trade Union Response* (Belfast: NICICTU, 2006).

15. Robert Beatty, Gillian Fegan, and David Marshall, *Long-Term International Migration Estimates for Northern Ireland (2004–5): Sources and Methodology* (Belfast: NISRA, 2006); *Long-Term International Migration Estimates for Northern Ireland (2005–6)* (Belfast: NISRA, 2007); *Long-Term International Migration Estimates for Northern Ireland (2006–7)* (Belfast: NISRA, 2008).

16. Northern Ireland Executive, "Population Grows by 10,000 New Migrants," press release, July 31, 2008, www.northernireland.gov.uk/news-dfp -310708-new-migrants.

17. NISRA notes, "Bulgaria and Romania joined the EU in 2007 and restrictions have been placed on their entry to the UK labour market. Home Office sources suggest that small numbers of Bulgarians and Romanians have

come to live in Northern Ireland" (Northern Ireland Executive, "Population Grows").

18. British Home Office, "A Points-Based System: Making Migration Work for Britain," press release, March 7, 2006.

19. Northern Ireland Executive, "Population Grows."

20. While net migration has fallen in the context of the world economic crisis, all indicators suggest a significant and permanent new BME population across the Six Counties. See NISRA, "Latest Figures Show Falling Net Migration to Northern Ireland," www.nisra.gov.uk/archive/demography/population/migration/Statistics%20Press%20Notice%20-%20Migration%20NI%202009.pdf.

21. Paul Connolly and Michaela Keenan, *Racial Attitudes and Prejudice in Northern Ireland* (Belfast: NISRA, 2000); Paul Connolly and Michaela Keenan, *The Hidden Truth: Racist Harassment in Northern Ireland* (Belfast: NISRA, 2001); Chris Gilligan and Katrina Lloyd, "Racial Prejudice in Northern Ireland," *Ark Research Update* 44 (2006).

22. Bill Rolston, "Legacy of Intolerance: Racism and Unionism in South Belfast," *IRR News,* February 10, 2004; Suzanna Chan, "Some Notes on Deconstructing Ireland's Whiteness: Immigrants, Emigrants and the Perils of Jazz," *Variant* 22 (Spring 2005): 20–22.

23. *Race Relations in Northern Ireland* (Belfast: Central Community Relations Unit, 1992), 1.

24. Martina Purdy, "Sectarianism Is Ulster's Racism: SDLP: Tensions Used by Enemies of Accord," *Belfast Telegraph,* July 21, 1998.

25. Connolly and Keenan, *Racial Attitudes,* 44.

26. Robbie McVeigh, "Irish Travellers and the Logic of Genocide," in *Encounters with Modern Ireland,* ed. M. Peillon and E. Slater (Dublin: IPA, 1997); Robbie McVeigh, *Travellers and the Troubles* (Donegal: Donegal Travellers Project, 2008); Robbie McVeigh, "'Special Powers': Racism in a Permanent State of Exception," in *Race and State,* ed. Alana Lentin and Ronit Lentin (Newcastle, UK: Cambridge Scholars, 2006), 127–44.

27. "Racism Growing in NI," BBC News, April 14, 2000.

28. Robbie McVeigh, "Racism and Sectarianism in Northern Ireland," in *Contemporary Ireland: A Sociological Map,* ed. Sara O'Sullivan (Dublin: University College Dublin Press, 2007), 402–16.

29. David McKittrick, "The Victims of Ulster's New Bigotry on a Disturbing Trend in Northern Ireland," *Belfast Telegraph,* July 16, 2003.

30. Jonathan McCambridge, "900 Per Cent Rise in Race Hate Crimes," *Belfast Telegraph,* October 30, 2003.

31. Angelique Chrisafis, "Racist War of the Loyalist Street Gangs," *Guardian* (London), January 10, 2004.

32. Lizette Alvarez, "Intolerance in Northern Ireland: Religion, and Now Race," *New York Times,* January 22, 2004.

33. Matthias Matussek, "The Madness of Belfast," *Der Spiegel* (Hamburg), February 28, 2005.

34. Kathryn Torney, "Northern Ireland: Hate Capital of Western World: Ulster Has Most Bigots, Shock New Study Reveals," *Belfast Telegraph,* July 2, 2007.

35. See Robbie McVeigh, "First They Came for the 'Gypsies,'" *Runnymede's Quarterly Bulletin* (September 2009).

36. See, for example, "Racism in Northern Ireland," *Raz Khan Show, Al Jazeera,* July 13, 2009; "Victimes de violences racistes, des Roms sont contraints de quitter l'Irlande du Nord," *Le Monde,* June 26, 2009; "Romanians to Leave NI After Racist Attacks," Reuters, June 23, 2009.

37. For example, the *New York Times* article explained that the rise in racism was "fueled in large part by the recent arrival of Asians, blacks, Indians and Pakistanis in Northern Ireland" (Alvarez, "Intolerance in Northern Ireland"). This was part of the story, but as we saw earlier, the *majority* of new migrants were (and are increasingly) white Eastern Europeans, and they too were subject to the rise in racism and racist violence.

38. Robbie McVeigh, *The Next Stephen Lawrence? Racist Violence and Criminal Justice in Northern Ireland* (Belfast: NICEM, 2006).

39. The Stephen Lawrence Inquiry was a British government–established inquiry into the murder of black teenager Stephen Lawrence and the subsequent shamefully incompetent police response to his death (William MacPherson, *The Stephen Lawrence Inquiry: Report of an Inquiry by Sir William MacPherson of Cluny* [London: The Stationary Office, 1999]). The resultant MacPherson report resulted in a fundamental challenge to and rethinking of British state policy and practice on racism with a particular focus on the role of institutional racism. This process never applied to Northern Ireland, however, despite its being arguably the area of the United Kingdom most in need of it, given its growing reputation as a race hate capital.

40. MacPherson, *Stephen Lawrence Inquiry.*

41. Quoted in McVeigh, *The Next Stephen Lawrence?,* 50.

42. Ibid., 44–45.

43. McVeigh, "Special Powers."

44. *Eighth Report of the Independent Monitoring Commission,* presented to the Government of the United Kingdom and the Government of Ireland, February 2006, 23, 24. These acronyms refer to illegal Loyalist paramilitary organizations—the Ulster Volunteer Force (UVF), the Red Hand Commando (RHC), the Ulster Defence Association (UDA)—and associated Loyalist

political organizations—the Progressive Unionist Party (PUP) and the Ulster Political Research Group (UPRG).

45. *Tenth Report of the Independent Monitoring Commission,* presented to the Government of the United Kingdom and the Government of Ireland, April 2006, 36.

46. See S. Jamison, "Islamic Centre Gets Bomb Threat," *South Belfast News,* July 2, 2009.

47. McVeigh, "Racism and Sectarianism"; McVeigh and Rolston, "From Good Friday to Good Relations"; Peter Shirlow and Brendan Murtagh, *Belfast: Segregation, Violence and the City* (London: Pluto, 2006).

48. For a developed analysis of this thesis, see McVeigh and Rolston, "From Good Friday to Good Relations."

49. "Four Jailed for McIlveen Murder," RTÉ News, May 1, 2009; "Family Says PSNI Failed to Protect McDaid," RTÉ News, May 29, 2009.

50. David Sharrock, "Catholic Man Kevin McDaid Beaten to Death 'by UDA Gang,'" *Times* (London), May 26, 2009; "McDaid Murder 'Not UDA'—Police," BBC News, May 26, 2009.

51. "Devlin Murder: A Mother's Fight for Justice," BBC News, February 24, 2010.

52. "Stab Family Believe 'PPS Failing,'" BBC News, August 11, 2008.

53. "Thomas Devlin Killer 'Might Never Be Freed,'" BBC News, April 30, 2010.

54. Robbie McVeigh, "Between Reconciliation and Pacification: The British State and Community Relations in the North of Ireland," *Community Development Journal* 37 (2006): 47–59.

55. *A Race Equality Strategy for Northern Ireland: A Racial Equality Strategy for Northern Ireland* (Belfast: OFMDFM, 2005); *A Shared Future: Policy and Strategic Framework for Good Relations in Northern Ireland* (Belfast: OFMDFM, 2005).

56. *A Shared Future and Racial Equality Strategy: Good Relations Indicators Baseline Report* (Belfast: OFMDFM, 2007), 34.

57. "NI Anti-Sectarian Proposals Criticised," BBC News, October 9, 2010.

58. Ian Pearson, "Race Attacks Shame Us All," *Sunday Life,* August 22, 2004.

59. *A Good Relations Framework: An Approach to the Development of Good Relations* (Belfast: CRC, 2004), 6–7.

60. "McGimpsey: McGuinness Altnagelvin Sectarian Jibe Hate," BBC News, April 7, 2011.

61. See, for example, Patrick Corrigan, "The Law Cannot Make a Man Love Me, But . . . ," *Belfast and Beyond* blog, Amnesty International, July 11,

2007, www2.amnesty.org.uk/blogs/belfast-and-beyond/law-cannot-make-man-love-me, and Chris Donelly, "What the Twelfth Means to Me," *Slugger O'Toole,* July 11, 2006, sluggerotoole.com/2006/07/11/what_the_twelfth _means_to_me.

62. Ronit Lentin and Robbie McVeigh, "Irishness and Racism: Towards an E-Reader," *Translocations: The Irish Migration, Race and Social Transformation Review* 1, no. 1 (2006): 22–40.

63. Robbie McVeigh, "The Specificity of Irish Racism," *Race and Class* 33, no. 4 (1992); Ronit Lentin and Robbie McVeigh, eds., *Racism and Anti-Racism in Ireland* (Belfast: Beyond the Pale, 2002); Ronit Lentin and Robbie McVeigh, *After Optimism? Ireland, Racism and Globalisation* (Dublin: Metro Éireann, 2006); Lentin and McVeigh, "Irishness and Racism."

64. *Kunqian Catherine Zhu and Man Lavette Chen v. Secretary of State for the Home Department,* Case C-200/02, European Court Reports, 2004. Lavette Chen moved to Belfast from Britain specifically to enable the child that she was expecting—Kunqian Catherine Zhu—to acquire the nationality of an EU member state. She was advised that giving birth in Britain would not give her new baby automatic residency rights because of the terms of the British Nationality Act but that choosing Northern Ireland guaranteed Irish nationality. This right granted to anyone born anywhere on the island of Ireland was underwritten by the Good Friday Agreement and enshrined in the Irish Constitution. Once the baby was born, she could live in the UK under EU rules that allow nationals of one member state the right to settle in another. The Chen family already had a child and could not have another under China's one-child rule. The case was referred to the Court of Justice by the British Immigration Appellate Authority after Chen appealed against the refusal of a residence permit in Britain ("Opinion of the Advocate General in Case C-200/02," press release, State Watch, May 18, 2004, www.statewatch.org/ news/2004/may/chen.pdf). In 2004, the court ruled that it was irrelevant that Lavette Chen had traveled to Belfast specifically to enable the child she was expecting to acquire the nationality of an EU member state (Clare Dyer, "Ruling Exposes Immigration Loophole," *Guardian* [London], October 20, 2004). The European Court allowed Lavette Chen as the mother of an Irish citizen the right to free movement within the European Union, provided she had adequate health insurance and enough resources to prevent her becoming a burden on the state.

65. Mary Fitzgerald, "BNP to Contest Seats in Ulster," *Belfast Telegraph,* October 31, 2002.

66. *Loyalist or Racist: You Can't Be Both* (Belfast: Loyalist Commission, 2006).

67. McVeigh and Rolston, "From Good Friday to Good Relations."

68. For a more detailed examination of this "genocidal logic," see Robbie McVeigh, "'The Balance of Cruelty': Ireland, Britain and the Logic of Genocide," *Journal of Genocide Research* 10, no. 4 (2009): 541–61.

69. "Romas Return After City Attacks," BBC News, August 6, 2009.

70. "Romas Made to Leave House in City," BBC News, August 26, 2009.

71. "Sammy Wilson: Give UK Citizens Jobs Before Migrants," *Belfast Telegraph,* January 26, 2009.

CHAPTER FIVE

THE LINGUISTIC CHALLENGE OF MULTICULTURAL IRELAND

Managing Language Diversity in Irish Schools

PÁDRAIG Ó RIAGÁIN

INTRODUCTION

Language differences are among the most difficult challenges for new settlers and receiving societies alike. Lack of necessary language skills can limit economic opportunity, access to social resources (shops, banks, the media), and the negotiation of societal institutions (education and health care facilities). Proficiency in the language or languages of the receiving society thus has profound effects on economic and social integration, as well as on newcomer well-being.[1] However, since immigration into Ireland until recently was made up primarily of returning Irish emigrants and other English speakers, language problems arose only in the case of numerically small groups. With the more recent increase in non-Irish and non–English-speaking immigration, these problems relate to much large numbers, and language issues have rapidly moved up the national policy agenda.

Because of the need to integrate migrant workers rapidly into the Irish labor market,[2] the language requirements of adult migrants was, from the outset, a major concern. The Organization for Economic Cooperation and Development (OECD),[3] among many other bodies, argued that language support for migrant children is also important in order to avoid perpetuating economic and social disadvantages into the future.[4] Schools have a central role to play in the integration of immigrants into Irish society—both for the immigrants themselves and for the native Irish population.

A full-scale appraisal of the Irish experience in educating the children of migrant communities is not yet possible. Even basic educational and language-related statistics are not available, and well-designed evaluative and comparative research is still awaited. Nonetheless, while details are lacking, the broad outlines of the situation can be established from official sources, and administrative and educational practice is relatively well documented.[5] The first part of this chapter presents a review of these sources.

The second part sets the Irish situation in a more comparative context in two respects. First, while the international research on educational programs for migrant children is by no means conclusive, some major studies raise concerns about the central thrust of current Irish policies. Second, and also pertinent, policy norms are emerging in European law concerning the language education of minorities. While historically these norms relate more to long-established minorities within national territories than to newly arrived immigrant minorities, the distinction between various minorities is weakening. Therefore, the opinions of the international monitoring bodies, set up as part of these international treaties, regarding specific elements of Irish policy are relevant to the present debate. The chapter concludes with a short discussion that highlights issues that require more attention than they have hitherto received.

DEMOGRAPHIC, SOCIAL, AND LINGUISTIC CHARACTERISTICS OF MIGRANT CHILDREN

The flow of immigrants increased from 33,000 per year in 1991 to 86,000 in 2006.[6] According to Hughes and Quinn, returning Irish made up the majority (68 percent) of immigrants as recently as 1991, but by 2004 non-Irish migrants accounted for nearly two-thirds of the total inflow.[7] Over half of these new arrivals were from the new member states of the European Union, and the remainder from other parts of the world.[8] By 2009, however, in-migration had peaked, and Ireland was clearly becoming a less popular destination for new immigrants. Nonetheless, the evidence suggests that immigrants with children in schools were not leaving the country in significant numbers.[9]

The Irish Census of 2006 estimated that there were 465,330 non-Irish nationals resident in the state—11 percent of the population. However, the proportion of non-Irish nationals among the under-fourteen age group is smaller at 7.5 percent. In part this reflects differences in age structure. While 44.2 percent of the native adult population is between twenty and forty-four, the corresponding figure for the immigrant population is 81.5 percent.[10]

Over half of immigrants (54.2 percent) have university qualifications, compared with just over a quarter (27.3 percent) of the native population. Although compared to the native population, immigrants are not employed in occupations that fully reflect their educational qualifications,[11] relatively high average levels of educational attainment are held by the parents of immigrant children.

There is no data on the languages spoken by immigrant children, by their parents, or in their homes. The 2006 national census did not include any questions about language proficiency or use. However, the 2011 Census of Population will, for the first time, include questions about the home language and ability to speak English of those whose normal home language is not English or Irish. In the meantime, some preliminary inferences can be based on the 2006 Census of Population data regarding the country of origin of children under fourteen years. In Table 5.1, this census data has been further divided between countries judged to be mainly or entirely English-speaking and those where "English is either a second language, or is rarely spoken at all."[12]

About 60 percent of the 52,500 children in the census came from countries where English is not widely spoken. Three of the largest groups came from Eastern European countries that joined

Table 5.1. Estimated Numbers of Non-Irish Children from Birth to
Age Fourteen by Country of Origin, 2006[13]

Country of Origin		Estimated Number
Britain and other English-speaking countries		22,500
Non–English-speaking countries		30,000
Examples:		
Poland	5,000	
Nigeria	4,000	
Lithuania	3,000	
Philippines	2,000	
Latvia	1,000	
India	1,000	
Romania	1,000	
Total		52,500

the European Union in 2004: Poland, Lithuania, and Latvia. Other
significant groups came from Nigeria, Philippines, and India. The
seven largest groups account for only slightly more than half of the
total originating in non–English-speaking countries; a large number of
immigrant communities have very small populations. While there is
evidence of some clustering among immigrant communities of the
same background, the general tendency is toward a dispersed distribution within the urban network. While there is a significant concentration in Dublin, there are also clusters within commuting distance
of Cork, Limerick, and Galway, and some fifteen other towns have at
least double the average proportion of non-Irish nationals.[14]

These conclusions are in broad accord with figures contained
in a recent (2011) report from the Department of Education and
Skills.[15] The report estimated that in 2007 there were 44,000 non-Irish
pupils in Irish primary schools (i.e., between the ages of four and
twelve). In addition, there were about 25,000 non-Irish pupils in Irish
postprimary schools (i.e., between the ages of twelve and eigh-

teen). Of this combined total of 69,000 pupils, an estimated 75 percent had limited or no ability to speak English. In total, 10 percent of primary pupils and 6 percent of postprimary pupils had limited skills in English (or none at all) when they began attending schools in Ireland.

Geographically, the spatial distribution of nonnational children follows the general pattern for all immigrants.[16] However, a nationwide survey of principals of primary and secondary schools conducted in 2007 showed that most immigrant students do not attend secondary schools with a high immigrant-student intake. There is a different pattern in primary schools; almost half of immigrant students attending primary schools are in schools with an immigrant student body of over 20 percent, and one in five are in schools with an immigrant-student intake of over 40 percent.[17]

EDUCATING IMMIGRANT STUDENTS IN IRELAND

The current approach of the Irish authorities to the education of migrant children has four elements.[18] First, all immigrant children are placed in regular mainstream classrooms in which instruction is in English or, in a minority of schools, Irish. Second, the Department of Education and Science authorized the use of assessment tests to assist in determining the language proficiency of pupils. The tests of English-language proficiency are compiled by Integrate Ireland Language and Training (IILT). The tests have been designed for use at the primary level but are being adapted to make them appropriate for use in postprimary schools. Third, additional teacher support is allocated to primary and postprimary schools according to the number of enrolled pupils for whom English is a second language and the associated assessed levels of pupils' language proficiency. Schools with between three and thirteen eligible pupils receive grant assistance toward the cost of employing a part-time teacher. Schools with fourteen or more such pupils are entitled to one or more full-time language-support teachers. In 2008–09, there were 1,650 full-time language-support teachers in Irish primary schools, and 560 "whole-time equivalents" in postprimary schools.[19] Fourth, the policy allows schools to be flexible in the deployment of language-support teachers. It is recommended that pupils receive language-support teaching in the classroom or in small groups, in addition to the support they receive from the class teacher. These specified periods of instruction, aimed at development of skills in English, continue for two years. Should these extra resources be required for individual pupils for longer than two years, support for an additional year can be requested, subject to some conditions. Because of the recent economic recession and its impact on public finances, the level of support was reduced to two additional teachers per school in 2009.[20]

This approach to the education of migrant children is followed in many countries. The National Council for Curriculum and Assessment has observed that

> the right to have one's own language is important in enabling people to develop a strong positive self-image. People also generally find it easier to develop complex thinking in their first language. For both ethical and educational reasons, then, it is important that the student's first language is valued and affirmed within the school context. . . . Learning in a bilingual environment can be a positive experience for all children, and it has long been a key feature of Irish primary education.[21]

This alternative perspective, also found in the international literature, is clearly espoused by some elements within Irish educational circles,[22] but it has yet to find meaningful expression in policy documents.

The postprimary system offers somewhat more support for immigrant children wishing to study their own language. The list of subjects for the Leaving Certificate curriculum includes the following language subjects: Irish, English, ancient Greek, Arabic, French, German, Hebrew, Italian, Japanese, Spanish, and Russian. Some of these languages are spoken by migrant children; in addition, the State Examinations Commission provides examinations in other language subjects. It should be stressed that these languages do not appear as part of the normal school curriculum, but students may opt to be examined in them if they meet certain criteria (which include the requirement that the language in question is the mother tongue of the student and that the student is also taking the state examination paper in English). Currently, these examinations are offered: Latvian, Lithuanian, Romanian, modern Greek, Finnish, Polish, Estonian, Slovakian, Swedish, Czech, Bulgarian, Hungarian, Portuguese, Danish, Dutch. However, apart from Arabic, Japanese, and Russian, this selection of language subjects is biased toward EU languages.[23]

IRISH POLICY IN AN INTERNATIONAL CONTEXT

One of the more useful surveys of international practice was conducted by the OECD in 2003 and published in 2006. Data was collected from sixteen states and ten regional governments. The goal of the survey was to capture policies and practices addressing the needs of students with limited proficiency in the language of instruction, and whose parents or grandparents had immigrated to the countries targeted in the survey.[24] The OECD classified the various responses to this survey within a scheme developed earlier by Kenji Hakuta.[25] See Table 5.2, which places national policies along an assimilation–maintenance scale with regard to the language of the migrant group. (All policies require the pupils to learn the language of the host country, but they differ in the terms of the scale and type of resources devoted to this objective.)

The OECD report concluded that "although all types of programmes are likely to be found in one form or another in many of the countries surveyed, the most prominent approach is clearly (B), i.e. 'immersion with systematic language support.' This is particularly the case within primary education."[26] The Irish approach is also best described as "immersion with systematic language support." The resources devoted to supporting the teaching of English are limited, and there is little formal attempt to use the languages of the migrant children within the schools. Although this is an approach widely used across the international spectrum, it is not without its critics. The OECD report is itself one of the most recent and

Table 5.2. General Approaches to Educating Immigrant Students
in the Language of Instruction[27]

---

*Note: L1 and L2 refer to first (mother tongue) and second language respectively. The second
language in this context is the language of instruction.*

A. Submersion/Immersion

Students with limited proficiency in the language of instruction are taught
in a regular classroom. Language skills in L2 develop as students participate in mainstream instruction. No systematic language support specifically targeted at immigrant students is provided.

B. Immersion with systematic language support in L2

Students with limited proficiency in the language of instruction are taught
in a regular classroom. In addition, they receive specified periods of instruction aimed at the development of language skills in L2, with primary focus on grammar, vocabulary, and communication rather than academic content areas. Academic content is addressed through mainstream
instruction.

C. Immersion with an L2 monolingual preparatory phase

Before transferring to regular classrooms, students with limited proficiency
in the language of instruction participate in a preparatory programme designed to develop language skills in L2. The goal is to make the transition to
mainstream instruction as rapidly as possible.

D. Transitional bilingual education

Most students in the programme have limited proficiency in L2. They initially receive some instruction through their native language, but there is
a gradual shift toward instruction in L2 only. The goal of the programme
is to make the transition to mainstream classrooms as rapidly as possible.

E. Maintenance bilingual education

Most students in the programme are from the same language background
and have limited proficiency in L2. They receive significant amounts of instruction in their native language. These programmes aim to develop proficiency in both L2 and the native language (L1).

---

comprehensive studies to raise questions about the effectiveness of this type of approach.

PROGRAM EFFECTIVENESS

PISA (Programme for International Student Assessment) is an internationally standardized assessment administered to large samples of fifteen-year-olds and conducted on an international basis by OECD at intervals. It assesses the skills of reading, mathematical, and scientific literacy. The survey analyzed in the 2006 report was conducted in forty-one countries in 2003. For statistical reasons, the immigrant study only focused on seventeen countries that had sizeable immigrant student populations, but it is still the largest comparative study yet undertaken in this field. The report assesses the success of immigrant students in school, in comparison to both their native counterparts and immigrant student populations in other countries.

The most common approach across the seventeen countries studied was "immersion with systematic language support." It is therefore of considerable concern, from an Irish viewpoint, to learn that in the OECD surveys, the average foreign-born student lags 48 score points behind his/her native counterparts on the PISA mathematics scale. This is the equivalent of an entire school year. In some states (e.g., Germany) immigrant students were up to three years behind their native counterparts. Second-generation immigrant students performed better, but in many countries more than 25 percent had still not acquired the necessary skills. Even after accounting for the occupation and education of parents, an average disadvantage of 30 score points remains. The performance gap associated with differences in languages used in the home and the language of instruction in the school was shown to be significant. OECD replicated this study three years later, using data from the 2006 PISA survey. This time it was possible to include Ireland in the analysis, and the results clearly indicate that the Irish experience conforms to the general international pattern. "English-speaking immigrant students [in Ireland] had mean reading scores exceeding those of their native peers, while non-English speaking immigrant students had mean scores about 60 points lower than their native peers."[28]

Tamar Levin and Elana Shohamy report findings obtained from another large-scale national study (299 schools; 2,761 students) that examined academic achievements of immigrants in Israeli schools.[29] It focused on two distinct groups of immigrant students (from the former USSR and from Ethiopia) in two subject areas—mathematics and language (Hebrew)—and in three grade levels—fifth, ninth, and eleventh. The scores of the immigrant students and those of a parallel group of students born in Israel were compared and analyzed. The results again demonstrated that the academic achievements of immigrant students in both mathematics and language (Hebrew) were significantly lower relative to their native Israeli counterparts, even after a long time of residence. It takes five to eleven years of residency and schooling to reach similar achievement in these two areas, if at all.[30]

Virginia Collier and Wayne Thomas studied US schools in which all instruction is given in the second language (English) for nonnative speakers of English, and no schooling was given in their first language.[31] It takes migrant students seven to ten years or more to reach the age- and grade-level norms of their native English-speaking peers. Furthermore, as in the case of the OECD study, this pattern of results is found across many student groups, regardless of the particular home language, country of origin, socioeconomic status, and other student-background variables.

CONVERSATIONAL AND ACADEMIC PROFICIENCY

All the studies reviewed in the preceding section agree that students who learn in a second language do not achieve the same outcomes as those learning in their first language until some later stage in their educational path, if at all. Furthermore, cognitive and academic development in the pupil's first language has an extremely important and positive effect on second-language learning and that academic skills and literacy development as well as learning strategies developed in the first language can transfer to the second language.[32]

In a more theoretical contribution, Jim Cummins draws a distinction between basic interpersonal communication skills and cognitive academic language proficiency.[33] Immigrant students can quickly acquire considerable fluency in the target language when they are exposed to it at school and in other environments. Despite this rapid growth in conversational fluency, it generally takes a minimum of five years (and frequently much longer) for them to catch up to native speakers in academic aspects of the language, since school-related knowledge demands proficiency in many areas, such as vocabulary specific to certain subjects, appropriate modes of writing, and the norms, values, and practices related to teacher–student classroom discourse and interaction.[34] During this period of language learning, therefore, academic performance suffers, while simultaneously (especially for younger students) conversational fluency in the home language tends to erode. This erosion retards rather than expedites academic progress.

One of the major problems of immigrants who enter primary school, when a second language is the medium of instruction, is that they have gained neither the necessary knowledge nor the skills in their first language to learn academic topics.[35] Significantly, a 2011 Department of Education report acknowledges the validity in Irish circumstances of the analysis offered by Cummins. "Given both the academic research and the practical application of language support on the ground, it is recommended that Departmental policy be revised to reflect the reality that language support does not end after two years in many cases. . . . [Migrant students] need to develop both communicative and, particularly, academic language proficiency. The latter takes time and continuous support."[36]

Not surprisingly, given the mounting evidence regarding the length of time taken for immigrant students to catch up with their native counterparts, attention has turned to bilingual education options as possible alternatives (Options D and E in Table 5.2). Bilingual education, by definition, involves the use of two languages as languages of instruction, one being the home language of the student and the other being the official language of the host country. Bilingual programs can vary enormously in terms of the duration of the programs, phasing, and allocation of time and subjects between the two languages of instruction.[37] Research found that there were "beneficial effects" from some bilingual programs.[38] But the results are sufficiently variable to suggest that bilingual education cannot be seen as the best or only solution in all circumstances.

EMERGING EUROPEAN NORMS IN MINORITY LANGUAGE EDUCATION

In any case, school effectiveness is not the only consideration. With the movement toward a new, more radical phase of European political integration, transnational organizations have become significant actors in the formation and implementation of language policy. Clearly, language policy has now to be considered and evaluated with a new postnational, polycentric politics. The more visible manifestations are found in international treaties such as the Framework Convention for the Protection of National Minorities (or FCNM, adopted by the Council of Europe's Committee of Ministers on November 10, 1994) and the European Charter for Regional or Minority Languages (1992). Complete agreement on priorities cannot be expected, but there is sufficient common ground to suggest that some broad policy norms are emerging against which the internal policies can be assessed.

The general thrust of this emerging consensus can be best seen in documents that, while not legally binding, nonetheless express a degree of political agreement. For example, the Council of Europe's Committee of Ministers issued recommendations related to multilingual areas, which are seen to include both "traditional" and "immigrant" minorities. They urged states to ensure that "there is parity of esteem between all the languages and cultures involved, so that children in each community may have the opportunity to develop full fluency and literacy in the language of their own community as well as to learn to understand and appreciate the language of the other."[39] As might be expected, the wording of specific international treaties and regulations themselves is more qualified and subject to the practicalities of political life, while espousing the same general principles. There is not space here to review all of the various initiatives that have been undertaken in this area.[40] Instead, the discussion will focus on three developments within the domain of international law that have a bearing on the Irish situation.

The Framework Convention for the Protection of National Minorities

The FCNM is the first legally binding multilateral instrument addressing the issue of minority rights.[41] It has been widely supported. Thirty-eight of the forty-six member states of the Council of Europe, including Ireland, have ratified it; it entered into force in 1998. The FCNM consists of a preamble and thirty-two articles. Articles 4–19 contain a set of principles that states are obliged to implement by means of domestic legislation and policies, and through bilateral and multilateral treaties. A number of provisions deal with language policy issues in the field of education. In Article 14, the countries that sign onto the convention "undertake to recognise that every person belonging to a national minority has the right to learn his or her minority language." Furthermore, "in areas inhabited by persons belonging to national minorities traditionally or in substantial numbers, if there is sufficient demand, the parties shall endeavour to ensure, as far as possible and within the framework of their education systems, that persons belonging to these minorities have adequate opportunities for being taught the minority language or for receiving instruction in this language." Although the principle of proportionality heavily conditions the applicability of these provisions, the FCNM leans heavily toward policies that provide the opportunity for students to study the languages of their minority groups or to be taught though the medium of their languages.

The convention also includes a monitoring mechanism, which regulates the relationship between the states and the Council of Europe. In accordance with this provision, the policies of the Irish state in this area were reviewed in 2002 and again in 2007. These reviews, particularly the second, focused on the status of minorities and their education. One weakness of the FCNM is that it does not define a "national minority." In particular, it does not provide any guidance as to whether the provisions are intended to cover the rights of "traditional" minorities within a state and/or immigrant minorities when they are present in "substantial numbers." In the absence of any definition, it is left to member states, when they ratify the convention, to formally declare the minorities they wish to include within the treaty's remit. In practice some, like the United Kingdom, have defined a minority as "a group of persons defined by colour, race, nationality (including citizenship) or ethnic or national origins." This includes ethnic minority communities (or visible minorities), as well as the Scots, Irish, and Welsh.[42] Others, like Germany, have restricted the definition in its case to "the national minorities of the Danes, of the Sorbian people and of the German Sinti and Roma, and the ethnic group of Frisians in Germany," thereby excluding immigrant groups.[43]

Ireland chose a middle position on this issue. In its initial statement in 2000, Ireland argued that "the definition of what constitutes a national minority is therefore dynamic." Therefore, while "Ireland has not made a declaration on the application of the Convention to any particular national minority or minority community," the special position of Ireland's Traveller community was recognized, and "groups that do not constitute national minorities may nevertheless benefit from the protection of the Framework Convention on an article-by-article basis."[44]

However, in its second report to the Council of Europe in 2006, Ireland acknowledged the existence of immigrant minorities and provided some detailed information, but stopped short of defining them formally as national minorities.[45] The council's Advisory Committee responded by welcoming "moves by the authorities towards acknowledgement of minority languages, including through possibilities to take minority languages as state examination subjects at senior cycle in second level education." However, the committee urged "the authorities to pursue their commitment in this area, including through provision of minority languages as education subjects."[46] Although the wording is diplomatic, Ireland is asked to begin implementing Article 14 of the Framework Convention in the development of its educational policies for migrant children.

An indication of how far the Council of Europe may ultimately press Ireland on this topic may be gleaned from its recommendations in 2007 in the case of the United Kingdom: "The Advisory Committee considers that the authorities should make concerted efforts to promote bi-lingual and multi-lingual education, including by stepping up funding for supplementary schools, and take a proactive approach in encouraging schools to expand the provision of minority ethnic languages."[47]

The European Commission against Racism and Intolerance

The European Commission against Racism and Intolerance (ECRI) was established by the first Summit of Heads of State and Government of the member states of the Council of Europe in 1993. ECRI is a monitoring body, combating racism and intolerance in greater Europe from the perspective of the protection of human rights. In this context, ECRI examines the situation in each of the member states of the Council of Europe and draws up reports containing its analyses and recommendations as to how each country might deal with the problems identified.

In its second report on Ireland (2002) ECRI encouraged Irish authorities to consider "ways of developing the provision of mother tongue teaching for children from other minority groups, while noting that the system of dispersal whereby asylum seekers and refugees are accommodated throughout the country, may make such provision difficult to organise in practice."[48] The Irish authorities were also encouraged to consider the possibility of recruiting teachers or teaching auxiliaries from among minority communities, as this "could represent a positive step in assisting the integration of minority pupils in the school system."

In its third report on Ireland (2007), ECRI further reiterated its recommendation that the authorities take measures to encourage members of minority groups to enter the teaching profession.[49] In addition, ECRI also recommended that the authorities establish a consistent system of data collection to assess minority pupils' performance in education and establish the necessary policies in this area.

The European Commission

The clearest indication of the policy of the European Commission is to be found in the *Council Directive of 25 July 1977 on the Education of the Children of Migrant Workers*. One article instructs member states to take "appropriate measures to ensure that free tuition to facilitate initial reception is offered in their territory to migrant children, including, in particular, the teaching—adapted to the specific needs of such children—of the official language or one of the official languages of the host State. Member States shall take the measures necessary for the training and further training of the teachers who are to provide this tuition." Another article, however, instructs member states to "take appropriate measures to promote, in coordination with normal education, teaching of the mother tongue and culture of the country of origin for the children."

This directive imposes positive requirements on member states. While it is disappointing to find, in a detailed examination of this directive, that implementation was "patchy and half-hearted," the directive nonetheless remains the commission's position on this issue.[50] Although the directive is restricted to the rights of children of EU member states residing in another EU member state, this obviously includes a large number of immigrant children in Ireland.

CONCLUDING DISCUSSION

A comprehensive review of Ireland's policy for the education of its migrant children is not yet possible. Basic sociolinguistic data and educational evaluations are not available, but the main features of Ireland's policy in this area can be established and set in comparative context. The preceding review of international research and practice suggests that, after a decade of high immigration, the Irish authorities need to reassess the educational policies and initiatives aimed at immigrant students. As the Department of Education and Skills has noted, "the current approach to the education of migrant children was initially developed in response to a limited need. When that need expanded significantly, the system responded by expanding what had been an initial ad hoc solution to a systemic solution. At no time were formal objectives for the programme articulated."[51]

Compelling evidence supports the view that low proficiency in the language of teaching is related to poor academic performance for considerable proportions of migrant students.[52] In several large-scale studies, these differences are repeatedly reflected in low scores, compared to native-born students, in reading comprehension and mathematics. The research evidence raises questions concerning the Irish approach in two respects. First, it clearly suggests that immigrants' difficulties in acquiring school knowledge persist for periods of time far longer than those encompassed by Irish support measures. Second, in the majority of these studies, the main educational program for immigrant children was similar, in all essential respects, to the "immersion with systematic language support" program adopted by Ireland. These studies' conclusions, therefore, clearly suggest that Ireland should be examining other interventions that will sustain immigrant pupils' long-term academic progress, rather than solely seeking short-term, "quick-fix" solutions to rectify these pupils' underachievement in English.

International monitoring bodies have been quietly taking stock of Irish immigrant policies over the past decade. Hardly noticed by the Irish media, they have been gently prompting the Irish authorities to formally incorporate the languages of immigrant communities into the Irish education system. The arguments rest partly on legal grounds and partly on an interpretation of international research. They have given some practical suggestions as to how a shift in this direction might be initiated. For example, Ireland has been asked to introduce minority immigrant languages as school subjects and to take measures to encourage members of minority groups to enter the teaching profession. These modest requests do not simply reflect the views of international bodies; there is also some evidence that the immigrant communities themselves would like policy to move in this direction. In 2007, the *Irish Times* carried a report that two weekend schools were to be opened in Waterford and Cork teaching exclusively in the Polish language.[53] While this is indicative of a demand for such programs, the schools are funded by the Polish, not by the Irish, government.

While these developments should be noted, I do not argue that the introduction of immigrant languages into the schools—either as curriculum subjects or as the language of instruction—can be a complete, once-and-for-all solution to the problems experienced by immigrant children. I concur with Diane August and Kenji Hakuta that the "key issue is not finding a programme that works for all children and all localities, but rather finding a set of programme components that works for the children in the community of interest, given the goals, demographics, and resources of that community."[54] Bilingual programs may be the appropriate policy response in certain circumstances, but obviously the minimum threshold numbers required for such programs will be present only in a limited number of schools. While international research and practice can be instructive, Ireland needs to develop an evidence-based approach deriving from, and applicable to, its own situation. This requires a collaborative process that uses the "knowledge and expertise of different stakeholders such as language experts in the native language of the immigrant groups involved, teachers of immigrants, students, and adults who know the cultural background characteristics of the immigrant groups."[55]

Many of the national and international reports reviewed in this chapter recommend that a far more comprehensive database needs to be established.[56] The data have to be sensitive to the high diversity that exists both among and within different immigrant groups regarding their cultural, language, and educational backgrounds. But as Levin and Shohamy note, "evaluation needs to go beyond assessing student achievement. It should simultaneously assess the educational programs and the school curricula as well as the appropriateness of specific instructional designs of learning and teaching to students' achievement and attitudes. Such models of evaluation need to be interpreted within the specific social, cultural and educational contexts."[57]

The Department of Education and Science's basic position on integration should be the greater cause for concern. When one looks behind the rhetoric about "accommodating cultural diversity,"[58] the

educational policies of the Irish government are actually assimilation-
ist in concept and effect. The fact that it is only the immigrant's proficiency (or lack of it) in English that is assessed and measured on entering Irish schools implies a deficit model of pupil development that
focuses on what immigrant students do not know. Notwithstanding
the acknowledgment in the 2011 report from the Department of Education that "achieving proficiency in mother tongue should also enhance their overall achievement in English,"[59] it is also observed that
school personnel "were largely unaware of the value of the purpose-
ful use of home languages in supporting the acquisition of new learning."[60] The report is extremely tentative in its recommendations as to
how this problem might be addressed. Although teachers are urged to
give due cognizance to the importance of the mother tongue of migrant students, it is not at all clear what this might mean in practice,
and the recommendation carries little conviction.

This contrasts markedly with the approach recommended in a report for the UK Department of Education and Science, which urged
that "community languages" (i.e., languages spoken by immigrants)
be seen as a "national asset"[61] and recommended an approach, previously supported by Ireland in the Council of Europe, that ensured
"parity of esteem between all the languages and cultures involved."[62]
Clearly, Ireland has not arrived at this position as yet; until it does so,
it is doubtful that the full cultural and linguistic potential of Ireland's
new immigrants will be realized.

NOTES

1. Feng Hou and Morton Beiser, "Learning the Language of a New
Country: A Ten-Year Study of English Acquisition by South-East Asian
Refugees in Canada," *International Migration* 44, no. 1 (2006): 135–65.

2. P. J. O'Connell and F. McGinnity, *Immigrants at Work: Ethnicity and
Nationality in the Irish Labour Market* (Dublin: Equality Authority, and Hor-
wath Consulting Ireland, 2008); *Final Report: Development of a National English
Language Policy and Framework for Legally-Resident Adult Immigrants* (Horwath
Report) (Dublin: Department of Education and Skills, 2008).

3. Claire Healy, *On Speaking Terms: Introductory and Language Programmes for Migrants in Ireland* (Dublin: Immigrant Council of Ireland, 2007).

4. *OECD Economic Surveys: Ireland* (Paris: OECD, 2008), 117.

5. *Language Support for Migrants: A Value for Money Review of Expenditure on the Education of Migrant Students at Primary and Post-primary Level Who Do Not Speak English (or Irish) as a First Language (2001/02–2008/09),* Department of Education and Skills, Dublin, March 2011.

6. Frances McGinnity et al., *Migrants' Experience of Racism and Discrimination in Ireland* (Dublin: Economic and Social Research Institute, 2006), 1; Alan Barrett and David Duffy, *Are Ireland's Immigrants Integrating into Its Labour Market?* (Dublin: Economic and Social Research Institute, 2007), 4.

7. Gerard Hughes and Emma Quinn, *The Impact of Immigration on Irish Society.* (European Migration Network). (Dublin: Economic and Social Research Institute, 2004), 6; McGinnity et al., *Migrants' Experience of Racism,* 4.

8. Barrett and Duffy, *Are Ireland's Immigrants Integrating,* 4.

9. *Language Support for Migrants,* 9.

10. Alan Barret, Adele Bergin, and David Duffy, "The Labour Market Characteristics and Labour Market Impacts of Immigrants in Ireland," *Economic and Social Review* 37, no. 1 (2006): 6.

11. Ibid.

12. Healy, *On Speaking Terms,* 7.

13. Data taken from *Census 2006,* vol. 4: *Usual Residence, Migration, Birthplaces and Nationalities,* Central Statistics Office, Cork, 2006, Table 41A, census.cso.ie/Census/TableViewer/tableView.aspx?ReportId=76491. Subtotals are rounded to the nearest thousand.

14. *Irish Times,* September 15, 2007.

15. *Language Support for Migrants,* 120.

16. *Irish Times,* May 24, 2007.

17. Emer Smyth, Merike Darmody, Frances McGinnity, and Delma Byrne, *Adapting to Diversity: Irish Schools and Newcomer Students* (Dublin: ESRI, 2009).

18. *Meeting the Needs of Pupils for Whom English Is a Second Language,* Circular 0053/2007, Department of Education and Science, Comamaddy, Athlone, Ireland, May 2007.

19. *Language Support for Migrants,* Table 6.6, 125.

20. *Meeting the Needs of Pupils Learning English as an Additional Language (EAL),* Circular 0015/2009, Department of Education and Science: Schools Division, Comamaddy, Athlone, Ireland, March 2009.

21. National Council for Curriculum and Assessment, *Intercultural Education in the Primary School* (Dublin: National Council for Curriculum and Assessment, 2004), 45.

22. For example, see E. Nowlan, "Underneath the Band-Aid: Supporting Bilingual Students in Irish Schools," *Irish Educational Studies* 27, no. 3 (2008): 253–66.

23. See www.examinations.ie.

24. *Where Immigrant Students Succeed: A Comparative Review of Performance and Engagement in PISA* (Paris: OECD, 2006), 118.

25. Kenji Hakuta, "The Debate on Bilingual Education," *Developmental and Behavioral Pediatrics* 20 (1999): 36–37.

26. *Where Immigrant Students Succeed*, 131.

27. Ibid., 120.

28. *OECD Reviews of Migrant Education—Ireland* (Paris: OECD, 2009), 24.

29. Tamar Levin and Elana Shohamy, "Achievement of Immigrant Students in Mathematics and Academic Hebrew in Israeli School: A Large-Scale Evaluation Study," *Studies in Educational Evaluation* 34 (2008): 9.

30. Ibid., 6.

31. Ibid., 8. See also Virginia P. Collier and Wayne P. Thomas, "Reforming Education Policies for English Learners Means Better Schools for All," *State Education Standard* 3, no. 1 (2002): 30–36.

32. Levin and Shohamy, "Achievement of Immigrant Students," 10. See also Virginia P. Collier, *Promoting Academic Success for ESL Students: Understanding Second Language Acquisition for School* (Elizabeth, NJ: New Jersey Teachers of English to Speakers of Other Languages—Bilingual Educators, 1995).

33. Jim Cummins, *Language, Power, and Pedagogy: Bilingual Children in the Crossfire* (Clevedon, UK: Multilingual Matters, 2000), 157–85.

34. See G. Valdes, "Between Support and Marginalisation: The Development of Academic Language in Linguistic Minority Children," *International Journal of Bilingual Education and Bilingualism* 7, no. 2–3 (2004): 102–32. Levin and Shohamy, "Achievement of Immigrant Students," 11.

35. Levin and Shohamy, "Achievement of Immigrant Students," 10.

36. *Language Support for Migrants,* 147.

37. Pádraig Ó Riagáin and Georges Ludi, *Bilingual Education: Some Policy Issues* (Strasbourg: Council of Europe, 2003), 22–30.

38. Diane August and Kenji Hakuta, eds., *Improving Schooling for Language-Minority Children: A Research Agenda* (Washington, DC: National Academy Press, 1997), 147.

39. *Recommendation No. R (1998) 6 of the Committee of Ministers* (Strasbourg: Council of Europe, 1998), par. 22, 2.

40. For a detailed review see M. Weller, ed., *The Rights of Minorities: A Commentary on the European Framework Convention for the Protection of National Minorities,* Oxford Commentaries on International Law (Oxford: Oxford University Press, 2005). See also N. Nic Shuibhne, "Minority Languages, Law

and Politics: Tracing EC Action," in *The Language Question in Europe and Diverse Societies: Political, Legal and Social Perspectives,* ed. D. Castiglone and C. Longman (Oxford: Hart, 2007), 123–47.

41. Council of Europe, *The Framework Convention for the Protection of National Minorities—Collected Texts,* 4th ed. (Strasbourg: Council of Europe, 2008).

42. United Kingdom, *Report Submitted by the United Kingdom Pursuant to Article 25, Paragraph 1 of the Framework Convention for the Protection of National Minorities,* Document ACFC/SR (1999) 013 (Strasbourg: Council of Europe, 1999), par. 2.

43. Germany, *Report Submitted by Germany Pursuant to Article 25, Paragraph 1 of the Framework Convention for the Protection of National Minorities,* Document ACFC/SR (2000) 001 (Strasbourg: Council of Europe, 2000), par. 1.

44. *Report Submitted by Ireland Pursuant to Article 25, Paragraph 1 of the Framework Convention for the Protection of National Minorities,* Document ACFC/SR (2001) 006 (Strasbourg: Council of Europe, 2001), 5.

45. *Second Report Submitted by Ireland pursuant to Article 25, Paragraph 1 of the Framework Convention for the Protection of National Minorities,* Document ACFC/SR/II (2006) 001 (Strasbourg: Council of Europe, 2006), 38.

46. Advisory Committee on the Framework Convention for the Protection of National Minorities, *Opinion on Ireland,* Document ACFC/INF/OP/II (2006) 007 (Strasbourg: Council of Europe, 2006), par. 102.

47. Advisory Committee on the Framework Convention for the Protection of National Minorities, *Opinion on the United Kingdom,* Document ACFC/INF/OP/II (2007) 003 (Strasbourg: Council of Europe, 2007), par. 220.

48. European Commission against Racism and Intolerance (ECRI), *Second Report on Ireland* (Strasbourg: Council of Europe, 2002), par. 44.

49. ECRI, *Third Report on Ireland* (Strasbourg: Council of Europe, 2007), par. 88.

50. Louise Ackers and Helen Stalford, *A Community for Children?: Children, Citizenship and Internal Migration in the EU* (Aldershot, UK: Ashgate, 2004), 264.

51. *Language Support for Migrants,* 9.

52. *Reviews of Migrant Education—Ireland.*

53. *Irish Times,* October 19, 2007.

54. August and Hakuta, *Improving Schooling,* 147. See also Ó Riagáin and Ludi, *Bilingual Education.*

55. Levin and Shohamy, "Achievement of Immigrant Students," 12.

56. See, for example, *Reviews of Migrant Education—Ireland,* 59, and *Language Support for Migrants,* 171–76.

57. Levin and Shohamy, "Achievement of Immigrant Students," 12.

58. Department of Justice, Equality and Law Reform, *Planning for Diversity — The National Action Plan Against Racism* (Dublin: Stationary Office, 2005), 109.

59. *Language Support for Migrants,* 188.

60. Ibid., 106.

61. Ron Dearing and Lid King, *Languages Review: Report Prepared for the Department for Education and Skills* (London: HMSO, 2007), 16.

62. Council of Europe, *Recommendation No. R (1998) 6 of the Committee of Ministers* (Strasbourg: Council of Europe, 1998), par. 22.2.

CHAPTER SIX

THE IRISH LANGUAGE IN TWENTY-FIRST-CENTURY IRELAND

Exploring Legislative and Policy Protections North and South

VERONA NÍ DHRISCEOIL

INTRODUCTION

Between 1999 and 2007, over 650,000 people immigrated to Ireland. Among those immigrating were returning Irish nationals, UK nationals, economic migrants, political refugees, and asylum seekers.[1] The pull factor was economic. Successful industrial relations and good investment incentives during this boom period made Ireland a viable location for establishing businesses and in turn an attractive location to earn a livelihood. Remarkable progress in the economy coupled with the influx of immigrants brought with it dramatic changes to the societal and cultural landscape of Ireland. Ireland became an increasingly multicultural and multilingual state during the Celtic Tiger era.[2] The transformation in social diversity brought with it many positive opportunities but also vulnerabilities and resistances, some of which have been highlighted in this volume. What has also been highlighted is the other dramatic transformation since the original conference in 2007:

the economic downturn and its effect on race and immigration. The new Ireland of wealth and cozy cartels, of immigration and construction has been replaced with recession, emigration, and ghost estates. The new has become the old, and the boom has become the bust.

Ireland is now in transition, experiencing change and crisis in every realm of society. In this political, social, and economic matrix, it is worth reflecting on the place of the Irish language and question what the future might bring. Indeed, the Irish-language question has long been a source of debate, but the nature of this debate has dramatically changed. In *A New View of the Irish Language,* Caoilfhionn Nic Pháidín and Seán Ó Cearnaigh note that "the Irish language question is entering a phase of unprecedented challenge and change." They note that "the results may be as startling as those which occurred at other historical watersheds like the Flight of the Earls or the revival movement of the late nineteenth and early twentieth century."[3] Such dramatic shifts are unparalleled, and therefore key questions are raised. Will the striking changes of contemporary Ireland have a positive or negative impact on the Irish language? Has the influx of migrants brought with it a new era in government language policy, or do remnants of nationalism remain? What impact will the economic crisis have on the future of the Irish language? Developing an understanding of the place of the Irish language in twenty-first-century Ireland and the influences that international language arguments have had on the legislative developments provides the central focus of this chapter.

I begin by exploring the relationship between the Irish language and national identity and how this relationship is continually changing. As noted by Michael Cronin in his seminal text *Irish in the New Century,* the ends are no longer the same. To declare the language simply as part of what we are makes little sense if we are no longer so sure of who or what we are.[4] This discussion will be followed by a brief examination of the international context and trends toward the protection of minority languages through positive obligations on states to guarantee language rights. This will provide a broader context within which to discuss the recent legal linguistic developments in the Republic of Ireland as well as in Northern Ireland. Such developments have arisen primarily because of the increased provision for minority languages at an international level, a changed Irish society, and a shift in the relationship between identity and the Irish language. Changes in Irish-language policy in Northern Ireland must be viewed within the context of the dramatic changes brought about by the Belfast/ Good Friday Agreement of 1998 and language, along with equality claims being made in a postconflict society. In this regard the approach to language policy in Northern Ireland differs substantially from language policy in the Republic of Ireland.

Given the current economic downturn, the chapter will conclude with some analysis on the future of the Irish language. At this stage it is impossible to fully understand the impact the recession will have on the Irish language in terms of cuts to government spending and, more importantly, whether the attitudes of the Irish people toward the language will shift. Nevertheless, the proposed policy changes for Irish put forward in the Towards Recovery: Programme for National Government 2011–2016 by the newly elected coalition government of Fine Gael/Labour does provide some insight into the government's viewpoint on the future of the Irish language.[5]

THE IRISH LANGUAGE AND NATIONAL IDENTITY

The state's relationship with the Irish language has always been complex—controlled and influenced by circles of historic and political influence. In 1922, Ireland became a newly independent state and thus entered a new political, social, and economic era. With its people having endured a recent civil war, colonization, and the Great Famine, a native government now at the helm sought to revive the Irish language. Free from the shackles of British rule, the rebellious political leaders were eager to establish and build a new Ireland and shape a separate national identity. In order to move forward, it was believed that Ireland and, more importantly, the Irish people needed to build—or perhaps more correctly reestablish—their identity. The Irish language was to become the key instrument in shaping this identity, and thus an intricate relationship between the state and the Irish language was born.

Since 1922, the Irish language has been regarded as a symbol of the Irish nation and thus reflected in state policy. The importance of Irish has been illustrated in the Irish constitution, in policies on education, and in the civil service.[6] That link between Irish national identity and state policy has, however, ebbed and flowed. Ó Riagáin describes the state's relationship with the Irish language as shifting from institutionalization to deinstitutionalization.[7] In the initial decades after independence, the state pursued a protectionist policy toward the Irish language, illustrated by the compulsory policies in the education system. During the 1950s and 1960s, political leaders were consumed by the economy, growth, and modernizing the state. Language policy shifted from Gaelicization to bilingualism, from institutionalization to deinstitutionalization, and in essence to a less coercive and perhaps more social democratic approach.[8] This shift was reflected in the removal of some compulsory elements relating to the teaching of Irish and the establishment of the first Irish radio station in 1972.[9] During the Celtic Tiger era, there was a further ideological shift to a neoliberal and individualist perspective.[10] This perspective is based on a rational choice model in which individuals are understood to act rationally to maximize their own advantage. Language policy shifted in favor of providing opportunities for speakers to use Irish should they choose to do so.

Thus shifts in language policy reflect the changing relationship between language and Irish identity. As Ireland has witnessed demographic, social, and economic change, the relationship between the Irish language and identity has changed. This is not surprising, given that identity is an ever-changing concept and in a continual process of construction. It can appear in various social contexts that manifest identity but simultaneously alter it.[11] Stuart Hall has argued that identity is built on the back of a recognition of some common origin or shared characteristic with another person or group, or with an ideal, but goes on to argue that identity formation is a process never completed— identity is always "in process."[12] In the end, identity is conditional, lodged in contingency, and changes can be either gradual or dramatic.

As Ireland experiences dramatic change in recent decades, the notion of national identity has been brought into sharp focus, where some common origin and reaffirmation of "us" and "our" is being explored through the Irish language and thereby simultaneously reinforcing the difference between "us" and "them." As Sara O'Sullivan points out, "issues of identity are highlighted at times of rapid social change."[13] Multiculturalism and multilingualism have become more common features in Irish society, in urban areas in particular. In response, subconsciously or consciously, Irish people have embarked on an exploration of identity, and the Irish language has formed part of that exploration. As a corollary, Irish has found a new lease on life.

It is hard to deny (despite contradictions in actual language use[14]) that the Irish language has seen an unprecedented revival in recent years. Irish-language classes are in demand, as are the ever-expanding Gaelscoileanna (Irish-medium schools), Irish names are in vogue, the Irish-language TV channel TG4 continues to prosper, and new Irish-language websites are continually being introduced.[15] On the airwaves, Irish can be heard daily. The revival of Irish in the last decade is particularly vibrant in urban Ireland. In this regard, the expansion in Gaelscoileanna in urban Ireland has formed the subject matter of much debate. Louise Holden calls the Gaelscoil movement "a post-Riverdance cultural zeitgeist."[16] David McWilliams asserts the view that the revival of the Gaelscoileanna, traditional music, and Celtic mythology could not have happened without the Brown Thomas credit card.[17] The elitist, middle-class tags often associated with Gaelscoileanna are refuted by others, most notably Gaelscoileanna Teo, the national voluntary organization supporting Irish-medium education. Nora Ní Loinsigh of Gaeilscoileanna Teo "rejects McWilliams' thesis that Gaelscoileanna are merely for the school of choice for the sophisticated elite. . . . Irish-medium education is available to all . . . from all classes and all backgrounds."[18]

The urban revival in Irish can be described as a countertrend to globalization known as "glocalization."[19] Glocalization acknowledges the importance of the local in the global. In the Irish context, this trend is reflected in the importance of the Irish language in contemporary Ireland—a marker of identity at a time of continuing change. While it may not transfer to increasing numbers of Irish-language speakers, this renewed interest at the grassroots level, especially in urban Ireland, has accordingly paved the way for dynamic measures at government level and a demand by Irish speakers and language activist groups for the implementation of measures to secure legal status for Irish. In this regard, Helen Ó Murchú in *More Facts about Irish* notes that the sociocultural changes have resulted in a more linguistically diverse environment and this in turn has had, to some extent, a widening and liberating effect on Irish-language planning and policy.[20]

THE INTERNATIONAL CONTEXT OF LANGUAGE RIGHTS

The issue of language rights and positive obligations to promote minority languages is a relatively new debate and a more recent feature in the broader framework of human rights discussions. Traditionally, the issue of language only featured in human rights standards, insofar as provisions prohibiting nondiscrimination or safeguarding freedom of expression. Language rights were seen as negative rights (the right to use one's language in the private sphere without persecution or prejudice).[21] The end of World War II brought about improvements, initially in a general and indirect nature but later more specific in various legal texts concerning the protection of fundamental language rights.[22] For example, Article 2 of the 1948 Universal Declaration of Human Rights states: "Everyone is entitled to all rights and freedoms . . . without distinction of any kind . . . including language."[23]

Similar nondiscriminatory provisions appeared in the European Convention on Human Rights 1950 (ECHR).[24] This convention includes two specific provisions on language in relation to persons arrested or persons before a court. Neither relates specifically to minority-language rights but instead provides procedural rights relating to due process when the official language of the justice system is not understood.[25] Furthermore, Article 14 of the ECHR provides a general clause prohibiting discrimination on any ground such as language.[26] The International Covenant on Civil and Political Rights (1966) goes further by specifically recognizing linguistic minorities in Article 27: "In those States in which ethnic, religious or *linguistic minorities* exist, persons belonging to such minorities *shall not be denied the right,* in community with the other members of their group, to enjoy their own culture, to profess and practice their own religion, or to use their own language" (emphasis added).[27]

Such provisions represent what Heinz Kloss describes as tolerance-oriented rights as opposed to promotion-oriented rights.[28] According to Kloss, tolerance-oriented rights are protections individuals have against government interference—in their homes, in the associations they are part of, and in the workplace. Promotion-oriented rights, on the other hand, involve "positive" rights—rights to use a particular language in accessing key public services such as education, government, courts, and public media through the medium of the minority language. For Kloss, immigrant languages should enjoy tolerance rights but not promotion rights. The state should not prevent immigrants from using their native language in the home, in civil society, and so on, but it should not accord immigrants the right to use of their languages by public institutions.

The international instruments mentioned above recognize tolerance rights and the traditional focus of language rights (and indeed human rights generally)—that is, on what the state *should not do* rather than on what the state *should* do. It is only in very recent decades that language rights in the form of positive or promotion rights have been increasingly advocated. Will Kymlicka and Alan Patten argue that this shift can be explained by several factors, including the rise of ethnolinguistic conflict in Eastern Europe; the resurgence of language-based secessionist movements in Catalonia, Flanders, and Quebec; the backlash against immigrant multiculturalism; the difficulties in building a pan-European commitment to European Union citizenship; and the global decline of language diversity and minority languages.[29] Around the world, concerns are being raised about the destruction of languages. Of 6,800 languages spoken at present, 90 percent will be dead within a century.[30] Minority languages have come under increased pressure to survive because of globalization and increased migration. According to Eric Garland, "as the world economy becomes more integrated, a common tongue has become more important than ever to promote commerce."[31] Linguists point out that such shifts are having devastating effects on language diversity. Linguistic loss is a symbol of a general crisis of biodiversity, since indigenous languages contain within them a wealth of ecological information that will be lost as languages are lost.[32] Countertrends can also be seen. Global prosperity and new technologies may allow smaller cultures to preserve their niches. Several modern examples (Québécois in Quebec and Welsh in Wales) show that a dying language can turn around and become vibrant again, depending on people's determination and the government policies that are put in place.[33]

From the 1990s onwards in particular, a shift away from mere tolerance of minority languages to positive action toward the promotion of minority languages can be witnessed in international instruments such as the UN Declaration on the Rights of Persons Belonging to National or Ethnic Religious and Linguistic Minorities 1992 and the European Charter for Regional or Minority Languages 1992.[34] Article 4 of the UN Declaration provides that states should take "appropriate measures" and "create favourable conditions" to enable persons to express their language.

The adoption of the European Charter for Regional or Minority Languages is seen as one of the most energetic measures in developing standards to support minority language protection.[35] The Charter came into force in 1998, but since then the geographical scope of its application has extended significantly. The Charter has now been ratified by twenty-four states and signed but not ratified by a further nine states.[36] As one of the key conventions of the Council of Europe, its aim is the protection and promotion of linguistic diversity in each of the contracting states (or Parties). It is the only binding international instrument specifically devoted to minority languages. Minority languages are defined as languages that are traditionally used within a given territory of a state by nationals of that state who form a numerically smaller group. Notably, this definition excludes languages of migrants and dialects of the official language(s) of the state.[37] On this basis, Ireland has not signed or ratified the Charter with regard to the Irish language, as Irish is the first official language of the state under the Irish constitution and thus does not come within the scope of the Charter. However, under the Charter the Irish language is recognized as a minority language in the United Kingdom. The United

Kingdom ratified the Charter in 2001 with respect to Irish in Northern Ireland, making a commitment to apply Part III (measures to promote use in public life) and accepted thirty-six actions, one more than the mandatory thirty-five. In general, it was the weakest action that was accepted in each of the following domains: education, judicial authorities, administrative authorities and public services, media, cultural activities and facilities, economic and social life, and transfrontier exchanges. Despite this weakness, the ratification of the Charter with regard to Irish is significant and an important basis on which arguments can be made for the continued protection and the United Kingdom's positive obligation toward the Irish language in Northern Ireland.

International and regional instruments such as the Charter have enhanced the status of minority languages and promoted greater recognition of language rights domestically. In line with the ethos and guiding principles of international instruments, the most recent trend in state recognition for language rights has been the adoption of domestic-language legislation. The rationale for language legislation is to recognize the validity of the aspiration of those who wish to use the protected language and the recognition that the language should be treated on an equal basis with the dominant language in the provision of public services. International trends in minority-language policy have paved the way for an extending appreciation of language rights claims in Ireland. The shift toward cultural rights and preserving culture heritage in international standards such as the UN Convention for the Safeguarding of the Intangible Cultural Heritage 2003 has received approval in government discourses. The 20 Year Strategy for the Irish Language 2010–2030[38] recognized the importance of preserving Irish on the basis of its contribution to language diversity internationally. "Safeguarding languages such as Irish" as a "crucial task in maintaining cultural diversity worldwide" recognizes the potential to move beyond Irish-language policy being rooted in support "couched in moral" terms and toward support on the basis of an "instrumental and functional perspective."[39] John Walsh's recent text *Contests and Contexts: The Irish Language and Ireland's Socio-Economic Development*[40] examines the links between the Irish language and positive economic development and thus the instrumental and functional value of the language. The functional value of the language and its potential contribution to economics and tourism may be more important than ever in these recessionary times.

LEGISLATIVE PROTECTIONS AND LANGUAGE POLICIES FOR IRISH

In the last decade and a half, much has been achieved in terms of governmental policy and legislative protection for the Irish language in Ireland and Northern Ireland, despite the differing contexts. The Belfast Agreement in 1998 guaranteed to "respect" and "promote" the Irish language in Northern Ireland and establish the cross-border body An Foras Teanga to promote Irish throughout the entire island of Ireland. In 2001, building on the commitments made in the Belfast Agreement, the United Kingdom ratified the European Charter for Regional or Minority Languages, with specific reference to Irish in Northern Ireland. In the Republic of Ireland the Official Languages Act 2003 was introduced, drawing on similar legislative initiatives in Wales (1993) and Canada (1985).

In the St Andrews Agreement 2006, the UK government promised to introduce language legislation with respect to Irish in Northern Ireland. In 2007, the Irish language, subsequent to a vigorous campaign by the Stádas committee, was granted status as an official language of the European Union. More recently, the 20 Year Strategy for the Irish Language 2010–2030 has been published, following the Irish government's Statement on the Irish Language in 2006. That statement affirmed the government's support for the development and preservation of the Irish language and the Gaeltacht and set out thirteen policy objectives to that end.

Given that the Statement on the Irish Language and indeed the 20 Year Strategy were brought to fruition under the stewardship of the previous Fianna Fáil/Green Party government, it will be interesting to observe the commitments of the newly elected government to the strategy and the Irish language generally.

The Republic of Ireland

The Official Languages Act 2003 in Ireland can be seen as a major milestone in Irish-language policy and the first instrument to give legislative effect to the constitutional provisions of Article 8.[41] While robust legal challenges to the position of Irish in the constitution have strengthened the legal status of Irish,[42] one must wonder how so much has been achieved in the last decade. While there is no simple answer, three factors in particular paved the way for the Official Languages Act.

First, the influence of international developments regarding language rights as well as the introduction of language legislation elsewhere (Wales, for example) provided a comparative context within which language rights claims for Irish could be made effectively. Second, the Irish-language debate has intensified as a result of the recent sociocultural changes in Ireland. Linguistic diversity in Ireland has had a liberating effect on Irish-language policy. Further still, an emerging liberal democratic consensus on human rights has allowed for increased acceptance of language legislation and increased language rights for Irish speakers. In general, there is widespread support for the Irish language. In a study undertaken by Micheál Mac Gréil and Fergal Rhatigan, it was shown that positive attitudes and aspirations for Irish have been maintained at very high levels. The results show overwhelming support for preservation of Irish: 52.5 percent want Irish preserved in the Gaeltacht and revived for use in arts and culture, while 40.9 percent want Irish revived and used for public purposes throughout the state.[43] However, there are also disputes on how best to support the language. For one, the cost of language translation of government documents as provided for under the Official Languages Act has received much criticism in recent years.[44]

Essentially, the primary objective of the 2003 act is to ensure better availability and a higher standard of public services through Irish. This objective will be achieved by placing a statutory obligation on departments of state and public bodies to make specific provision for the delivery of services in the Irish language in a coherent and agreed fashion through a statutory planning framework, known as a "scheme."[45] The language schemes of public departments will be agreed on a three-year renewable basis between the head of the public body and approved by the minister. Public bodies for the purposes of the act are those categorized or listed in the schedule and include government departments, local governments, and various state agencies. Section 20 of the act also provides for the appointment of a commissioner of official languages to supervise and monitor the implementation of the act. The commissioner will have the power to advise public bodies and independent citizens regarding their rights under the act as well as the power to investigate complaints and take legal action against any public body when requested information is not provided or when there has been a failure to produce a language scheme or update an old scheme. The ultimate sanction available to the language commissioner is to publish adverse findings in annual reports.[46] Besides the language schemes and the appointment of a language commissioner, the act ensures the unrestricted right of persons who communicate with public bodies to receive a reply in the same language. Furthermore, public bodies furnishing information to the public are required to do so in Irish or bilingually. The act also provides specifically for the *right* to use the Irish language in the courts and the Oireachtas (the Irish parliament).[47]

In terms of the legal status of the Irish language, the 2003 act is highly significant. In contrast to the plight of minority languages elsewhere, the act represents a major achievement in language policy. Nevertheless, despite the fact that many of the state's public bodies have made progress in relation to the quantity and quality of services provided through the Irish language, and the awareness of language rights has increased among the public, the extent to which the act challenges the long term belief that Irish is less appropriate than English in conducting business with state bodies is restricted on a number of grounds. In other words rhetoric does not match reality. The findings of the annual reports from the language commissioner are an invaluable source in providing an insight into the gaps between theory and practice.

Similar gaps are evident when one reflects on the official status of the Irish language in the European Union. In terms of status and employment, while its recognition has been a positive development for the Irish language, there has been a shortage of translators at the necessary level of competency to take up employment as EU language translators. Third-level institutions, like the Dublin Institute of Technology and the National University of Ireland Maynooth, have responded by providing diploma- and master-level courses in translation in order to meet the demand. Aside from the employment benefit, it will be interesting to monitor the long-term impact of official status for the Irish language in Europe.

Northern Ireland

Since the signing of the Belfast Agreement in 1998, the Irish language has become a central issue in human rights and equality debates in Northern Ireland, as a result of the commitments made by all parties to the agreement to respect and tolerate linguistic diversity. Drawing heavily on the language of the European Language Charter, the agreement provided that: "All participants recognise the importance of respect, understanding and tolerance in relation to linguistic diversity, including in Northern Ireland, the Irish language, Ulster-Scots and the language of various ethnic minorities, all of which are part of the cultural wealth of the island of Ireland."[48] The inclusion of this clause and respect for both Irish and Ulster-Scots specifically has been seen by some as a type of "conflict management."[49] In recent decades Ulster-Scots gained prominence in cultural discourses in response to the growth and revival of the Irish language in Northern Ireland, since the establishment of the Shaw's Road Gaeltacht and growth in Irish-medium education. The inclusion of Ulster-Scots and "languages of various ethnic minorities" in the agreement came at the behest of the Ulster Unionist Party. The reference to "other" ethnic languages does, however, represent the potential to elevate the language discussion in Northern Ireland beyond Irish and Ulster-Scots, to one based on the recognition and importance of language diversity in the light of international standards.

Under paragraph 4 of the agreement, the Irish language is given further recognition. The UK government declared that it would take "resolute action" to promote the language by facilitating and encouraging the use of the language in speech and writing in public and private life. Furthermore, commitments were made to facilitate Irish-medium education and explore ways of extending the availability of Irish-language television, "where appropriate," in the context of "active consideration" being given by the United Kingdom to signing the Council of Europe Charter for Regional or Minority Languages.[50] In the immediate years following the Belfast Agreement, the commitments made to the Irish language caused political controversy. Speaking in 2000, David Trimble, then first minister, described "language" and more generally "cultural matters" as a "political battleground."[51] Evidently, there was deep concern that the commitments to equality and recognition of the importance of the Irish language would in fact reinforce traditional political tensions rather than reduce them.

In terms of giving substantive legal recognition to the Irish language in Northern Ireland, the commitment made by the UK government under the St Andrews Agreement 2006 amounts to the most significant development. Within the agreement, the UK government promised to "Introduce an Irish language Act reflecting the experience of Wales and Ireland and work with the incoming Executive to enhance and protect the development of the Irish language."[52] Legislation arising from the St Andrews Agreement was passed in Westminster in 2006. No reference to a language act was included; instead, it placed a duty on the Northern Ireland Executive to adopt strategies "to enhance and protect the development of the Irish language."[53] To date, language legislation for Irish in Northern Ireland has not transpired, despite the publication of two consultation papers by the Department of Culture, Arts and Leisure in Northern Ireland.[54] In 2007, then minister Edwin Poots decided against introducing a language act. After reviewing the responses to both consultation processes and reflecting carefully on all the relevant issues, he "remained un-persuaded that there is a compelling case for bringing forward Irish language legislation at this time." He asserted that the actual proposal to introduce an *Irish Language Act* is "divisive" throughout the community: "the proposal to introduce Irish language legislation at this time is unlikely to command the necessary support in the Assembly on the grounds of being incapable of securing sufficient consensus."[55]

The primary obstacle to the introduction of language legislation for the Irish language is the political tension surrounding the issue. The issue is completely submerged within identity politics. Furthermore, this hostility and politicization of the issue has intensified as a result of the UK government's failure to fulfill the promises made within the St Andrews Agreement within an appropriate time frame. In 2010 the Irish-language debate and the demand for increased legal status for Irish in Northern Ireland were drawn into sharp focus once again, following two language-related developments: the publication of the *Third Report from the Council of Europe on the Implementation of the European Charter for Regional or Minority Languages in the United Kingdom*[56] and the dismissal of a case in the Court of Appeal concerning the use of Irish in court proceedings in Northern Ireland.[57]

The Committee of Ministers from the Council of Europe following the *Third Report* recommended that the authorities of the United Kingdom as a matter of priority "adopt and implement a comprehensive Irish language policy, preferably through the adoption of legislation" in Northern Ireland.[58] The council recommended the implementation of the "commitments" made by the UK government in St Andrews in 2006. The Court of Appeal case concerned a request to apply for an occasional liquor license through the medium of Irish. This request was refused on the basis of the Administration of Justice (Language) Act (Ireland) 1737, which prohibits the use of any language other than English in courts in Northern Ireland. The act provides that "all proceedings in Courts of Justice within this Kingdom shall be in the English Language."[59] This applies to all forms of oral hearings in open court and also to all official documents filed in connection with the proceedings.

Justification for Legislative Protections

According to the 2006 census figures, 160,000 people spoke Polish in Ireland every day, in comparison to the 85,076 speaking Irish daily.[60] The most anomalous aspect of gaining further status for Irish in the context of an increasingly linguistically diverse state is that there is no move to significantly expand this shift toward granting status or legislative support to minority immigrant languages. Though translation services are provided in public bodies such as in the courts[61] and the health service, government commitment to protecting the use of immigrant minority languages in Ireland is weak.[62] The overall climate regarding the retention of immigrant languages is, according to Kymlicka, "generally hostile," despite well-intentioned rhetoric of unity in diversity and equal rights claims.[63] Is it not a contradiction to have language policy and more specifically language legislation protecting Irish—a minority language—but not all minority languages? As the census figures in 2006 show, it cannot be attributed to size. Equally, in the UK several immigrant groups outnumber Gaelic speakers in Scotland and Irish speakers in Northern Ireland.[64]

One justification is linguistic survival. Although immigrant languages may disappear in the host country, the language survives in the mother country. If historic minority languages are lost in the homeland, they are lost for good. For this reason, special protection should be granted to languages in their historic homeland. The state also has an obligation to protect the national minority language because of historic injustices. In the Irish context, Kymlicka's justification theory would apply in the general sense. The notion of linguistic survival in the mother country is particularly relevant. For the immigrants that have come to Ireland—Polish, Chinese, Russian—their languages will continue to survive in their mother countries. However, if Irish does not continue to receive legal protection and government support in Ireland, the chances of its survival are lower.

In the context of the broader trends in language discourse in Ireland and internationally, cultural heritage as the justification for legislative protection and language-policy initiatives is stronger than historic injustice. Justifications for protecting the Irish language on the basis of historic injustice and nationalism have long been replaced in Ireland with arguments based on cultural heritage and cultural diversity. The aim is no longer one of Gaelicization but bilingualism. Recent language legislation and policy developments suggest greater links to concepts of equal opportunity, cultural heritage, and diversity. A shift in political vocabulary can be witnessed toward the importance of language as a part of cultural heritage and away from narrow nationalist ideology and the notion of Irish as a political tool. Rhetoric surrounding the government statement on Irish in 2006 identifies this shift in policy well: "The aim of 20th Century Government policies was to reinstate Irish as the main language spoken by the people, but the Government now plan to focus firmly on the practical development of a bilingual society where as many people as possible use both Irish and English with ease."[65]

Language rights and the protection of Irish as a part of cultural heritage are also evident in the 20 Year Strategy for the Irish Language, which recognizes that "safeguarding languages such as Irish is . . . a crucial task in maintaining cultural diversity worldwide."[66]

THEORY AND PRACTICE IN IRISH-LANGUAGE POLICY

Despite the enhanced legal status and recognition for the Irish language in recent decades, gaps remain in terms of its future as a viable and sustainable language. The gaps between theory and practice are clearly illustrated in the annual reports of the Office of the Language Commissioner, which oversees the implementation of the Official Languages Act 2003. The annual report of 2009 claimed that on a national level, the native language was secure and protected by state laws, but it went on to say that "the future of Irish as a living community language, even in the strongest Gaeltacht areas, is currently at its most vulnerable level."[67] In the 2010 annual report, the commissioner claimed that (despite an increase in the quality and quantity of services available in Irish) there were still significant gaps between the level of service provided in Irish and the same services offered in English. According to the 2010 report, that "alarming" gap was painted by the Department of Education and Skills in 2010, which reported that only 1.5 percent of the administrative staff of the department had the ability to provide a service in Irish of an equivalent standard to the service provided in English.[68]

Such statistics clearly illustrate the disparity between the ability to provide services in English and Irish as a result of a lack of bilingual competency among staff in the state sector. The supply of state services in Irish is dependent, above all else, on the language capacity of staff in the state sector. Until this fact is addressed in a realistic and measured way, the gaps will not easily be filled and the rights as provided for in the Official Languages Act will not be recognized as equal. Providing rights without the means to ensure those rights is not truly acknowledging rights and is thereby illustrating a contradiction in Irish-language policy and planning. The dynamics of reform in the past decade has brought forth fine intentions, but it is in the application that the full implementation of language rights for Irish speakers will be realized.[69]

The 20 Year Strategy for the Irish Language can assist in shortening the gap between theory and practice in Irish-language policy: it represents a newfound level of relativism and realism, illustrating a shift away from the essentialist claims based on cultural nationalism. The strategy refers to the elements that make up the modern-day context for the Irish language: "We know from the situation that faces Irish that language use does not follow automatically from ability to speak the language. *Actual language use results from the co-presence of ability, opportunity, and positive attitudes.* This Strategy seeks, therefore, to create positive circumstances for greater use by our people of the language ability that they have and for a real increase in that ability over time" (emphasis added).[70] Such relativism however, must be viewed in the context of the drastic economic downturn in Ireland and the advent of a new government in 2011.

Within the document *Towards Recovery: Programme for National Government,* the newly elected Fine Gael/Labour government furnished seven pledges to the Irish language. The government *now* fully supports the 20 Year Strategy. Fine Gael stated during the election campaign that it would support *many* (thus suggesting not all) of the provisions of the strategy. This support has now been extended to *all* provisions of the strategy, but on the condition that it will only deliver on the "achievable goals and targets proposed." In terms of the

Irish curriculum, the government has promised to undertake a thorough reform of the Irish curriculum and the way in which Irish is taught at primary and second levels of education. Regarding second-level teaching in particular, the government has also retracted the arguments advanced during the election campaign about making Irish an optional subject for the Leaving Certificate. Forceful criticism of the proposal during the election has resulted in a changed tack on the issue. It now states that a review of whether Irish should be optional will be carried out. On the implementation of the Official Languages Act 2003, the Government intends to carry out a review "to ensure expenditure on the language is best targeted towards the development of the language and that obligations are imposed appropriately in response to demand from citizens."[71]

Overall, the newly elected Fine Gael/Labour government appears to be committed to the Irish language. However, the inclusion of such phrases as "to ensure expenditure is targeted" and "achievable goals" suggests that the new coalition will not be unduly swayed by moral sentiment. Its stance will be influenced by economics, output, and results. The pledge made "to review current investment and funding programmes that benefit Irish language organisations in order to achieve visible value for money for citizens and tangible outcomes on a transparent basis" illustrates this point well.[72] Once more, the position of the Irish language is inseparable from the changing political and more specifically economic landscape of Ireland.

In Northern Ireland, the gaps between theory and practice in Irish-language policy arise as a result of the polarization of the language issue since the St Andrews Agreement. The 2010 developments epitomize the extent of the gap between rhetoric and reality within the language issue in Northern Ireland: the rhetoric of the UK government in St Andrews as opposed to the reality of the stance on the issue in the Northern Ireland Assembly. The Republican/Nationalist parties and Irish-language organizations however, continue to exert pressure on Westminster and the National Assembly. In light of the *Third Report* from the Council of Europe in 2010, Margaret Ritchie of the SDLP sponsored a motion on January 26, 2011 (no. 1348), which called on

Westminster to agree to a time scale to enact the Irish-language legislation that was promised in the St Andrews Agreement. The Irish-language advocacy group Pobal met with the new minister of state, Hugo Swire, on April 7, 2011, to discuss the ongoing stalemate situation in Northern Ireland. The position in Northern Ireland as regards minority-language recognition and status is completely out of step with developments in Wales and Scotland. Language legislation has been implemented with regard to Welsh and Scots Gaelic that allows for the use of these languages in the courts. Without full implementation of the commitments made to the Irish language in the Belfast Agreement and the St Andrews Agreement, the change sought by such agreements fails to fully materialize. The failed governance, on the part of the UK government in particular, discredits the ideals of equality and human rights as envisaged through "respect, understanding and tolerance" in the Belfast Agreement.

CONCLUSION

The last two decades have been extremely positive for the Irish language, with the growth of Gaelscoileanna, the launch of TG4, the implementation of the Official Languages Act, and recognition of the importance of the Irish language in the Belfast Agreement. Simultaneous to the suggested threats to language diversity and language survival brought about by globalization, energetic movements to "halt, counter and reverse linguistic convergence"[73] can be seen in contemporary Ireland. Peader Kirby, Luke Gibbons, and Michael Cronin note that "the Irish language which had been consigned along with Faith and Fatherland to the trash-can of late modernity not only did not do the decent thing and die, but actually expanded, developed and was taken over by a new generation."[74] Manuel Castells notes that the globalization of local economies can affirm local identities.[75] An appreciation for the importance of the Irish language at grassroots levels coupled with increased state resources and wealth paved the way for legislative and Irish-language policy developments. In Northern

Ireland, the signing of the Belfast Agreement announced a new era in Irish-language policy.

Nevertheless, complexities and contradictions in Irish-language policy remain. Measures introduced to protect the Irish language during the boom period will be tested in the current economic downturn, when there are fewer resources available and increasing pressure on the government to allocate spending in the "right" direction. Though the Irish language has never been in a better position in terms of legislative support, it remains vulnerable; this vulnerability, as with every other aspect of Irish society, is exposed by the economic crisis. The language commissioner in his 2010 report acknowledged that "one could hardly expect the Irish language to be ring-fenced while every other sector of society was suffering."[76]

Ireland is in a period of major transition. Nothing is certain; everything remains contingent on recovery. As a corollary, the Irish language is also facing a period of transition with the future uncertain. The current stance of the government leans in favor of prudence and a cautious approach to spending. The utilitarian focus is on "visible value for money" and "tangible outcomes." In this regard, Irish-language policy could find itself far down the pecking order of the balance sheets of the European Union, International Monetary Fund, and European Central Bank, and language developments achieved during the boom could fall by the wayside.

NOTES

1. *Population and Migration Estimates,* Central Statistics Office, Cork, 2010.

2. In its study of linguistic diversity in Europe, the Council of Europe's VALEUR Project listed Ireland among its "most multilingual countries." The project identified 158 additional languages in Ireland, defined as "all languages in use in a society, apart from the official, national or dominant language(s)," thus including regional or minority languages, migrant languages, nonterritorial languages, and sign languages. Joanna McPake and Teresa Tinsley, *Valuing All Languages in Europe* (Graz: European Centre for Modern Languages, 2007), 7, 27.

3. Caoilfhionn Nic Pháidín and Seán Ó Cearnaigh, introduction to *A New View of the Irish Language* (Dublin: Cois Life, 2008), x–xi.

4. Michael Cronin, *Irish in the New Century* (Dublin: Cois Life, 2005), 10.

5. Following a general election in February 2011, Fine Gael and Labour formed a coalition government for the sitting of the Thirty-first Dáil. The National Plan for Recovery (see www.finegael.ie) was released on March 7, 2011, following coalition talks between Fine Gael and Labour.

6. Article 8 of Bunreacht na h-Éireann (the current constitution) states that Irish is the first official language of the Republic of Ireland. The First National Programme for Education 1922 recommended that Irish be taught or used as a medium of education for at least one hour a day. In 1925, Irish became a prerequisite to enter the civil service. See Seán Ó Riagáin, *Language Policy and Social Reproduction: Ireland 1893–1993* (Oxford: Clarendon, 1997).

7. Ibid.; see also Diarmait Mac Giolla Chríost, *The Irish Language in Ireland: From Gíodel to Globalisation* (New York: Routledge, 2005).

8. Iarfhlaith Watson, "Identity, Language and Nationality," in *Contemporary Ireland: A Sociological Map,* ed. Sara O'Sullivan (Dublin: University College Dublin Press, 2007), 361.

9. Ibid., 361.

10. Michael Mays, "Irish Identity in an Age of Globalisation," *Irish Studies Review* 13, no. 1 (2005).

11. Watson, "Identity, Language and Nationality," 352.

12. Stuart Hall, "Introduction: Who Needs Identity?" in *Questions of Cultural Identity,* ed. Stuart. Hall and P. Du Gay (London: Sage, 1996), 2.

13. Sara O'Sullivan, Introduction to *Contemporary Ireland: A Sociological Map* (Dublin: University College Dublin Press, 2007), 9.

14. Micheál Mac Gréil and Fergal Rhatigan, *The Irish Language and the Irish People: Report on the Attitudes towards, Competence in and Use of the Irish Language in the Republic of Ireland in 2007–'08,* Survey and Research Unit, Department of Sociology, National University of Ireland Maynooth, 2009.

15. In 2010 in the Republic of Ireland there were 139 Irish-medium education primary schools and 36 secondary Irish-medium education schools in existence. In 1990, there were 64 Irish-medium primary schools and 11 Irish-medium secondary schools. Gaelscoileanna Teo, a national, voluntary organization in Ireland supporting the development of Irish-medium schools at primary and at postprimary level (founded in 1973), gathers statistics every year; see www.gaelscoileanna.ie. For more on the TV channel TG4, see its *Annual Report 2009,* 2010, 9, www.tg4.ie.

16. *Irish Times,* April 17, 2007.

17. David McWilliams, *The Pope's Children: Ireland's New Elite* (Dublin: Gill & Macmillan, 2005).

18. For more, see C. MacMurchaidh, "Current Attitudes to Irish," in Nic Pháidín and Ó Cearnaigh, eds., *A New View of the Irish Language.*

19. For more, see D. Mac Giolla Chríost, "Globalisation and Transformation: Language Planning in New Contexts," in *Language, Power and Identity Politics,* ed. Máiréad Nic Craith (New York: Palgrave Macmillan, 2007), 21–42.

20. Helen Ó Murchú, *More Facts about Irish* (Baile Átha Cliath, Ireland: Coiste na hÉireann den Bhiúró Eorpach do Theangacha Neamhfhorleathana Teoranta, 2008), 42.

21. Sue Wright, "The Right to Speak One's Own Language: Reflections on Theory and Practice," *Language Policy* 6, no. 2 (2007): 203.

22. Manuel Rodriguez, "The European Convention on Human Rights and Minority Languages," in *Minority Language Protection in Europe: Into a New Decade,* Regional or Minority Languages, No. 8, Council of Europe, April 2010, 13–28.

23. United Nations General Assembly, Universal Declaration of Human Rights, Resolution 217A (III), Article 2, December 10, 1948.

24. European Convention on Human Rights, ETS No. 005, 1950.

25. European Convention on Human Rights, Article 5 (2) and Article 6 (3).

26. Article 14: "The enjoyment of the rights and freedoms set forth in this Convention shall be secured without discrimination on any ground such as sex, race, colour, language, religion, political or other opinion, national or social origin, association with a national minority, property, birth or other status."

27. International Covenant on Civil and Political Rights, 999 UNTS 171, Article 27, adopted December 16, 1966, entered into force March 23, 1976.

28. Heinz Kloss, *The American Bilingual Tradition* (Rowley, MA: Newbury House, 1977).

29. Will Kymlicka and Alan Patten, "Language Rights and Political Theory," *Annual Review of Applied Linguistics* (2003): 3.

30. James McCloskey, "Irish as a World Language," in *Why Irish?: Irish Language and Literature in Academia,* ed. Brian Ó Conchubhair (Syracuse, NY: Arlen House and Syracuse University Press, 2008).

31. Eric Garland, "Can Minority Languages Be Saved?: Globalisation v Culture," *Futurist* (July–August 2006). See also N. Rassool, "Language Maintenance as an Arena of Cultural and Political Struggles in a Changing World," in *Rights to Language: Equity, Power, and Education: Celebrating the 60th Birthday of Tove Skutnabb-Kangas,* ed. Robert Phillipson (Mahwah, NJ: Lawrence Erlbaum Associates, 2000), 57–61.

32. Countertrends can also be seen. See Giolla Chríost, "Globalisation and Transformation."

33. Garland, "Can Minority Languages be Saved?."

34. UN Declaration on the Rights of Persons Belonging to National or Ethnic Religious and Linguistic Minorities 1992, Resolution 47/135, UN General Assembly, December 18, 1992; European Charter for Regional or Minority Languages (ECRML), Council of Europe Treaty Series no. 148.

35. Sue Wright, *Language Policy and Language Planning: From Nationalism to Globalisation* (Houndmills, UK: Palgrave Macmillan, 2004), 192.

36. This list is regularly updated on the website of the Council of Europe Treaty Office: conventions.coe.int.

37. *European Charter for Regional or Minority Languages: Collected Texts, Regional or Minority Languages,* No. 7, 5, Council of Europe, January 2010.

38. "20 Year Strategy for the Irish Language 2010–2030," Government of the Republic of Ireland, December 21, 2010, www.ahg.gov.ie/en/20Year StrategyfortheIrishLanguage.

39. Colin H. Williams, "Governance Without Conviction," in *Rights, Promotion, and Integration Issues for Minority Languages in Europe,* ed. Susanna Pertot, Tom M. S. Priestly, and Colin H. Williams (New York: Palgrave Macmillan, 2009), 4.

40. John Walsh, *Contests and Contexts: The Irish Language and Ireland's Socio-Economic Development* (Oxford: Peter Lang, 2010).

41. The Irish constitution states the following: "The Irish language as the national language is the first official language" (Article 8[1]); "The English language is recognized as a second official language" (Article 8[2]).

42. See further the leading case on the right to use Irish in courts in Ireland: *Ó Beoláin v Fahy* [2001] 2 I. R. 79. For a detailed discussion on legal challenges to the constitutional status of the Irish language, see Tomás Ó Máille, *The Status of the Irish Language—A Legal Perspective* (Dublin: Bord na Gaeilge, 1990).

43. Mac Gréil and Rhatigan, *The Irish Language,* 6, 110.

44. "Mind Your Language: More Than €6 Million Lost in Translation," *Sunday Tribune* (Dublin), February 15, 2009.

45. Official Languages Act 2003, no. 32 of 2003, Section 11.

46. To date, the commissioner has furnished six annual reports that provide detailed findings on the implementation of the act.

47. Official Languages Act 2003, no. 32 of 2003, Sections 9(2), 10, 8, 6.

48. "Economic, Social and Cultural Issues: Rights, Safeguard and Equality of Opportunity," par. 3, The Belfast Agreement, 1998.

49. See S. McMonagle, "Deliberating the Irish Language in Northern Ireland: from Conflict to Multiculturalism," *Journal of Multilingual and Multicultural Development* 31, no. 3 (May 2010): 257.

50. "Rights, Safeguards and Equality of Opportunity," par. 4, The Belfast Agreement.

51. *Irish Times,* October 7, 2000.

52. Annex B, St Andrews Agreement, October 13, 2006. The St Andrews Agreement (Comhaontú Chill Rímhinn) was an intergovernmental treaty between the British and Irish governments. The agreement resulted from multiparty talks held in St Andrews, Fife, Scotland, October 11–13, 2006, between the two governments and all the major parties in Northern Ireland, including the Democratic Unionist Party (DUP) and Sinn Féin. It resulted in the restoration of the Northern Ireland Assembly and the formation (on May 8, 2007) of a new Northern Ireland executive and a decision by Sinn Féin to support the Police Service of Northern Ireland, courts, and rule of law.

53. Northern Ireland Bill, St Andrews Agreement, November 21–22, 2006.

54. *Consultation Paper (13th March 2007) on Proposed Irish Language Legislation for Northern Ireland: Summary of Reponses,* Department of Culture, Arts & Leisure, Belfast, October 2007.

55. Statement by Edwin Poots, MLA, Minister of Culture, Arts and Leisure, to the Northern Ireland Assembly, on the proposal to introduce Irish language legislation, October 15, 2007, www.northernireland.gov.uk/news/ news-dcal/news-dcal-october-2007/news-dcal-161007-a-statement-by.htm.

56. *Third Report of the Committee of Experts on the Application of the European Charter for Regional or Minority Languages, in the United Kingdom,* Council of Europe, April 2010, 4, 21.

57. *Caoimhín Mac Giolla Catháin v The Northern Ireland Court Service* [2010] NICA 24.

58. *Third Report of the Committee of Expert,* 6.

59. Administration of Justice (Language) Act (Ireland) 1737, Chapter 6, 11 Geo 2, Section 1.

60. Central Statistics Office, *Census 2006 Principal Demographic Results* (Dublin: Stationary Office, 2007).

61. In 2008, seventy-one languages were used in Irish courts. For more, see *Irish Times,* October 28, 2009.

62. Government policy initiatives regarding immigrants include the National Action Plan Against Racism (2005–2008) (NPAR) and the Health Services Executive's National Intercultural Health Strategy 2007–2012. Over the last decade it has been recognized that translation and providing interpretation services are major challenges for Ireland today. The National Consultative Committee on Racism and Inter-culturalism (NCCRI)'s paper *Developing Quality Cost Effective Interpreting & Translating Services,* published in 2008, makes clear that in government policy there is no specific provision for interpreting and translation services for government service providers but there are references to supporting those minorities with little or no English, in the context of worker's rights, asylum and integration, and education policy.

63. Will Kymlicka, "Language Policies, National Identities," in *Language and Governance,* ed. Colin H. Williams (Cardiff: University of Wales Press, 2007), 507.

64. Ibid., 3–21.

65. An Taoiseach Bertie Ahern, December 19, 2006, at the launch of the Government Statement on the Irish Language.

66. "20 Year Strategy," 6.

67. *Annual Report 2009,* An Coimisinéir Teanga, Office of the Language Commissioner, Republic of Ireland, March 2010, 3.

68. Teanga, *Annual Report 2010,* An Coimisinéir Teanga, Office of the Language Commissioner, Republic of Ireland, February 2011, 6.

69. Williams, "Governance Without Conviction," 118.

70. "20 Year Strategy," 3.

71. *Towards Recovery: Programme for National Government 2011–2016,* Government of the Republic of Ireland, 2011, 55.

72. Ibid.

73. Wright, *Language Policy,* 181.

74. Peader Kirby, Luke Gibbons, and Michael Cronin, "The Reinvention of Ireland: A Critical Perspective" in *Reinventing Ireland: Culture, Society, and the Global Economy,* ed. Peader Kirby, Luke Gibbons, and Michael Cronin (London: Pluto, 2002), 14.

75. Manuel Castells, *The Rise of the Network Society* (Oxford: Blackwell, 1996).

76. *Annual Report 2010,* 5.

CHAPTER SEVEN

INTEGRATION THROUGH SPORT

The Gaelic Athletic Association and the New Irish

MIKE CRONIN

A group of teenage girls shouted "kill the fucking nigger"
at an under fourteen GAA player in Carlow last week,
and were encouraged to do so by adults.[1]

That Ireland has changed since the mid-1990s is indisputable. Outward emigration all but ceased for a period, peace came to the North, prosperity arrived in the Republic and then faded once more, and, for the first time in the history of the state, Ireland experienced large-scale immigration. The effect of the New Irish has been felt in all areas of Irish life. The world of sport has not been immune from the challenges laid down by the New Irish. Whether in soccer, rugby, or Gaelic games, the various ruling bodies have developed policies to encourage the New Irish to play their games. These policies have been driven not only by the demands for integration that exist at government level but also by sporting bodies that are in intense competition: one more young Brazilian or Latvian playing Gaelic games is one less who will succumb to soccer. Sporting bodies are in competition with each other for players and spectators. Catch them young, and they will be yours for a lifetime; lose them before they are teenagers, and you will struggle to win them back. With upwards of 10 percent of the population classed as nonnational in the 2006 census, the New Irish became one of the most significant groups in the battle for sporting hearts and minds.

This chapter explores how one sporting body, the Gaelic Athletic Association (GAA), responded to the New Irish. The GAA, founded in 1884 and at the heart of the cultural revival, is the largest and single most important sporting body across the thirty-two counties.[2] It is not merely a sporting body but rather a cultural organization, imbued with Irishness and underpinned by a community ethos that defines what it is to be Irish. The games are indigenous, rooted in the historical struggle—North and South—to create an independent Irish Republic, and located, through the 2,500 parish clubs, at the heart of the community. While some, such as many Ulster Unionists, often perceive the GAA as a backward-looking force championing an exclusive nationalism, the association has been more active than any other sporting body to win over the New Irish and to get them involved in Gaelic games.

This chapter, while acknowledging and applauding the GAA's efforts to welcome the New Irish into its organization, seeks to problematize the policy of integration through sport. The experience of the GAA, and other Irish sporting bodies, is located in a comparative context, and this chapter looks at how other sports organizations across the world have coped with the challenges of immigrant groups. It asks whether a policy of integration through sport is indeed desirable and whether, given the resources that are poured into reaching out to the New Irish, it is a worthwhile policy. Does the search for integration through sport drain limited resources from areas where equivalent spending would be more effective (such as attempting to slow the rates of rural emigration or to encourage sport among socially deprived groups) and contribute more to the creation of a mutually beneficial civil society?

Sport, since the days of the "games ethic" in the nineteenth-century British public schools and the emergence of Olympism as championed by Baron Pierre de Coubertin, has always maintained that it has distinctive, and positive, philosophical values. Sport, or so it is argued, is not simply a leisure pursuit (or, in the context of Premier League soccer or American football, a form of mass entertainment) but a force for good within society.[3] A society that embraces sport will have better cross-community relations, people will be fitter, their codes of conduct will improve, their levels of obesity will reduce, and their sense of responsibility to others (the ideal of the "team") will be heightened. All of this is true in certain contexts.

But sport also has an ugly side. It is an arena within society where racism and sexism are rife, it favors the strong over the weak, and most centrally, it excludes as many as it includes.[4] Many of the New Irish arrived in Ireland with a history of sporting participation. For some, their needs were instantly met by forming or joining soccer teams (that most international of games); others wanted to belong to a community whose sporting lingua franca was a peculiarly specific Irish game of which they had no knowledge. The GAA has reached out to those communities, but why is it that sport is held up so readily by media commentators, and others, as the public venue where attitudes toward newcomers and issues of race are to be interrogated? Sport, particularly the GAA, is one area of public life that has been regularly scrutinized by commentators as a means of deciding whether the Irish have been welcoming and inclusive.

The GAA is the most Irish of sporting bodies. It organizes its games across the whole of Ireland. Its rules contain commitments to the creation of a united Ireland, a devotion to the Irish language, and a promotion of Irish culture in all its forms. In terms of size and scale, the GAA outlasted and had more importance than the other great organization of the revival period, the Gaelic League, and it has a greater representation and active membership across the contemporary island than the Catholic Church. It has embraced the corporate ideals of sport (marketing and sponsorship), while maintaining its commitment to community-owned, grassroots, participatory sport. Despite its popularity among sections of the Irish diaspora and attempts at internationalism through its test series with Australian rules football, it has found no global outlet. They are Irish games, played on Irish pitches, by Irish men and women. The GAA has a mental landscape that stretches from parish to county and ends, every season, with the possibility of All-Ireland glory. It is localism set in a national context. It is about knowing where you are from.

And herein lies a problem for the GAA. Historically it has championed the very idea of being and belonging to Ireland. It is part of the establishment that created the independent Irish state and resisted British rule in the North of Ireland. In many ways the GAA creates difficulties for itself. It defines Irishness and a sense of place like no other organization on the island. Yet what happens if you are not born into the GAA family? How then do you access this association? Traditionally the question of exclusion has always been played out in the context of contested Irish identities. To be a Protestant, especially one from the North of Ireland, was to accept that the GAA (in most cases) was not for you. Explicit GAA bans excluded those who were members of the security forces or who played "foreign" games.[5] The association supported a specific ideal of what it meant to be Irish (and what Ireland might be), and therefore Protestants steered clear of it. In the changing context of Northern Ireland since the Belfast/Good Friday Agreement of 1998, the GAA has changed key rules that excluded non-Catholics and nonnationalists.[6] Yet how to face the challenge of the New Irish, those people who were not part of a historic binary division but who simply want to make Ireland their home and see their children play the games that their school friends play? By courting and encouraging the inclusion of the New Irish, is the GAA challenging its historic sense and definition of what it is to be Irish (and everything that the association has stood for), or is it seeking to ensure that all those who join are integrated into exactly the type of Irishness that the GAA historically represented?

The major waves of emigration from Europe, in the second half of the nineteenth and into the twentieth century, coincided with the establishment of codified, organized, and modernized sports across the Western world. The second half of the nineteenth century was the key period in the organization, and then explosion, of sport. With origins in elite British public schools and universities, sport spread rapidly.[7] The diffusion of sport was enabled by the trade and military routes of the British Empire, middle- and upper- class support for the sporting ideal as something that would "improve" the working classes, the advent of regular leisure time for industrial workers, and the railway revolution that transformed the sporting landscape in allowing fixtures (and rivalries) to be played across ever-larger geographical areas. Such macro forces worked similarly across the world, and in some countries the games of Britain were adopted.[8] Cricket found a home in Australia, South Africa, India, and the West Indies. Other countries, most notably the United States, adapted British games and produced their own sports, namely baseball, American football, and basketball. Ireland resisted the colonial impulse behind the sports of Britain and reinvented ancient pastimes, such as hurling and Gaelic football, so that they stood as Irish games for Irish people.[9]

The diffusion of games and the part that immigrants played in supporting the games of their new home are instructive for understanding what is happening in Ireland today. When the Irish left home in the later decades of the nineteenth century, their sporting minds would have been familiar with the newly established Gaelic games, as well as those British games of soccer, rugby, and cricket. Arriving in settler nations such as Australia, they would have found much that was familiar, and in the ranks of the great players in all the codes of Australian sport many Irish immigrants are to be found. The largest number of Irish immigrants headed to the United States, and it is here they would have found an unfamiliar sporting landscape. American football was, at that stage, largely the preserve of college athletics, and it was thus inaccessible to many Irish on the basis of wealth and class. The most common and popular game was baseball; played in both urban and rural spaces, it was *the* American game. For the Irish, however, the sport was one of which they knew nothing. They had a choice: stay with the games of their home and remain as outsiders, or adopt the new game as their own and integrate into the sporting customs of their new home.

The newly arrived Irish chose to go native. While the GAA has always had grounds and teams in the main "Irish" cities (Boston, Chicago, New York), these clubs have relied on fresh waves of immigrants to sustain themselves. (Indeed, during the years of the Celtic Tiger and with the recent problems of the status of undocumented Irish in the

United States, inward emigration has been so low that many American GAA clubs struggled to survive, a trend that has continued as the new wave of Irish emigrants have chosen to settle in countries such as Australia that have made visas more readily available than the United States.) The Irish largely chose to embrace the new sports that they found: they opted for sporting integration over cultural exclusivity. Accordingly, the Irish dominated baseball in the later years of the nineteenth century and, in doing so, became part of the fabric of American life. The same was true at the turn of the century in basketball, when Irish players and teams came to dominate. Their decision to embrace the sports of their new homes and to become Americans on the playing field was a key part of their transformation from outsiders to insiders.

By playing the games of the nation, the new immigrant group, despite any initial racist reactions from the locals, set themselves up to be included—something that they did without a plethora of state or sporting policies to encourage integration. They began to share the same rhythms of leisure time, the same fixtures, the same gossip, and the same favorites and rivals as their fellow Americans. To remain exclusively within the confines of their own sports, Gaelic games, would have marked the Irish as separate, as a group that did not wish to integrate or to become American. The very success of the Irish experience of integration into the American mainstream through sport had a profound effect on the viability of their own games in its new home, and the decision of most of the Irish to go native has always restricted the growth of the GAA in North America.

The Irish experience of sporting integration above isolation, which we can consider the norm of the immigrant, was echoed in Britain during the second half of the twentieth century. After the arrival of large numbers of New Commonwealth workers from the late 1940s, and the agreements that allowed the Irish free access, Britain became a multicultural and multiethnic society.[10] The last half century has not lacked incidents of racism, the presence of anti-immigrant political parties, and mainstream political and media comment about what stance should be taken toward the newcomers. That said, the

British experience of immigration (perhaps because of shared colonial cultures) has, for the most part, been positive.

One of the measures of the immigrant groups' success, especially favored by the media, has been the sporting achievements of the new arrivals and their descendants. What is instructive here has been the success of immigrants and their children. In the 1950s legendary West Indian cricketers such as Learie Constantine and Frank Worrell plied their trade in the Lancashire Leagues.[11] By the 1970s, the first black, British-born players were appearing for England, and by the 1990s Nasser Hussain became the first nonwhite captain of the national cricket side. Similarly in soccer, a lineage extends from Arthur Wharton, the first black professional footballer in the 1880s, to Paul Ince, the first black captain of the English national side and, in 2008, the first black Briton to briefly manage a Premier League side. All these processions, from point of arrival to a time of sporting leadership, were closely watched, and many people reacted to the sight of black soccer and cricket players in a hostile and racist manner. That said, it is in the arena of sport, more than any other part of British society (with the exception of the media and popular music), where immigrants and their descendants have visibly succeeded. It was through participation in sport, in playing the national games and becoming part of the nation's narrative, that the immigrant communities marked their arrival and announced their success. Sport, because it is so high profile and dominates large sections of the media, offers an entrée into society that is neither initially closed (like electoral politics) nor obviously visible to mainstream society (like the business world).

In the case of immigrant and outsider communities and sport, whether in North America, Europe, or Australasia, integration—although it might take generations to achieve—is key. To succeed, to announce one's arrival, and to be visible is to perform at the highest level in the sports of the host community. The challenge facing Ireland and the New Irish in recent years is whether native pastimes are open to outsiders, how far racism is an abhorrent but inevitable by-product of the initial stages of sporting integration, and whether sport should be the lens through which society judges if integration is working. Clearly racist incidents involving the New Irish and sport are eagerly reported by the press, and some of them will be discussed here, but other arenas, such as physical attacks in public, verbal abuse in the workplace, and discriminatory practices in the arena of employment, while monitored by several agencies and against the law, are, by comparison, seldom reported.

All the major sports bodies in Ireland have attempted to tackle racism in their organizations and on the field of play. In 2003, the Irish Football Association (IFA) launched its World United football initiative as a way of bringing together newly arrived immigrants in a single team that would play in local leagues. In celebrating the inclusion of Indian players in the team in 2007, the former Northern Ireland football manager, Lawrie Sanchez, noted that the scheme was "making a positive contribution to the development of football in Northern Ireland, encouraging people from different backgrounds to become involved in the sport of football in a culture based on respect."[12] The World United team currently includes players from Somalia, India, Ivory Coast, Qatar, Portugal, Zimbabwe, Brazil, Poland, and Iran. Similar initiatives have taken place in the Irish Republic with the support of the Football Association of Ireland (FAI) and have been promoted by one of the key agencies in the area, SARI (Sport Against Racism Ireland).

SARI was established in 1997 and has as its key aim the promotion of cultural integration and social inclusion through sport. SARI works closely with the major Irish sports bodies and has involved 50,000 New Irish people in various sports at different levels. This is done through a series of fun days, annual Soccerfest weekends (where an "international" competition is staged), and its SARI intercontinental league. This league contains twenty senior teams drawn from various national groups. The aim is to encourage involvement in soccer and introduce players to domestic leagues and teams. SARI has been successful, but there is a gulf between the grassroots involvement of New Irish sportspeople and a changing mindset at the top levels of sports administration. For example, in 2002, the world governing body of soccer, FIFA, gave €30,000 to all national federations to develop antiracism projects. The FAI failed to even apply for the money.

The FAI has developed projects relating to the New Irish in recent years, working closely with SARI and the Show Racism the Red Card scheme since 2006. In 2007, the FAI also introduced multilingual coaching and employed a series of locally based development officers who had integration and multiculturalism as one of their key objectives.[13] The national rugby body, the IRFU, has introduced a range of schemes promoting the involvement of anyone with an interest in rugby and a raft of rules that prohibit the use of racist language.

Despite the positive steps taken by the soccer authorities on the island, racism has still been an issue for New Irish players. Emeka Onwubiko, who played for Bray Wanderers and has played for Ireland at the under-nineteen level, witnessed racism as part and parcel of the game, especially when he was playing in the lower levels of the league. He recalled, "during the game one of their players [from Crumlin United] called me a nigger and a black cunt. Sometimes these things are said under the breath so [you] mightn't be sure, but this was straight to my face. The referee heard it too, but didn't do anything."[14] Despite reporting the abuse to the FAI, Onwubiko was told that without a personal witness (which never materialized), nothing could be done.

Soccer is an international game, and many of the New Irish arrive with experience of the game and are keen to continue their involvement. This has been a key reason behind the "international" teams and tournaments promoted by SARI and others. Since it is familiar, soccer lends itself to a degree of integration; while the problem of racism remains, soccer is, as much vocalized by its supporters, an international game. While SARI is supported by a range of sporting bodies, the bulk of its work has been with soccer. Rugby, while making a contribution to the debate and bringing in rule changes and supporting initiatives to welcome the New Irish, has not developed a player base from among the New Irish. Historically the strength of rugby has largely been in settler nations, and as such it has not, with some notable exceptions, worked outside its traditional recruitment base. In the Irish setting, rugby has been largely focused on fee-paying schools. Despite some notable successes with new clubs in urban areas under the guidance of the IRFU's community officers, the schools have remained the main feeders for the games. As fee-paying institutions, such schools are unlikely to have a large cohort of New Irish students, and as such, the game remains largely unchanged in terms of class and ethnic background.

This is why the GAA comes under more intense focus than other sporting bodies in Ireland. It is geographically spread across the whole country; it has received, in recent years, government grants to support its operations; and there is a sense (at least in the media) that it should be reaching out to the New Irish because it prides itself on its community appeal. So what has the GAA done about the New Irish question? The feeling that the GAA has a special role, given the central place of community in its activities, was not lost on Conor Lenihan, the former minister of state with special responsibility for integration: "The GAA is so wrapped up with our identity and habits as a people, it is no exaggeration to state that it is probably the most important social and sporting organisation ever to have come into existence in Irish life." Lenihan was certain that the involvement of the New Irish in the GAA was centrally important to the process of integration, as the association defined what it is to be Irish: "Hopefully there will be great voices and roars from the terraces in the years ahead for young men and women, the children of immigrants, who will in time excel at our native games. Immigrants who really want to find out what makes the Irish tick should make the effort to get those valued tickets for Croke Park over the summer. On a good Sunday, the electric atmosphere of a GAA crowd tells you virtually all that you need to know about Ireland."[15]

Despite there not being an international team in Gaelic games that is regularly involved in world and European tournaments, the GAA is seen as the most important definition of Irishness through sport: more rooted and expressive even than the men in green who line up for Ireland in soccer or rugby. The GAA has recognized this fact over recent years and has made strides to welcome New Irish communities into their clubs. This is not an easy task, as the hand of welcome is inviting the New Irish into a specifically Irish space where indigenous games are played. This is different from the experience of soccer, or even cricket, where many of the New Irish will have an instant familiarity with what is on offer. The GAA has pursued integration by staging family days at clubs across the island; the New Irish are brought into clubs, introduced to the games, and have the whole phenomenon of the GAA explained to them. A number of clubs have received state and council grants to appoint part-time staff and support schemes that reach out to the New Irish in a structured fashion.

The most important step forward for the GAA came in 2008, when it launched its strategy document, *GAA Strategic Vision and Action Plan 2009–2015*. In addition to planning the future of the games and the organization at various levels, the association made commitments toward the process of inclusion and integration. Specifically, the GAA appointed a full-time inclusion officer to plan and implement strategy for the whole island. Schools and clubs have had material made available in a number of languages for the New Irish, so that they can access the GAA more readily, and by 2015, it is envisaged that 30 percent of all clubs across the country will be staging "Have-a-go" days for immigrants and migrants. The aim of the strategy was to offer an inclusive and open environment for everyone and to be able to "welcome people of all nationalities, religions, ages and abilities into our Association and make it easy for everyone to take part."[16]

One of the most regularly cited success stories for the GAA has been the integration of the Brazilian population of Gort into the association. The original expectation was that the Brazilians would be more comfortable with soccer than Gaelic. The key issue in all this is schooling. Rugby and soccer are represented in the Irish schooling system, but Gaelic games dominate. While the adult New Irish may arrive with fixed sporting affiliations, their children, like all children, are attracted to those games they play at school with their peers. So while New Irish adults may remain outside of the GAA, and possibly not well informed about its games and ethos, their children have been ready converts. They have no choice about what games they play, and they have to take part in school lessons. Hence, if the school plays Gaelic games, then it is an obligation. The networks afforded through playing at school, along with the chatter on the playground about games on television and local sport heroes, results in New Irish youth being as conversant with the GAA as their peers. Scoil Eoin in Gort has a large number of Brazilian students, and Gaelic games are the core physical activity in school. The children are encouraged to write about the games (in Portuguese), and these reports, along with photographs of the matches, are sent to family members in Ireland and in Brazil. The transition from school-level participation to membership in the local club is supported by grants that ensure youngsters bitten by the Gaelic bug at school continue at club level as they grow older. However, with the downturn in the economy, many Brazilians who had made Gort home have returned to Brazil, and the number of Brazilians in school, and hence on the GAA pitch, has fallen.

Despite the past successes of the GAA in Gort and across the school system, it has not all been plain sailing. In July 2008 an under-fourteen GAA match in Carlow made national headlines for all the wrong reasons. Playing for Éire Óg was a then recent immigrant from South Africa, Teboga Sebala. During the match he was subjected to racist abuse from a group of teenage girls. What stunned most onlookers was not simply the abuse from the girls but the fact that their actions appeared to be condoned, even encouraged, by a group of adults. Father Brendan Howard, chair of the local board responsible for underage competitions, stated: "This has never emerged before. And I'd be very disappointed if it did. There's no place for that here. We have always tried to embrace other cultures and give them all a welcome, be they rich or poor or whatever. I wouldn't tolerate that kind of behaviour, it's totally unacceptable." Teboga had been subjected to similar racist abuse in the past and argued in the press following the game that it was entirely normal: "It's just the usual, people are racist against my colour. It just happens."[17] The GAA was quick to set up an investigation into the matter and unequivocally condemned the racist taunts aimed at Teboga.[18]

Clearly the issue of how to deal with racist abuse in sport taxes all sporting organizations in Ireland today (and indeed, around the world). Given the integration agenda, and the money available to sporting bodies that take positive and public steps to encourage integration, the majority of sporting organizations are working hard to develop strategies to welcome and include newcomers. But the problem of how to include all sectors of the island's population in sport is nothing new. Given Ireland's history, especially the conflict in the North in the last three decades, sporting spaces are not always shared spaces where everyone is welcome or respected. In soccer, in Northern Ireland, there was always a sense that the game, while played by both sides of the community at the grassroots level, was open only to Protestants at the elite and national level. The two leading Catholic teams were forced from the league because of sectarian violence and mistrust—Belfast Celtic in 1948 and Derry City in 1972. Windsor Park, the home of the Northern Irish national side, was seen, until recent years, as a bastion of Loyalist identity, and Catholic players, such as Neil Lennon, had suffered sectarian abuse and death threats at the hands of those who were "supporting" him. The IFA has invested much time, effort, and money into transforming this situation and removing the more obvious sectarian flags and chants from the terraces of Windsor Park. But sectarianism, in this case, is simply a historic manifestation of contemporary sporting racism: it is the mistrust and demonization of the outsider. In the past the outsider was an Irish Catholic; in modern times it is more likely to be a black or Eastern European player.

The GAA has always organized its games on the basis of a thirty-two-county Ireland. Given its historic bans on the security forces and foreign games, and its open embrace of "Amhrán na bhFiann" and the Irish tricolor as a prelude to every game in Northern Ireland, the GAA is not natural territory for the Protestants of Northern Ireland. So while the association works hard to welcome the New Irish into its ranks, it also has to face the historical difficulty of what to do about welcoming members of the Protestant and Unionist community. In its 2008 strategic document, the GAA makes clear that the work on inclusion and integration, primarily aimed at the New Irish, also has to reach out, in Ulster at least, to the Unionists: "In Ulster, the Association will establish cross-community hurling and football teams, urban focused cross-community Gaelic games camps, and continue to develop links with the Unionist community."[19]

In 2007 the GAA faced a great deal of criticism after sectarian abuse was directed at Fermanagh hurler Darren Graham. In a local match "someone from the opposing team called him a 'black cunt'.

'Black', in this case, was a reference not to the colour of his skin but to his religion. It is short for 'Black Protestant', a long-standing term of sectarian abuse. 'It just came to a head,' he told the *Belfast Telegraph*. 'Something bad [was said] on the field: "You're a black cunt." Then another ran by and said: "It's the truth, you're nothing but that."'[20] That Graham was a Protestant in Northern Ireland on the receiving end of sectarian abuse was nothing unusual. But Graham was also a Protestant playing Gaelic games, and his father, along with two of his uncles, had been killed by the IRA during the Troubles. In response to the abuse, Graham stated he would never play GAA again. Subsequently Graham rejoined the ranks of the association after the leadership of the GAA supported his stance and stated that they would not allow any further incidents of sectarian abuse to go unpunished. For many in the Unionist community, the Graham incident proved everything they felt they knew about the GAA: it is a closed organization for people from a Catholic/nationalist heritage, and not for them.

The historic and contemporary issues surrounding who plays which sport on the island of Ireland are complex. In an age of fiscal, governmental, and popular accountability, sports bodies have to be seen to be doing the right thing. This has resulted in all major sports bodies having policies and procedures on integration and racism/sectarianism and all of them appearing in a rush to throw open their doors. In itself, this is a noble cause and one that echoes the British government's sporting mantra of the 1970s: "Sport for All." Indeed, anyone who wants to should be allowed to access sporting organizations. However, this is not a level playing field. Private sports clubs across the island, be they golf, tennis, or leisure, do not come under the same scrutiny. Since 2004, Portmarnock Golf Club has been locked in a legal case as to whether their stated men-only membership rules contravene equality legislation. Simplistically their defense is that, as a private members' club to which fees are paid, they can admit or exclude anyone or group as they see fit. Equally, the finances of joining most private sporting clubs mean that they can never be truly open, especially to those from poorer backgrounds, from the "wrong" class, or from the ranks of the New Irish.

It is the large-scale, mass-membership, and publicly funded sports that have come under most scrutiny with respect to accessibility issues. Rugby is insulated to a degree from the debate because of its link with fee-paying schools. Soccer and cricket can most easily point to successes: they are international and familiar games that can absorb newcomers who readily understand the rules and the social structures. The GAA, which prides itself on its history and heritage as an Irish cultural and sporting organization, has historically sought to support the needs of one strain of Irish identity. While it has to have an open-door policy with respect to the New Irish and Unionist communities, it is questionable whether the resources being spent and the pressure to achieve results are desirable.

The historic experiences of integration through sport, whether in the United Kingdom, United States, or Australia, show that this process cannot be forced. Sporting assimilation takes place gradually. From the current crop of New Irish GAA players, who are being introduced to the games through their schools, star players will undoubtedly emerge. But that will take a decade or so, and with the ebb and flow of emigrants dependent on the fortunes of the economy, the numbers of the New Irish will not be stable. Once established, these stars will be able to act as the role models for the next generation. In an era of economic uncertainty, when the numbers of the New Irish are being radically transformed by decisions to return home or to move on, the predictions of even a few years ago of how large the New Irish population would be are difficult to stand by. As such, planning becomes difficult, if not impossible. While the GAA is accountable to its membership and the public, is a large expenditure of resources on inclusion and integration desirable? Will money spent in Ulster really turn large numbers of Unionists into fervent GAA members? Surely it is better to develop plans that support the games in urban areas, for example; by their nature these include large numbers of New Irish and socially deprived. This could be seen as a benefit for whole communities and bring them together around a vibrant GAA club, instead of targeting one group whose sporting allegiance is not clear-cut and whose long-term presence in that community is not fixed.

These are all complex challenges for the GAA and other sporting bodies. Doors have to be open, support has to be given where necessary, and incidences of racism/sectarianism have to be stamped out. However, we should not be unrealistic. Sport is predicated on choices. Individuals have to choose whether to play at all and, if so, which game to play. Policies and expenditure are not guaranteed to make either the New Irish or Unionist populations GAA players and followers. They have the right to choose to stay with sports they know, such as soccer, gymnastics, or rugby, or reject sport altogether. Equally, the GAA has to be respected if it makes the decision to function as a supporter and embodiment of a specific cultural and sporting identity (Irish) and is mindful of the interests of its majority population, so long as it is open to allowing others to enter and embrace that culture.

NOTES

1. Brendan Lawrence, "Fans at U14 Match Shouted 'Kill the Nigger,'" *Carlow Nationalist,* July 23, 2008.

2. Mike Cronin, *Sport and Nationalism in Ireland: Gaelic Games, Soccer and Irish National Identity* (Dublin: Four Courts, 1999).

3. Nyla R. Branscombe and Daniel L. Wann, "The Positive Social and Self Concept Consequences of Sports Team Identification," *Journal of Sport and Social Issues* 15, no. 2 (1991): 115–27; John Sugden, "Belfast United: Encouraging Cross-Community Relations Through Sport in Northern Ireland," *Journal of Sport and Social Issues* 15 (1991): 59–80.

4. Andre Krouwel, Nanne Boonstra, Jan Willem Duyvendak, and Lex Veldboer, "A Good Sport?: Research into the Capacity of Recreational Sport to Integrate Dutch Minorities," *International Review for the Sociology of Sport* 41 (2006): 165–80; Kristin Walseth, "Sport and Belonging," *International Review for the Sociology of Sport* 41 (2006): 447–64.

5. Paul Rouse, "A History of the GAA Ban on Foreign Games, 1884–1971," *International Journal of the History of Sport* 10, no. 3 (1993): 333–60.

6. David Hassan, "The Gaelic Athletic Association, Rule 42 and Police Reform in Northern Ireland," *Journal of Sport and Social Issues* 29, no. 1 (2004): 60–78.

7. Richard Holt, *Sport and the British: A Modern History* (Oxford: Clarendon, 1989); J. A. Mangan, *Athleticism in the Victorian and Edwardian Public School: The Emergence and Consolidation of an Educational Ideology* (London: F. Cass, 2000).

8. Allen Guttmann, *Games and Empires: Modern Sports and Cultural Imperialism* (New York: Columbia University Press, 1996).

9. Mike Cronin, William Murphy, and Paul Rouse, eds., *The Gaelic Athletic Association, 1884–2009* (London: Irish Academic Press, 2009).

10. Enda Delaney, *The Irish in Post-War Britain* (Oxford: Oxford University Press, 2007).

11. Jeffrey Hill, "'Connie'—Local Hero, National Icon: Cricket, Race and Politics in the Life of Learie Constantine," *Sports Historian* 22, no. 1 (2002): 79–99.

12. Robert Caryy, "Sanchez Hails NI Anti-Racism Through Football Initiative," *Metro Éireann,* June 7, 2007.

13. Catherine Reilly, "Nothing's Black and White with the FAI," *Metro Éireann,* April 21, 2006.

14. Sandy Hazel, "Racist Abuse Straight to My Face," *Metro Éireann,* July 31, 2008.

15. Conor Lenihan, "Gaelic Games the Key to Integration," *Metro Éireann,* July 17, 2008.

16. *GAA Strategic Vision and Action Plan 2009–2015* (Dublin: Gaelic Athletic Association, 2008), 34.

17. Lawrence, "Fans at U14 Match."

18. Fiach Kelly, "Race Taunts Won't Put Me Off GAA, Says Young Player," *Irish Independent,* July 25, 2008.

19. *GAA Strategic Vision,* 35.

20. Fintan O'Toole, "Diary," *London Review of Books,* September 6, 2007.

CHAPTER EIGHT

REFLECTIONS ON RACE IN CONTEMPORARY IRELAND

STEVE GARNER

Any reflection on the category "race" in the contemporary world is inevitably framed by the cumulative layers of meanings and practices attached to bodies and cultures over the previous centuries. If the idea of race resembles anything, it is a palimpsest,[1] with past interpretations leaking through to make the ink of the present run. Accordingly, I present some historical notes not as a distinct prelude to the "real" story, positing a rupture of past and present, but as the beginning of the story proper.

I want to begin by establishing three elements of the analysis set out here, and to which I shall return throughout. The first is about shifting the understandings of the scope of racism, away from its attribution to aberrant and deviant individuals and also away from the notion that these are old ideas and practices that no longer apply in North America or Europe. The place to which we are moving these understandings is where racism (as a set of ideas and practices) is also embedded in the structures of society. This functions in the ways people routinely think about groups of people who are "not like us," in how the "us" is imagined, in the way laws operate, and in the way people have differential access to resources and services. In brief, racism is about power differentials encapsulated in social systems. All of this necessarily has a historical dimension—hence the talk of the past, but, I reiterate, it is not located only in the past.

The second point is that to fully understand racism, we have to grasp that it embraces not merely physical differences but culture and, equally as important, that this has always been the case. Think of the nineteenth-century obsession with bodies as expressions of cultural superiority and inferiority as the anomaly, or blip, in the story of race. The element of continuity has been the reliance on understandings of innate cultural difference, that what lies beneath the skin, fat, bone, and muscle is determinant and distinctive. Thus, what is referred to as the "new racism,"[2] "cultural racism,"[3] or, at a stretch, "color-blind" racism[4] represents an ideological "return to normalcy" as far as presentations of race are concerned.

Third, the way in which power relations and cultural understandings are wedded is through processes involving the material (practices) and the ideal (ideas). One of these spheres alone is not enough. As in the cases of class and gender, the dominant group normalizes its dominance in the world of the material through the realm of ideas, so that this domination becomes natural and unremarkable. There are advantages and disadvantages to be gained from the system of structural discrimination: some are winners, and some are losers. From this understanding of racism, individuals can disagree with the ideas that constitute racism while still benefiting from the material outcomes their society produces for them. Structural racial discrimination is a form of social contract, and while some whites are not signatories to it, they still derive material and cultural advantage from it.[5] To apply this strictly to the Irish case, in which racialized others are also white, focusing too much on the color line leads us to a misleading picture of the actors. However, not focusing on it enough leads us to a misleading picture of the complexity of the situation. Finally, focusing only on migrants and only on contemporary Ireland loses the specificity of the story of race.[6]

Our mission, therefore, is to begin addressing epistemological ignorance: "Whites will then act in racist ways *while* thinking of themselves as acting morally. In other words, they will experience genuine cognitive difficulties in recognizing certain behavior patterns *as* racist."[7]

Social scientists in particular should seek to avoid making the starting point assumptions that are actually outcomes of racism. These might include the assertion that racism no longer exists; that racism only exists elsewhere; that only odd people, rather than normal, nice people, can be racist; or that race is only about skin color. Instead, we must take into account the full spectrum of ideas and practices that constitute racism and recognize that ways of knowing (epistemologies) are not neutral. Here I am going to focus on the racialization[8] of social relations in the Republic of Ireland and of Irishness in relation to its specific historical and material location: that is, a once-booming economy. I will include a discussion of Travellers, a long-standing, indigenous Irish minority whose omission from the story would render this study seriously skewed. Beginning with some brief historical notes, I then identify the racialization of the Travellers before moving on to the new demographic configuration brought about by the migration of the 1990s onwards. Finally, I will analyze how the booming economy structured the racialization of Irishness, Travellers, and new migrants in particular ways, and indicate the roles of the state in this process.

HISTORICAL NOTES

The streams of history influence the creation of a discourse that depicts the actors as members of culturally distinctive groups and whose social relations are hierarchically organized. In the case of the Irish, this process took the form of attributing a set of characteristics to Irish society and the individuals who comprised it, and it covers the period from about the twelfth century to the second half of the sixteenth century.[9]

By the 1570s, the question for colonial rulers in Ireland[10] was not "Are the Irish a distinct group with a backward culture?" but rather "What are the consequences of this fact?" They were either redeemable heathens, who could be civilized by exposure to English rule, or nonredeemable savages who could be treated as such (slaughtered with impunity, land stolen, etc.). Vacillation between these poles can be identified, for example, in Spenser's *A View of the Present State of Ireland* (1596).[11] The background to our story of race in Ireland thus lies squarely within the context of colonial rule; the division of subjects into civilized and uncivilized, superior and inferior. Yet until the late eighteenth and early nineteenth centuries, reference to physical difference is absent from the discourse: everything is culture. English historian Edmund Campion's 1633 description of the Gaelic Irish encapsulates this duality through the colonizer's eyes: "Clear men they are of skin and hue, but of themselves careless and bestial."[12]

A major distinguishing point of the cultures was their capacity for productivity. There is particular emphasis on the Irish people's perceived incapacity to turn land to profit at the expected rate. Irenius, in Spenser's *View of the Present State of Ireland,* stresses that "though Ireland is by nature counted a great soil of pasture, yet had I rather few cows kept and men better mannered than to have such huge increase of cattle and no increase of good conditions." Moreover, Sir John Davies notes triumphantly in 1612: "The lands of the Irish in Ulster were the most rude and unreformed part of Ireland, and the centre of the last great rebellion. They are now better organized and established, than any of the lands in the other provinces. . . . The organization of those lands happened with the special providence of God, who cast out those wicked and ungrateful traitors, the enemies of the Reformation in Ireland."[13] The drive to make Irish soil more productive lies at the heart of the English initiatives from the mid-sixteenth century, and this is underscored by the projection of the Irish as being congenitally slothful and unproductive.

THE ROLE OF DIASPORA

Between the plantations of the 1550s and the 1641 rebellion, the three-way split between Old Irish, Old English, and New English gave way to the binary of Irish Catholic/Gaelic and English and Scots/Protestant.[14] Irish people thus learned about race at home in the colonial setting: an unequal power relationship. They did not learn about race through physical *and* cultural distinctions until they encountered people outside Europe from the 1600s. These encounters occurred with the Irish protagonists in a far greater range of positions than those involving the majority of English, French, and Spanish, for example, in the New World, because they were prisoners of war and indentured laborers as well as missionaries, landowners, administrators, and soldiers (and not only in the British Empire). The earliest collective encounters of this nature took place in the Anglophone Caribbean islands in the seventeenth century, at a time when the Irish were still considered threatening and potentially disloyal to the Crown. Yet by the end of that century, the overriding social identities within those colonies were whiteness and blackness, which by then corresponded exactly with the distinction between free and enslaved labor status. The Irish, in that context, had become unquestionably white.

In North America, the story was different. The Catholic waves of immigration that are now thought of as the mainstream replaced numerically superior waves of earlier Protestant emigration that had occurred throughout the eighteenth century. The Catholic Irish arrived from the 1830s onward, and their numbers peaked in the aftermath of the Famine. The world of social relations into which they disembarked bore a number of similarities and dissimilarities to what they were used to.

The dominant ethnic group was still Protestants of Northern European stock, who organized North American institutions as a reflection of Protestant cultures. Catholics were viewed as a lower level of European civilization, and the Irish were the first European Catholics to immigrate to the United States in any numbers. Popular images of these Irish immigrants (linked to inferior culture, poverty, and urban dwelling) were so negative that Protestant Irish Americans began to refer to themselves exclusively as "Scotch-Irish" to distinguish themselves from "Irish" (which meant "Catholic") by the middle of the nineteenth century.[15]

However familiar the domination of Protestantism may have been, two other connected aspects of American society were new to the Catholic Irish. First, American society was divided into slaves and freemen. Some of the latter were former slaves. The stakes of not being slaves greatly influenced the development of Irish American identity. The party that sought to organize them politically in the eastern seaboard cities and Chicago was the pro-slavery Democratic Party. In the mid-nineteenth century, the Democrats created anxiety among working-class whites by focusing on the projected consequences of abolition for them: a drop in wages, greater employment competition, and the disappearance of the white race in a wave of "amalgamation."[16]

This leads us to the second major difference: color and culture were dividing lines that had serious impacts on people's life chances. After living in a context in which whiteness and blackness had little relevance in terms of ordering society, nineteenth-century Catholic Irish immigrants were now embedded in one in which color and culture determined whether one could be made a slave, whether one could be considered a person or an object in the eyes of the law, and one's access to a variety of rights and resources. The only way in which the Catholic Irish were not unproblematically part of white America was culture: they had the right to citizenship and the vote through their European origins. Nevertheless, they still had to demonstrate that they were not going to jeopardize the Protestant secular public sphere through their allegiance to Rome. The passage to mainstream American whiteness would be greatly facilitated by the removal of black Americans from the areas where the Irish lived and the economic niches in which the Irish worked. Irish Americans proceeded to do so frequently and successfully in the middle decades of the nineteenth century.[17]

AMBIVALENT RELATIONSHIP TO EMPIRE

The ambivalent Irish participation in empire produced varied responses from a range of roles.[18] Some of the latter, such as slave owner, administrator, soldier, and missionary, gave Irish people executive power over those seen as members of other, inferior races across Asia,

Africa, Australasia, and Latin America.[19] These roles enabled negative evaluations of others to be accrued and transmitted within and across the diaspora.[20] Just as sixteenth-century accounts of exposure to Africa and colonial America provoked comparisons between the indigenous people and the Irish,[21] so too did the Irish enjoy access to the dominant discourse of empire in the eighteenth and nineteenth centuries.[22] Moreover, despite the colonial relationship between England and Ireland, the latter was (unevenly) a material beneficiary of empire. The experiences of internalizing norms of domination, according to which the colonized peoples were lesser breeds, cannot obviously be generalized to a unitary position of racial superiority held by all Irish people. However, by the mid-nineteenth century it was frequent for groups to be labeled as "races" and for the understandings of "race" to legitimize the material relations of slavery and colonial rule. Within the hierarchy of social Darwinian readings of world development that emerged in the final quarter of the nineteenth century, Irish nationalists, like other nationalists of that time, saw their destiny as Europeans in a world of European nation-states defined by superior culture and forms of government.

CONFRONTATION OF HIERARCHICAL NATIONALISMS

Ireland has been the site of ongoing confrontation between three nationalisms (British, Irish, and Unionist) for nearly a century, and between Irish and British for a lot longer. This is not to say that they each have equivalent power to construct social relations or impose their views of the world. Clearly the most compelling power for a long time has been British, and this has been backed by the military might of the state. Irish and Unionist nationalisms have been dominant for different periods in different places. The relevance of this point is not to begin a debate about what is distinct about each, or their precise lineage, but to note that nationalisms are, on the whole, exclusive by their very nature. In saying "we," nationalisms implicitly define a "they." The dynamic of racialization similarly depends on the injection of one set of interpretations of difference, to do with

culture and/or inherited features or traits. Racialization is a two-way
process. At different periods in Ireland's history these nationalisms
told different stories about their proponents.

The nationalism of the New English Protestants from the 1570s
posited the distinction between Protestantism and Catholicism as
the major dividing line.[23] Three centuries later, the focus on the racial
terms "Anglo-Saxon" and "Celt" did not necessarily banish the religious divide from the field of racialization; indeed, the latter was pre-
sumed by the former. The Gaelic revival put forward a Gaelic heritage for Catholic Celts, a further cultural manifestation of a profound
difference permeating the blood and the air that the authentic Irish
breathed. The Unionists' twentieth-century stress on a particular form
of Protestantism (as well as allegiance to the Crown) as the correct
manifestation of Britishness seems to bring us back full circle. But
that would be simplifying what has been historically a multilayered
struggle over meanings for which nationalist ideologies have been
the mutually antagonistic vehicles.

The racial discourse of Irishness has been at least partly the un-
predictable outcome of a set of competing exclusions. Different elements of identity get emphasized as distinguishing points, and membership in the nations imagined by the British, the Irish nationalists,
and the Unionists (with overlapping territories) is predicated on cultural understandings, inheritance, and the capacity to mobilize symbols. This process has been undergirded by military and paramilitary
violence. The circulation of ideas between dominant and subordi-
nate groups can be exemplified in the way that Travellers have been
represented as marginal to the nation through their nomadism.

TRAVELLERS

In the Renaissance period the English pointed to the seminomadic
settlement patterns of the Gaelic Irish as evidence of their uncivilized
nature. Civilization was constituted in this view as, among other things,
being sedentary and centered in urban areas. Traveller activist Sinéad
Ní Shuínéar argues that the anti-Traveller racism in contemporary

Ireland continues this colonial view.[24] Jim McLaughlin asserts that antinomadism flourished as a result of the Irish nationalist movement's espousal of modernity.[25] Attachment to land, in the form of individual (not communal) property relations, was posited as the lynchpin of the modern.

Irish Travellers are an indigenous minority who comprise between 22,000 and 30,000 (about 0.7 percent) of the Irish population at the 2006 census. According to a variety of indices such as levels of education, mortality rates, life expectancy, and income, Travellers are a disadvantaged group in Irish society.[26] In the mid-1990s, they attained "ethnic minority" status, which we might conceptualize as "recognition" of difference as the basis of equal rights though not always equal treatment.[27] A question in the census now allows for people to identify themselves as members of the "Travelling community." This made them collective actors in the corporatist social partnership model— represented on the board of the National Consultative Committee on Racism and Interculturalism (NCCRI) and the Equality Authority, the bodies set up to monitor and advise the government on racism.

Attitudes toward Travellers seem to have remained unflinchingly hostile across the last few decades. While opinion polling is problematic, it does tell us some broad things about people's views.[28] In the attitudinal survey work done between 1972 and 2001 (but mainly since the late 1990s), Travellers were the subject of the most hostile attitudes of any Irish racialized or ethnic minority.[29] This is despite the presence of refugees and black people in growing numbers, antipathy toward whom is clearly identified in the Eurobarometer 1997 and 2000[30] and sporadic newspaper polls. In the 1996 follow-up to his work from the early 1970s, McGréil found that Travellers were the most "socially distant" of the *ethnic* groups in his survey, and fifty-second out of fifty-nine out-groups.[31] Travellers also report the highest frequency of physical and verbal attacks among the minorities in the 2001 Amnesty International survey.[32]

The racialization of Travellers in Ireland has not differed greatly from that of nomadic people elsewhere in Europe. They are characterized as unproductive, thieving, uncivilized, and nomadic bearers of disorder and, above all, dirt.[33] Since the 1960s, when the first commission report was written, Irish authorities have officially treated Travellers as a problem whose solution is assimilation out of their culture and into sedentary life. By the mid-1990s, Travellers had fought for and achieved a space in which they could pursue the nomadic element of their culture.[34] This development came into conflict with the commodification of land in booming Tiger Ireland.

However, before this boom, Travellers had been discriminated against by both individuals and authorities. Bryan Fanning explores the institutionalization of anti-Traveller racism in one local authority: Clare County Council, in the West of Ireland, between 1963 and 1999.[35] Local councillors made it difficult for Travellers to access housing in a number of ways, such as failing to comply with the statutory obligation to provide accommodation for Travellers. The use of distinctions between "local" and "outsider" was also used to the Travellers' detriment. Even if individual Travellers felt they were from Clare, they were likely to be categorized as being from another county, because proof of residence within the council's jurisdiction was difficult for Travellers to provide. Moreover, councillors actively contributed to creating a climate of antipathy toward Travellers, sometimes supporting settled residents' fears of Traveller settlement in their areas. They also criticized voluntary sector initiatives for improving Travellers' living conditions, and what they saw as Travellers' behavioral norms, rather than the authority's responsibility to house its clients, frequently became the subject of discussion.

In recent years, the most significant intervention in the field of Traveller relations with the Irish state has been the transformation of nomadic culture into a potentially criminal offense. As in the case of Britain (through the 1994 Criminal Justice and Public Order Act), the Irish state has effectively shrunk the space available for the enactment of a core element of Traveller culture: mobility. The most important of the state's instruments are Section 32 of the 1998 Accommodation Act and the Amendment to the Criminal Justice Act 2002. These make "trespass" a criminal (rather than a civil) offense.[36] Yet local authorities have consistently failed to follow the government's actions plans when it has come to providing the required number of "halting places"—that is, officially sanctioned roadside sites. A growing proportion of Travellers are thus left no option but to use unofficial sites, therefore putting themselves in jeopardy of prosecution and open to physical attacks. While antagonism to Travellers has a long history, Ireland's established identity as a country of emigration has only recently undergone transition to a country of immigration.

"NEW" MIGRATION

Beginning in 1996, the Republic shifted to a country of net immigration. While the majority of the immigrants in the first few years of that period were "returning emigrants" and a substantial minority were European Union nationals, there was an increasing number of workers on temporary visas from outside the European Union.[37] The majority of those (until 2004, when the European Union expanded to include a number of Eastern and Central European nations) were from Eastern Europe, particularly, Latvia, Lithuania, Poland, and Romania.[38] There were smaller numbers from other countries in Africa, Latin America, and Asia. Indeed, the profile of contemporary migration is the ever-broadening spectrum of countries of origin. Over 120 nations were represented annually among work permit holders in the 1999–2005 period. The distinction between EU nationals and non-EU nationals is now the key one in European nations' immigration policies. EU nationals now have the right to residence in each other's countries and usually the right to work there, as well as the right to vote in European elections. They thus no longer require visas for employment. In effect, there are completely separate immigration regimes for EU and non-EU nationals now in operation.[39]

The result of a decade of net immigration is a substantial tilting of demographics. The 2006 census records that 14.68 percent of the 4.1 million population of the Republic was foreign-born, a high figure for the European Union.[40] However, 10.5 percent of the 14.68 percent (i.e., 71 percent of the foreign-born population) are EU nationals, and only 1 percent are from Africa, 1.3 percent from Asia, and less than 1 percent from the Americas.

So before we pursue the relatively hostile responses to immigration, we need to put the numbers into perspective. The largest ethnic minority group in the Republic of Ireland are UK nationals! Immigration per se is not the subject of discourse; only particular categories of immigrants are seen as problematic (often but not exclusively from outside Europe). Not recognizing this phenomenon would be an illustration of epistemological ignorance. Moreover, this discursive focus on "problematic" immigrants has reracialized the Irish population. On Amnesty International's survey of racial abuse, the "Black Irish" group reports the highest levels of racist experiences.[41]

Moreover, while the immigration issue is an important turning point for the configuration of racism in Ireland, it is not the only factor. Ireland has been "multicultural" (in descriptive terms) for centuries, not just since 1996. In addition to antinomadic racism, a history of Jewish settlement as well as anti-Semitism extends back to the sixteenth century.[42] Indeed, the racial discourse in Ireland since the mid-1990s has not neglected Jews or Muslims, identifying them as not belonging to the nation and singling out individuals for abuse. Ireland may well have specific characteristics in its construction of race in the early twenty-first century, but this development is also part of a wider pattern, framed by the world economy's shifting cores and peripheries, and the neoliberal governance that is currently hegemonic in the West.[43]

THE ROLES OF THE STATE

It is now established within the sociology of racism that the state plays a particular set of roles in the process of racialization. This has been theorized in relation to the United States and contemporary Europe, including Ireland.[44] The gamut of the state's interventions can run from creating and sustaining categories (through the census, legislation, and immigration regimes) to defining or redefining citizenship in terms of bloodlines to responding to different social movements.

Tighter control of permits (for non-EU nationals only) has been one tool for responding to the slowdown in economic growth since 2008. Talk of changing the rules surrounding work visas first surfaced in summer 2001, in a speech by Mary Harney, the influential minister for enterprise, trade and employment (responsible for migrant workers) and the Progressive Democrat (PD) leader and Tánaiste (deputy prime minister).[45] She then raised the cost of work permits twice before finally subjecting the scheme to reform in 2003. From that date, the categories of unskilled and semiskilled posts open to the work-permit scheme have been reviewed and amended on a regular basis. This is aimed at making the scheme more responsive to labor-force shortages. However, this approach provoked criticism from employers' organizations, which argued that Ireland's economy was still characterized by a skills shortage rather than an immigrant-fueled labor surplus. Moreover, since 2004 employers have been instructed by the Department for Enterprise, Trade and Employment to first seek labor from the EU accession states[46] and only venture outside this when there are special requirements or no labor supply in that quarter can be attracted.[47]

The state's rationalization of regulations governing employment demonstrates how migrants are being constructed primarily as bodies making the Irish economy more productive. The rationale for short-term, mainly employer-centered permits and a focus on EU labor are ostensibly technocratic issues, but the principles are discriminatory, founded, like all EU immigration regimes, on turning the EU/non-EU distinction into a fetish. Irish immigration regimes are now the product of intergovernmental EU partnerships and agreements, as well as national regulations. The rules forged in the EU section of the policy-making world determine which countries can be in the EU, who needs a visa to get into the EU, and who can live in an EU country. The Irish state alone governs the rules on employment visas: the regulation of conditions under which movement occurs (access, length of stay, industry); the defense of borders; who is Irish (and how this status is arrived at); who is counted (and how). Over the last decade, Ireland has thus witnessed an adjustment of the state's definition of Irishness. With the 2005 Citizenship Act, this definition saw a *jus soli* republican principle giving way to a strategic *jus sangui-nis*.[48] More prosaically, early studies of migrant organizations demon-strate the norms that are imposed on them. Failure to implement leg-islation on employment has allowed widespread abuse of contracts and has led to demonstrations—for example, by Polish workers—over pay and conditions.[49]

From the outset of the Celtic Tiger phenomenon, the state em-ployment agency, FÁS, ran campaigns trying to attract Irish emi-grants and people of Irish descent back to Ireland. The notion of "home" in the Irish diaspora is a prominent theme. The definition of "Irish descent" stretched back centuries in some cases, to include Newfoundlanders.[50] The private sector also participated, which in-volved a presence at trade and employment fairs as well as media tar-geting of likely recruits.[51] Such workers were urged to "return" home. Katy Hayward and Kevin Howard note the emphasis on a mystical connection between culture and place.[52] In the promotional material, a bond between Irish soil and culture and the people disconnected from it through diaspora is depicted as a puzzle waiting to be fitted together.

BOOMING TIGER

The phenomenon of the latest stage of racialization of Irishness oc-curred in the midst of the Celtic Tiger, drawing a parallel with the Asian Tigers of Singapore, Hong Kong, Taiwan, and South Korea. This economic background locates the racialization of Irishness in the 1990s and the turn of the twenty-first century in a particular neo-liberal migration regime. Even if we take Gary Murphy's argument that according to the strict technical criteria, Ireland cannot be cate-gorically labeled "neoliberal," it is approaching that designation.[53] In terms of the free movement of labor, the neoliberal understands mi-gration to be purely a strategic instrument for temporary use in cru-cial areas of the economy at the stages of development: immigrants are thus primarily (if not exclusively) agents for increasing produc-tivity rather than subjects with rights or prospects of long-term integration. Ireland's immigration regime has therefore been based on labor market requirements and regulated by short-term work permits and a small work visa scheme (with slightly more entitlements) for highly skilled migrants. The neoliberal path, if we can put it in these terms, was followed by Fianna Fáil (FF) administrations since 1997, under the aegis of its coalition partner, the PD, thus fueling the growth of the Tiger economy in the second half of the 1990s: the moment when Ireland became a country of immigration.[54]

Ireland also provides a countercase to the plentiful social science literature on the pathology of anti-immigrant attitudes, which are linked systematically with shrinking economic opportunities.[55] Moreover, the dynamics of the boom have drawn Travellers into the racialization process in a way that differs from previous patterns, an example that demonstrates how deracialized spaces can be racialized.

The boom period of 1994–2008 has received relatively little critical attention in terms of its disparities.[56] Its roots lie in the expansion of US multinationals into Europe and the attraction of low corporate taxation, an aggressively business-friendly state apparatus, and a young skilled workforce within the European Union.[57] While the gross indices of production and income soared, the distribution of the benefits of this boom present a more complex picture. While unemployment across the state dropped, there were still some important local, regional, and above all class-based distinctions.[58] Places where the software, pharmaceuticals, and data-processing industries settled (especially the greater Dublin, Cork, Limerick, and Galway areas) benefited considerably more financially through this presence than other areas, particularly the border and northwestern counties of the Republic. The type of employment offered also drew people toward these areas. Moreover, opportunities in the service industry, call centers, and a range of assembly and data-processing work left two types of gaps in the workforce: one at the specialized level and one at the unskilled level. People were thus brought in to fill specific niches in industries for which there is an international market (health care, software, civil engineering) and also for the low-wage jobs increasingly deserted by Irish workers taking advantage of the better paid and plentiful semiskilled jobs.

The resulting map of the correspondence between employment type and nationality of origin is only beginning to emerge. So far, catering and the service industries have accounted for the majority of immigrant work permits issued. Those issued with work permits have come principally from Eastern Europe (until 2004), South Africa, and Brazil, for example, with significant numbers of permits also going to health care professionals from Asia, especially the Philippines and India. However, the pattern of distribution of minorities into specific economic niches has not yet become particularly clear.

The other key theme within the economic boom was the rise in the price of land and the cost of housing. Ireland's housing boom saw prices roughly triple in the 1995–2005 period and continue to rise until 2008. This hugely benefited the land and/or home-owning middle classes and property developers at the expenses of the working classes.[59] As a result, undeveloped land around towns rapidly acquired higher value. Since Travellers' temporary settlement patterns have historically included the margins of towns, which allowed them access to both rural and urban casual labor markets, the pressure on Travellers' space increased. The hunger for development land engulfed common or waste land on the edge of urban areas. Travellers were moved away from new residential and business developments, which occupied places where they had previously stopped unharrassed. As land accrued value, Traveller culture thus became further devalued.

In turn-of-the-twenty-first-century neoliberal society, marked by an increased obsession with production and output, people seen as nonproductive (Travellers, asylum seekers, the long-term unemployed) are correspondingly seen as unfair competitors for space whose needs can be deprioritized. This unproductive land, runs the logic, can be used more productively to create housing and leisure space for the spending of new capital. When families have to use the parents' home as a guarantee for the children's mortgage (if the value of the property even makes this possible), and the majority simply cannot afford to buy a first home regardless of how hard they work, then people who "don't work" and thus "waste space" become targets for displaced hostility.

"WHITE FLIGHT" AND "BLACK SCHOOLS"

Figures from the 2006 census indicate that the spatial concentration of minorities is at its highest in some inner-city Dublin and northwest electoral divisions. One high-profile outcome of rapid population growth in Blanchardstown (northwest Dublin, postal code Dublin 15) was the opening of what was described as Ireland's "first all-black school" in September 2007. In the early part of that year, schools in Balbriggan (an area within Blanchardstown) were receiving high numbers of applications at both primary and secondary levels.

The vast majority of public education in the Republic is still provided through the church bodies—mainly Catholic but also Protestant—and prospective new pupils were being refused admission based on the criterion that places were reserved for Catholics only. Over the summer holidays, a new school was established very quickly by the nondenominational charity Educate Together.[60] Its first intake was comprised of around eighty black children (primarily those of Nigerian and Congolese migrants) who had been unable to find school places elsewhere in the area. Two major reports have since addressed the issue of school admissions in Ireland: Enda McGorman and Ciaran Sugrue, who focus on Dublin 15, and the Economic and Social Research Institute report, which has a national scope.[61]

The area around Blanchardstown experienced rapid population growth between 2002 and 2006: the population in the school's electoral division increased by more than three times the national average. Indeed, in terms of gross numbers, Blanchardstown-Blakestown increased more than any electoral division in the country—by nearly 8,000 from a starting point of 24,400, or greater than 33 percent. Other, smaller wards saw their populations treble or multiply by two and a half. Amid this population increase also came local settlement of nonwhite migrants in the area (at least 13 percent overall in 2006) and, in some electoral divisions, between 1,000 and 2,000 people. Using "qualification for rent supplement" (a welfare benefit) as a proxy, estimates are that 60 percent of the claimants are non-Irish nationals, and by far the largest group of the latter are African (61 percent), especially from Nigeria and Democratic Republic of Congo, followed by Central and Eastern Europe (28 percent). The overall younger demographic is, according to McGorman and Sugrue, an urgent educational issue because the number of school-age children also rose dramatically between 2004 and 2006.

Attention to the proportion of children with English Language Support (ELS) for the area's schools shows highly demarcated patterns; some have fewer than 20 percent in this category, while two schools have more than 50 percent. Moreover, more than one in four ELS pupils are from Central and Eastern Europe, so it should be borne in mind that the correspondence between ethnic background and English-language support requirements is more complicated than white children not needing help and black children needing help— it is frequently the opposite. Indeed, around one in three visible minority residents is Anglophone (including Nigerian) and therefore does not require ELS. The Dublin 15 report also notes a high turnover in movement from schools with an ethnic base. "In relation to Irish children," write McGorman and Sugrue, "82 pupils left in the period while only 40 joined these classes. This represents a movement of 2:1 out of Dublin 15 by Irish pupils. By contrast, the number of newcomer children joining theses classes was 152, which represented 79 percent of the total cohort of new children joining."[62] The corresponding ratio for foreign national children was 5:3 into Dublin 15 (i.e., for every three who left, five came in).

Picking up on Balbriggan, the *Sunday Tribune* ran a series of articles on ethnic segregation in November 2007, suggesting that the phenomenon of segregated schooling and housing is the Irish version of "white flight."[63] In relation to McGorman and Sugrue's report on Dublin 15 and the Balbriggan school incident, interviewees who were head teachers in Cork, Dublin, and Roscommon suggested that some schools were deliberately excluding non-Irish children (by hiding behind sibling and Catholics-only policies), and that there was a current of white flight to these schools. McGorman and Sugrue's figures certainly indicate discrepancies in the proportions of minority children in different schools and between who was moving into and out of Dublin 15 schools. Moreover, in the more critical ESRI report, Emer

Smyth and colleagues conclude that current criteria for admissions implemented by Irish schools—siblings, date of application, religion, children of past pupils or current staff, primary school attended— combine to discriminate against newly arrived families.[64] They go on to argue that there is more clustering of "newcomer children" at the primary than the secondary level, and there is a trend of parents removing white Irish children from what are known as "newcomer schools."[65]

A variety of social changes were thus occurring simultaneously in northwest Dublin, such as large-scale building development without the corresponding infrastructure, increased capacity for private rented accommodation that attracts migrant families, a demographic bulge in the young school-age children cohort, and the state's failure to plan for demographic shifts. This story is clearly not only about racial discrimination. Nevertheless, it is an excellent case study exactly because it demonstrates interconnected processes and how institutional racism functions in the middle of processes that are not necessarily about race at all.

THE POSTBOOM SITUATION

As the bailout by the European Union, International Monetary Fund, and European Central Bank and Fianna Fáil's historic defeat at the March 2011 elections usher in a new, postboom period, where are we in relation to race in the Republic? The ethnic breakdown of the Republic's population, as of the 2006 census, stood at 87.4 percent white Irish, 6.9 percent "other" white, and 0.5 percent Travellers—an overall total of 94.3 percent white. The figures for other groups are: 1.1 percent "other" (including multiracial people), 0.97 percent African, 0.4 percent Chinese, and 0.85 percent "other Asian." Given the numbers of work permits issued and asylum applications made by nationals from the Philippines, India, Malaysia, and Pakistan, we might speculate that the "other Asian" group is dominated by these nations. In a separate census table, by nationality, 90 percent are Irish (hyphenated or otherwise). The discrepancy of 2.6 percent (the difference between 90 percent Irish and 87.4 percent white Irish) can be seen as an indicator of ethnic-minority Irish. Significantly, the demographic balance of that nonwhite Irish group favors the younger end of the scale: in the birth-to-age-four group, only 88 percent are white (in all the other cohorts, this proportion is between 90 and 98 percent).

Another way to interpret the story of post-1996 changes is to see shifts in Irish ethnic demography as more to do with a diversification of whiteness than the overall diversification of the population. This is bound up with the changing frontiers of the European Union in the late twentieth and early twenty-first centuries. Before 2004, the majority of work permits were issued to either "returning migrants" (from the Irish diaspora) or Central and Eastern European nationals. We can assume these groups are virtually all white. After the accession of the Eastern and Central European countries to the European Union, their nationals no longer required work permits and, significantly, are no longer counted in the official statistics under that heading. Later research based on social security numbers gave rise to estimates of the number of such nationals in Ireland.[66] Whichever way you look at these figures, the only conclusion is that white Europeans from other EU member states are by far the largest group of migrants to the Republic of Ireland in the period when that country became a net importer of labor. As a result of the shrinking, recession-hit labor market, these numbers are now falling: the Central Statistics Office's estimates for the year ending April 2010 indicate a drop from more than 50,000 EU migrants in 2006–07 to 5,000 in 2009–10.[67]

What are the consequences of this decade of net immigration? One is that there is increasing religious diversity.[68] This means not only the introduction (or extensions) of observance of Islam and Hinduism but a diversity of Protestant churches (many African-dominated) and forms of Catholicism (following Central and Eastern European norms). The diversification of the Irish population in terms of ethnicity and religion (and diversity within Christian churches) affects the dominance of Catholicism and the Protestant-Catholic binary in the country. Moreover, the question of residential and educational integration has been broached in public discourse, notably with negative framing by the media as white flight. The key national event was the emergency response to a shortage of school places in northwest Dublin in September 2007.

The Irish state's response to diversity is still equivocal. The much-vaunted 2010 Immigration, Residence and Protection Bill (aimed at ironing out the many outstanding issues in the immigration and asylum processes) appears not to have achieved its object. The Irish Council on Immigration's numerous criticisms include the introduction of summary deportation, insufficient protection for victims of human trafficking, and a continuing failure to provide a permanent immigration status. Indeed, continuing the cross-party tradition of slow compliance with EU equality directives, Ireland has not opted into the European Council Directive 2003/109/EC on the status of third-country nationals who are long-term residents.[69]

As the Republic embarks on the turnaround into net out-migration again, those who are staying to make their lives in Ireland are doing so in a situation vastly changed from what was the case in the first decade of the twenty-first century. This is postboom, contracting-labor-market, bailout, public-service-cuts Ireland, in which there is an outflow of graduates as well as less well-qualified young people, but the previous decade's migrants and their children—the first generation of new "hyphenated" Irish—are settling in. Even more than before, people will identify migrants as an unwarranted drain on resources that they believe should be focused on Irish recipients. The tiny far-right parties are stepping up the criticisms of ongoing levels of migration, but they are not alone in identifying this as a problem. Neither are the migrant groups alone in seeing their integration into Irish society as desirable and ongoing. The discussion about what it means to be Irish in the twenty-first century can no longer omit the possibility that it includes having genealogies that begin in different European countries and on continents other than Europe, North America, and Australasia.

CONCLUSIONS

The specific historical development of the idea of race and the practices of racism in Ireland mark it out as distinctive: a colonized white

European nation whose members participated at a variety of levels in colonial enterprises as well as in the development of the slave-based economy in the United States. There is no simple monolithic interpretation of these experiences. The complexity should alert the reader to the error of consigning the Irish, en masse, to the position of either solely victim of racism or solely perpetrator. Many have found themselves simultaneously in both roles. The Catholic Irish experience is highly pertinent to contemporary Ireland. The conditions of their mass emigration, generated by the ravages of the forces of international economics (cores and peripheries) in the context of colonial underdevelopment, are parallels to the forces now pushing people from developing world countries and newly liberalizing former Eastern bloc nations to Ireland. The Irish were historically also to be found in a variety of social positions in the countries to which they emigrated, ranging from indentured laborer to bishop. Contemporary migrants to Ireland from the same country might well have different statuses, such as asylum seeker, refugee, labor migrant, or student, each with different rights and resources attached.

The Irish administration is a nationalist and neoliberal one, a fact that has certain impacts on the immigration regimes and on ideas about who can and can't be Irish and why.[70] The Irish state is not the only governmental actor: intergovernmental agreements under the aegis of the European Union have bonded the Republic to a set of EU-wide immigration norms. It determines, for example, the mutual rights of EU nationals to live and work without requiring visas in each other's countries. The knock-on effect for Irish immigration patterns is, as elsewhere in Europe, that the scope for non-EU immigration is shrinking all the time, making white European migrants the staple for the future outside of specialist areas of employment.[71]

The role of the "new migrant" communities (i.e., those established in the 1990s) and their leadership appears crucial in shaping the trends. The developing alliances and the relationships between the state and these bodies, as they take over from the white Irish-dominated advocacy groups that preceded them, will have the greatest effect on anti-racist and integration-focused initiatives within the state. Yet this micro-level negotiation of roles takes place within the larger macro-economic context, as the international economy transforms particular places into magnets for migrant workers at particular moments. Cores and peripheries are not fixed geographical points. Places can start as peripheral and become cores, as the island of Ireland has done over the last decade. Moreover, this process carries within it the proposition that the reverse could also happen. As patterns of development and investment shift in different directions, Ireland could lose its core status, and this would have important ramifications for the way race gets played out there. A decrease in migration and a longer-standing ethnic minority population stabilizing during a period of economic slowdown presents a different scenario from one that features increasing temporary migration in the midst of a boom.

Stepping back from this level of detail, the question for people involved in antiracist struggle is how and where do counterhegemonic voices make themselves more powerful? One approach is to remain focused on the role not only of migrant groups but, as a necessity, of sedentary society's relationship with the indigenous Travellers, who were present before the Tiger and are still there now, in the postboom era. The patterns of hierarchical social relations that generate anti-Traveller racism are the same as those that generate the racialization of new migrants and Irish people of color, and it is essential that neither set of outcomes is neglected. The two foci should be seen as complementary rather than of differing priorities. This calls for a long, historical view as well as action in the present. One area that appears to cry out for development is the organic linking of new migrants and Travellers around opposing the neoliberal project, which casts both of those internally diverse groups as at best a necessary evil and at worst an obstruction to progress, just as the sixteenth-century Gaelic Irish were seen as inherently incapable of productivity before the idea of neoliberalism had been invented.

NOTES

1. Matthew Jacobson, *Whiteness of a Different Color: European Immigrants and the Alchemy of Race* (Cambridge, MA: Harvard University Press, 1998).

2. Martin Barker, *The New Racism: Conservatives and the Ideology of the Tribe* (London: Junction Books, 1981).

3. Pierre-André Taguieff, "The New Cultural Racism in France," *Telos* 83 (1990): 109–122; Tariq Modood, "Difference, Cultural Racism and Anti-Racism," in *Debating Cultural Hybridity: Multi-Cultural Identities and the Politics of Anti-Racism,* ed. Pnina Werbner and Tariq Modood (Atlantic Highlands, NJ: Zed Books, 1997), 238–54.

4. Eduardo Bonilla-Silva, *Racism Without Racists: Color-Blind Racism and the Persistence of Racial Inequality in the United States,* 2nd ed. (Lanham, MD: Rowman and Littlefield, 2006).

5. Charles W. Mills, *The Racial Contract* (Ithaca, NY: Cornell University Press, 1997), 6.

6. Robbie McVeigh, "The Specificity of Irish Racism," *Race and Class* 33, no. 40 (1992): 31–45.

7. Mills, *Racial Contract,* 93.

8. Ronit Lentin, "Responding to the Racialization of Irishness: Disavowed Multiculturalism and Its Discontents, *Sociological Research Online* 5, no. 4 (2001), www.socresonline.org.uk/5/4/lentin.html.

9. Dating from the twelfth century is based on Giraldus Cambrensis's treatise *History and Topography of Ireland* (1189). Nicholas P. Canny, *The Elizabethan Conquest of Ireland: A Pattern Established, 1565–76* (Hassocks, UK: Harvester, 1976).

10. David B. Quinn, *The Elizabethans and the Irish* (Ithaca, NY: Cornell University Press, 1966); Canny, *Elizabethan Conquest.*

11. Patricia Coughlan, "'Some Secret Scourge Which Shall by Her Come unto England': Ireland and Incivility in Spenser,'" in *Spenser and Ireland: An Interdisciplinary Perspective,* ed. Patricia Coughlan (Cork: Cork University Press, 1989), 50.

12. Edmund Campion, *History of Ireland* (1633). For greater coverage of this racialization of the Irish in the colonial period, see Steve Garner, *Racism in the Irish Experience* (London: Pluto, 2004), chapter 3, particularly the excellent historical and cultural studies referenced in it.

13. John Davies, *Discovery of the True Causes Why Ireland Was Never Entirely Subdued . . . Until the Beginning of His Majesty's Happy Reign* (1612).

14. D. George Boyce, *Nationalism in Ireland,* 2nd ed. (London: Routledge, 1991).

15. "Scotch-Irish" had been used since the mid-eighteenth century, but as only one of the ways in which this group identified itself.

16. Theodore W. Allen, *The Invention of the White Race,* vol. 2 (New York: Verso, 1994).

17. Albon Man, "Labor Competition and the New York Draft Riots of 1863," *Journal of Negro History* 36, no. 4 (1951): 375–405; Iver Bernstein, *The New York City Draft Riots: Their Significance for American Society in the Age of the Civil War* (New York: Oxford University Press, 1990); Noel Ignatiev, *How the Irish Became White* (New York: Routledge, 1996).

18. Andy Bielenberg, "Irish Emigration to the British Empire, 1700–1914," in *The Irish Diaspora,* ed. Andy Bielenberg (Harlow, UK: Longman, 2000), 215–34; Piarás Mac Éinrí, "'A Slice of Africa': Whose Side Were We On? Ireland and the Anti-Colonial Struggle," in *Race and State,* ed. Alana Lentin and Ronit Lentin (Newcastle, UK: Cambridge Scholars, 2006), 255–73.

19. This is not to argue that there were no Irish people in these positions who challenged colonial domination, but these were exceptions to the rule.

20. Robbie McVeigh, "The Specificity of Irish Racism," *Race and Class* 33, no. 40 (1992): 31–45.

21. Quinn, *Elizabethans;* Patricia Coughlan, "Counter-Currents in Colonial Discourse: The Political Thought of Vincent and Daniel Gookin," in *Political Thought in Seventeenth-Century Ireland: Kingdom or Colony?,* ed. Jane H. Ohlmeyer (Cambridge, UK: Cambridge University Press, 2000), 56–82.

22. This may well have been more problematic and ambivalent for individual Irish people.

23. Canny, *Elizabethan Conquest.*

24. Sinéad Ní Shuínéar, "Othering the Irish (Travellers)," in *Racism and Anti-Racism in Ireland,* ed. Ronit Lentin and Robbie McVeigh (Belfast: Beyond the Pale, 2002), 177–92.

25. Jim McLaughlin, *Travellers and Ireland: Whose Country? Whose History?* (Cork: Cork University Press, 1995).

26. See fact sheets provided by Pavee Point: www.paveepoint.ie/pav _factsh_a.html.

27. Charles Taylor, *Multiculturalism and "The Politics of Recognition": An Essay,* ed. Amy Gutmann (Princeton, NJ: Princeton University Press, 1992).

28. Respondents are often asked whether they are racist with no definition offered as to what that means. Moreover, the overwhelming social taboo against racism pushes people not to define themselves as racist. People are often asked to answer questions that cover racist assumptions, such as "Do you think immigration is too high?" How would you assess how many is "too many," or who is an immigrant and who is not just by looking at them, if there were no racialized understandings of difference? Other social topics become proxies of race: immigration and asylum notably have assumed this position in the last ten to fifteen years in Europe, so that questions about these themes become inextricably entwined with race. Questions can be loaded by

their context (asking about immigration after a series of questions about in-
equalities in resource distribution); by wording (such as "Parts of this country don't feel like Britain any more because of immigration," and asking to
what extent they agree with the statement); finally, immigration can be placed
on a list and people asked to say which are the most important topics, instead
of asking, "What do you think are the most important issues facing the
country?" with no prompts.

29. Garner, *Racism in the Irish Experience.*

30. *Eurobarometer 2000* (Brussels: European Commission, 2001); *Eurobarometer 1997* (Brussels: European Commission, 1998).

31. Micheál McGréil, *Prejudice in Ireland Revisited* (Maynooth, Ireland:
Survey and Research Unit, St Patrick College, Maynooth, 1996).

32. *The Views of Black and Ethnic Minorities* (Dublin: Amnesty International, 2001).

33. David Sibley, *Geographies of Exclusion: Society and Difference in the West*
(London: Routledge, 1995).

34. Government of Ireland, *Task Force Report on the Travelling People*
(Dublin: Stationary Office, 1995).

35. Bryan Fanning, *Racism and Social Change in the Republic of Ireland*
(Manchester, UK: Manchester University Press, 2002), 112–51.

36. "Trespass" is the generic legal term for the offense of entering private property without permission in the United Kingdom and Ireland. Powers conferred on the police in the cases of what is interpreted as "illegal en-
campment" allow on-the-spot fines and confiscation of vehicles. So it is
possible for Travellers to lose their home and means of transport just for
parking temporarily in an unofficial roadside site.

37. Garner, *Racism in the Irish Experience*; Katy Hayward and Kevin Howard, "Cherry-Picking the Diaspora," in *Immigration and Social Change in the Republic of Ireland,* ed. Bryan Fanning (Manchester, UK: Manchester University
Press, 2007), 47–62.

38. Figures on work permits are obtained from the Department of Enterprise, Trade and Employment's annual reports.

39. Cf. Steve Garner, "The European Union and the Racialization of
Immigration, 1985–2006," *Race/Ethnicity: Multidisciplinary Global Contexts* 1,
no. 1 (2007): 61–87.

40. Cf. 2005 figures for France, 8.4 percent; United Kingdom, 9.7 percent; Sweden, 12.4 percent. *Stocks of Foreign-Born Populations in Selected OECD
Countries,* Organization for Economic Development and Cooperation, 2005,
www.oecd.org/dataoecd/25/55/39331322.xls.

41. *Views of Black and Ethnic Minorities.*

42. Katrina Goldstone, "Christianity, Conversion and the Tricky Business of Names: Images of Jews in Nationalist Irish Catholic Discourse," in *The Expanding Nation: Towards a Multi-ethnic Ireland,* proceedings of a conference held in Trinity College Dublin, 22–24 September 1998, ed. Ronit Lentin (Dublin: Department of Sociology, Trinity College Dublin, 1999), 31–33; Ronit Lentin, "At the Heart of the Hibernian Post-Metropolis: Spatial Narratives of Ethnic Minorities and Diasporic Communities in a Changing City," *City* 6, no. 2 (2002): 229–49.

43. Emmanuel Wallerstein, *The Capitalist World Economy: Essays* (Cambridge, UK: Cambridge University Press, 1979).

44. Michael Omi and Howard Winant, *Racial Formation in the United States: From the 1960s to the 1980s* (New York: Routledge & Kegan Paul, 1986); David Theo Goldberg, *The Racial State* (Malden, MA: Blackwell, 2002); Alana Lentin and Ronit Lentin, eds., *Race and State* (Newcastle, UK: Cambridge Scholars, 2006).

45. "900 Jobs Lost at Gateway as Company Closes Base," *Irish Times,* August 9, 2001.

46. Accession states are those that became members of the European Union on May 1, 2004. These are chiefly from the former Communist bloc.

47. Ronit Lentin and Robbie McVeigh, *After Optimism? Ireland, Racism and Globalisation* (Dublin: Metro Éireann, 2006), 67.

48. Ronit Lentin, "From Racial State to Racist State: Ireland on the Eve of the Citizenship Referendum," *Variant* 20 (2004); Steve Garner, "Ireland and Immigration: Explaining the Absence of the Far Right," *Patterns of Prejudice* 41, no. 2 (2007): 109–30.

49. Paul Conroy and Aoife Brennan, *Migrant Workers and Their Experiences* (Dublin: Equality Authority, 2003); Kieran Allen, "Double Speak: Neo-Liberalism and Migration," in Fanning, ed., *Immigration and Social Change,* 84–97.

50. Garner, *Racism in the Irish Experience,* 52.

51. Garner, *Racism in the Irish Experience.*

52. Hayward and Howard, "Cherry-Picking the Diaspora."

53. Gary Murphy, "Assessing the Relationship between Neoliberalism and Political Corruption: The Fianna Fáil/Progressive Democrat Coalition, 1997–2006," *Irish Political Studies* 21, no. 3 (2006): 297–317.

54. Murphy states that the crucial element has the economic ideology of the Progressive Democrats dragging the more social-spending oriented Fianna Fáil supporters toward ever freer markets.

55. Lincoln Quillian, "Prejudice as a Response to Perceived Group Threat: Population Composition and Anti-Immigrant and Racial Prejudice

in Europe," *American Sociological Review* 60, no. 4 (1995): 586–611; Christian Dustman, "Racial and Economic Factors in Attitudes to Immigration," IZA Discussion Paper no. 190, 2000; M. Coenders, M. Guijsberts, and P. Scheepers, "Resistance to the Presence of Immigrants and Refugees in 22 Countries," in *Nationalism and Exclusion of Migrants: Cross-National Comparisons,* ed. M. Guijsberts, L. Hagenddorn, and P. Scheepers (Aldershot, UK: Ashgate, 2004), 97–120.

56. Peadar Kirby, *The Celtic Tiger in Distress: Growth with Inequality in Ireland* (London: Palgrave, 2001); Kieran Allen, *The Celtic Tiger: The Myth of Social Partnership in Ireland* (Manchester, UK: Manchester University Press, 2000).

57. Denis O'Hearn, *Inside the Celtic Tiger: The Irish Economy and the Asian Model* (London: Pluto, 1998).

58. Allen, *Celtic Tiger*; Garner, *Racism in the Irish Experience.*

59. Indeed, investment patterns of wealth creation show that over recent decades, the proportion of national wealth created through investment has outstripped that accrued through wage and salary earning (Cf. Allen, *Celtic Tiger*; Garner, *Racism in the Irish Experience*).

60. D. Sharrock, "Ireland Opens Its First All-Black School," *Times* (London), September 24, 2007.

61. Enda McGorman and Ciaran Sugrue, *Intercultural Education: Primary Challenges in Dublin 15: A Report Funded by the Social Inclusion Unit and the Department of Education and Science* (Dublin: Department of Education and Science, 2007). See also E. Smyth, M. Darmody, F. McGinnity, and D. Byrne, *Adapting to Diversity: Irish Schools and Newcomer Children* (Dublin: Economic and Social Research Institute, 2009), www.esri.ie/UserFiles/publications/20090529124035/RS008.pdf.

62. McGorman and Sugrue, *Intercultural Education,* 59.

63. "The New Class, *Sunday Tribune* (Belfast), November 4, 2007; C. McMorrow, "Immigrant Communities Are Living in Isolation," *Sunday Tribune* (Belfast), November 11, 2007; A. Bracken, "The Ghettos That Are Dividing the Nation," *Sunday Tribune* (Belfast), November 11, 2007; S. McInerney, "We Are Not Making It Easy for Migrants to Settle Here and Achieve Their Full Potential," *Sunday Tribune* (Belfast), November 11, 2007.

64. Smyth et al., *Adapting to Diversity,* 60.

65. Ibid., 68.

66. T. Krings, A. Bobek, E. Moriarty, J. Salamonska, and J. Wickham, "Migration and Recession: Polish Migrants in Post-Celtic Tiger Ireland," *Sociological Research Online* 14, no. 2 (2009), www.socresonline.org.uk/14/2/9.html.

67. *Population and Migration Estimates 2010* (Cork: Central Statistics Office, 2010), www.cso.ie/releasespublications/documents/population/current/popmig.pdf.

68. A. Feldman, "Beyond the Catholic-Protestant Divide: Religious and Ethnic Diversity in the North and South of Ireland," Working Papers in British-Irish Studies 31, www.ucd.ie/ibis/filestore/wp2003/31_fel.pdf.

69. *The Immigration, Residence and Protection Bill 2010: A Critical Overview,* Immigrant Council of Ireland, 2010, www.immigrantcouncil.ie/images/stories/IRP_Bill_2010_overview.pdf.

70. Garner, "Ireland and Immigration"; Kieran Allen, "Neither Boston nor Berlin: Class Polarisation and Neo-Liberalism in the Irish Republic," in *The End of Irish History?: Critical Reflections on the Celtic Tiger* ed. Colin Coulter and Steve Coleman (Manchester, UK: Manchester University Press, 2003), 56–73.

71. Garner, "The European Union."

CHAPTER NINE

CONCLUSION

Ireland, Immigration, and the Ethics of Memory

LUKE GIBBONS

*Ireland's confidence and cosmopolitanism is a mask
hiding deeply etched and historically rooted anxieties
and insecurities. In its new prosperity, "commonsense"
Ireland has been quick to forget its own emigrant
past and the hostilities and hardships Irish emigrants
faced abroad as largely unwanted arrivals.*[1]

In a dinner party scene in Irving Welsh's short 2007 film *Nuts*, which features a caustic view of Celtic Tiger Ireland, one of the characters remarks with a casual certitude that the Irish can't be racist: "How can we be? We're the original economic migrants." To which another guest counters, in case the parallels with the past are too close for comfort: "We contributed wherever we went. They don't."

In this short exchange, it is possible to see some of the double standards that have informed responses to immigration and cultural memory in the new multiethnic Ireland, exemplified by the decision of the Irish government to abolish the official bodies it set up to counter racism in Ireland: the National Consultative Committee on Racism and Interculturalism in Ireland (NCCRI) and the National Action Plan Against Racism (NAPAR).[2] On the one hand, there is an uncritical claim to high moral ground with respect to racism on account of Ireland's own colonial and diasporic history, as if the experience of injustice in the past automatically prevented its perpetuation in the present. On the other hand, an equally suspect hollowing out of history denies any analogies between Ireland's past and the condition of immigrants in the Ireland of the Celtic Tiger. All analogies are founded on difference, not just similarity, and such particularities have to be borne in mind when making comparisons between past and present. Yet, in a basic sense, ethics itself is founded on analogy: the individual putting him or herself in the place of another, imagining the world through others' eyes.

I will argue that the measure of a culture's engagement with its past is not always to be found in its museums or even its archives, but in its "moral histories" (to appropriate James Joyce's phrase), or narratives produced by memory that extend the range of the moral imagination in the present. These narratives are not always ready to hand and may be submerged until (re)activated through an encounter with "the other"—a factor that may help to explain the latent hostility often shown toward reminders of an unwelcome past of poverty and emigration, a past that may well return in the future. This engagement with the past not only is of benefit to the host culture but may also assist in turning acclimatization into a dynamic cultural exchange. This is evident, for example, in the remarkable 2006 production of Jimmy Murphy's play *The Kings of the Kilburn High Road* by the Nigerian director and playwright Bisi Adigun, in which African actors based in Dublin played the roles of Irish laborers in London. The ordeal of the forgotten Irish in Britain was no less harrowing for being a reminder that it could just as easily be the plight of Africans—or other immigrants—in the Ireland of today. Through casting alone, the production functioned as a two-way mirror, allowing both Irish and immigrant cultures to see each other through the same darkened glass.

MORAL HISTORIES

Sadly perhaps, we are not "all on the same side": a simple appeal to Irish race memory does not turn all Irish people into good anti-racists.[3]

In a report on immigration in rural Ireland, the Mayo Intercultural Action committee expressed as one of its framing principles the wish "that no stranger arriving in our county will have to face what so many Mayo emigrants faced when they were forced to leave home for an uncertain reception in foreign lands in the past." The report continues:

> The diversity of people and cultures coming to Ireland, which for so long has known only emigration, has the potential to enrich our society both socially and culturally. Ireland's history has given the Irish a unique understanding of what it is like to be an immigrant in a foreign country. This should inform the way in which we respond to people from other countries who come here to work and live. It should allow us to understand the importance of building a society which values the social inclusion of people from diverse backgrounds, and also recognizes the need to promote integration.[4]

The report stresses that integration is a mutually interactive process and quotes the Irish government's own definition of integration "as placing duties and obligations on ethnic minorities and on the State to provide for a more inclusive society."[5] But this obligation on the host culture to present qualities that welcome rather than alienate the stranger places an even greater emphasis on the importance of Irish people linking with their own diasporic pasts. The majority of countries in the West that have drawn in immigrants have done so in the wake of colonial power, with attendant histories of condescension and hostility, often masked under the guise of civility and tolerance. Ireland, by contrast, offers the prospect of a host culture that was historically on the receiving end of colonialism, and while it has much to borrow from the best practice of its European neighbors, it is clear that undue harmonization in EU immigration laws, particularly in the intensified security climate and intrusive policing of the War on Terror, endangers not only existing traditions of civil liberties in Britain and Ireland, as Piaras Mac Éinrí has argued, but also the very status of Irish neutrality.[6]

As has been frequently observed, Ireland's uneven development is not without its own examples of the "gratefully oppressed." The inclusion of the Irish diaspora in host cultures abroad was often achieved by participating in the very structures that led to domination in the first place. This is evident in the espousal of racial conceptions of whiteness to hasten assimilation in the United States; the willingness (if such it was) of the "Fighting Irish" to act as the foot soldiers of empire in the British or American armies; the role of more upwardly mobile Irish in the administration of the colonies (though not always with the loyalty and discipline expected of them); the self-proclaimed mission of the Catholic Church to propagate Ireland's own "spiritual empire" abroad; and, not least, back in Ireland itself, the cultural isolationism that turned its back on the plight of Jewish and other refugees since the founding of the state.

These examples of participation in oppressive systems underline the facility with which the Irish could disavow memories of underdevelopment to further "inclusion" or social advancement, a form of amnesia that lent itself under the Celtic Tiger to the exploitation of foreign workers in the vulnerable economic position once experienced by Irish emigrants themselves. The national outcry over the revelation of gross exploitation of Turkish road workers on the GAMA construction site in County Clare in 2005 and the decision of Irish Ferries in November 2005 to replace an Irish workforce with Latvian seamen at a third of the minimum wage were only the more visible manifestations of practices throughout lower-paid sectors of the Irish economy. The massive demonstration through the streets of Dublin organized by the trade union movement to challenge Irish Ferries, and other less visible initiatives to counter discriminatory practices, can be seen as part of an overall determination to prevent history repeating itself, albeit with the Irish now in the driving seat. RTE News reported in 2007, in relation to a labor dispute at a food distribution center, in which foreign nationals were paid half the rate of "native" workers: "[The Irish workers] were agitated about this. . . . They feel it is simply wrong. A lot of these men in their own day, in the 80s, worked abroad, and they've seen it from the other side. They also feel their jobs and conditions will be eroded."[7] Drawing on their own experiences as foreign nationals, the Irish workers were in a position to contest the racial divisiveness that set workers with common interests against each other. The sudden onset of new outflows from Ireland with the collapse of the Celtic Tiger is a salutary reminder that the plight of emigration is not just a thing of the past but remains a recurrent feature of Irish uneven development.

The capacity to see the stranger "from the other side" by virtue of one's own cultural (and not always distant) memory replaces the abstract category of the nonnational (as designated in the Immigration Act, 2004) with the more particular address of the "foreign" national—a person migrating from a particular culture, often with deep, enduring attachments. It is with this in mind that the Mayo Intercultural Action report highlighted the need for a more nuanced approach to the cultural texture of migration, on both sides of the immigrant experience. As one local respondent noted: "We need to understand the different cultures: apart from language, a lot more sensitivity is required: asylum seekers and refugees could educate us . . . we need a 'Cultural Mediation Service' like the one they have in Dublin."[8] It is not just that the host culture makes itself more amenable to the immigrant: it is also a matter of recognizing the cultural energies contributed by newcomers to a society in transition. For the most part, however, the debate about immigration has been conducted in narrow economic terms, gauging the contributions made by immigrants along crude, cost-effective lines. When the loneliness and depression faced by Polish and other East European migrants in Ireland became a matter of national controversy in 2005, it was attributed, among other factors, to the cultural void in which they found themselves, cut off from their families back home and yet adrift in their new environment.[9] Such conditions led Philip Watt of NCCRI to compare their difficulties with that of Irish emigrants during the last major wave of Irish emigration: "Polish and other migrants from the 10 EU accession countries were experiencing the same problems young Irish migrants to Britain and the US experienced in the 1980s. 'There is a vulnerable minority, mainly young single men and, to a lesser extent, women,' he said."[10]

In surveys conducted in 2006 and 2007 by the Irish Immigrant Council (IIC), three-quarters of Irish people believed that migrant workers from outside the European Union should be entitled to have their families with them when they work in Ireland, and almost nine out of ten people surveyed felt that migrant workers from outside the European Union should have the right to be visited by close family who have the proper documentation.[11] Commenting on these findings, the IIC chief executive, Denise Charlton, noted that "the Irish public's positive attitudes, demonstrated by the polls, showed compassion and good economic sense. Government policy is clearly lagging behind public sentiment on the issue of family rights for migrant workers." That government policy is lacking on this front is clear from the anomaly that refugees applying for Irish citizenship are prevented from being united with immediate family members, a sundering of familial and cultural ties given constitutional force in the exclusionary Citizenship Referendum of 2004.[12]

It is precisely these affective zones, the cultural spaces for both intracultural and intercultural contact, that were highlighted by former Irish president Mary McAleese in her wide-ranging address, "The Changing Faces of Ireland: Migration and Multiculturalism," delivered to the British Council in London in 2007: "The Irish have a ready understanding of the need emigrants have for the comfort of the familiar, for places and associations where they can meet their fellow countrymen, speak their own language, express and continue to develop their identity. We also understand their need to belong to the wider Irish community in ways that are fulfilling and meaningful."[13]

The subordination of a integrated reception policy to short-term market needs, as in the work permits scheme that governs non-EU and central European migrant labor, is part of a wider tendency to see migrants as a transient phenomenon, mere "guest workers," passing through on their way elsewhere or making fast money before their eventual return home. It is not simply that culture and history are absent from the mix: rather, cultural and political "asset stripping" of the migrant facilitates the exploitation of groups whose relationship to society is reduced to the most instrumental economic level.

THE "HISTORICAL DUTY" ARGUMENT

The weight of the past, the researches of our local interpreters and the start of the remembrance of the famine, in my view, point us towards a single reality: that commemoration is a moral act, just as our relation in this country to those who have left it is a moral relationship. We have too much at stake in both not to be rigorous.[14]

More than any other public figure, Mary McAleese has given voice to what has come to be known as the "historical duty" argument in relation to Irish responses to immigration. This was given its most succinct formulation in her "Changing Face of Ireland" address:

The Irish know better than many other races how valuable the emigrants to our shores are. We know these things because of our own extensive history of being emigrants. . . . Of all people on the planet we have no excuse for getting it wrong and a lot of work is going into trying to get it right. What is perhaps unique to the Irish situation now is the speed and scale of change for we have absorbed in one decade what many other so-called "countries of immigration" absorbed over many decades if not centuries.[15]

Such pronouncements acquired a new relevance with the rise of immigration in the past decade, but related sentiments were also part of former president Mary Robinson's attempts in the early 1990s to link a historical awareness of the Irish diaspora to human rights and developmental issues in the third world. She formulated this reflexive turn in memory in a 1994 speech, having been the first Western head of state to visit famine-stricken Somalia two years earlier: "It is also our sense as a people who suffered and survived that our history does not entitle us to a merely private catalogue of memories. Instead it challenges us to consider . . . with compassion and anger those other children to whom we can give no name who are dying today in Rwanda and whom I saw in the camps in Somalia."[16]

There is an "ethics of analogy" at work here, but unlike the standard argument that moves from the proximate and familiar to the distant and the strange, it may have been memory itself that was endangered in the Irish public sphere in the 1990s. This was due to the readiness with which an economy, in the first surge of affluence, was willing to displace its past, not least by institutionalizing it onto the heritage industry, but also due to the protracted crisis in national memory precipitated by three decades of conflict in Northern Ireland. As the furious critical response to Neil Jordan's *Michael Collins* (1996) and to Ken Loach's *The Wind That Shakes the Barley* (2006) indicated, it is not so much the past that unsettles the official historical narrative but its echoes in the present—indeed, the very notion that cultural memory is part of a society's continuing dialogue with itself. Such amnesia often surfaces in liberal antiracist discourse intent on establishing a more refined pedigree for its undifferentiated notions of tolerance and integration. Cultural memory is invariably cited as a negative influence, the heavy "hand of history," as in the recourse to the concept of atavism to explain away pathologies of violence that erupt in civil society, whether in Northern Ireland or the Balkans in the 1990s. It is readily conceded that memory can traverse generations or even centuries when there is "great hatred, little room," but legacies of solidarity, struggle, or hope are not accorded the same long shelf-life.

That the past could have other than a baneful influence is suggested by the philosopher Avishai Margalit's concept of an "ethics of memory," whereby an acknowledgment of the injuries of history leads to a determination that others will not have to suffer them again.[17] An ethics of memory raises the question of whether there are obligations on communities to remember those who have gone before, particularly the casualties of injustice and inhumanity, or those who have given up their lives for the betterment of future generations. It may be the case that a certain kind of forgetting—a refusal to draw analogies between past and present—perpetuates the original injustices.

As Nancy Wood observes in *Vectors of Memory,* contemporary forms of amnesia prompt the question "whether historical memories, including memories of the Holocaust, have indeed become encased in an entropic system where, to invoke its physical analogy, the energy devoted remembering the past has proved itself incapable of being 'converted' into relevant action in the present."[18] To speak of an ethics of memory is to resolve that others will not have to relive one's own tribulations in the past, but there is nothing inevitable about such an outcome. Expressions of solidarity are not automatic, but they may be appropriate, and they are no less binding on this count if they are to do justice to the past.

In a trenchant critique of Irish cultural remembrance, Susan Kelly and Stephen Morton have taken issue with President Robinson's linking of the Irish experience of emigration with enlightened attitudes toward race and immigration in the present—"a shift from the public memory of a national trauma to a celebration of diversity." Drawing on President Robinson's address at the unveiling of the Annie Moore statue on Ellis Island in 1993, they write:

> Implicit in Robinson's public address was the assumption that Irish immigrants had necessarily developed a social consciousness of cultural and racial difference as a logical consequence of their own experience of colonial oppression, economic hardship, and labor migrancy. Indeed, it was perhaps this tacit assumption that led her to encourage a spirit of hospitality among Irish people at home. Such an appeal is symptomatic of a liberal narrative of victimhood that equates the traumatic historical experience of colonialism and economic migration with an unconditional spirit of tolerance and hospitality towards other migrant groups.[19]

This critique justifiably challenges the assumption that memory "necessarily" generates "a social consciousness of cultural and racial difference" (though it is far from clear that either former president Robinson or McAleese is committed to such a simplistic position). It is also justified in raising doubts about eventual redemptive outcomes of trauma, as if "evil" can be mitigated by the later appearance of "good," thus drawing a veil over the original scenes of horror and immiseration. Such occlusions of the past are related, in Kelly and Morton's eyes, to the erasure of cultural and historical difference, to the radical "discontinuities between the economic context of immigration from Europe to the United States in the nineteenth century and from many Eastern European and North African countries to Ireland in the present."[20]

Yet it is precisely for this reason that the recognition of difference, of sympathy across discontinuities in experience, is crucial to a culturally sensitive response to immigration. As Jonathan Boyarin has pointed out, the problem with certain kinds of empathy is an undue emphasis on sameness, the assumption that we are all similar or human underneath (which is to say, human in the same way). Such expressions of empathy, however well intentioned, amount, in effect, to an obliteration of otherness, as is evident, for example, in popular responses to the Holocaust: "We might say that this occurs where humanism demands acknowledgement of the Other's suffering humanity, but where . . . the paradoxical linkage of shared humanity and cultural Otherness cannot be expressed. In popular-culture representations of the Holocaust, the particular horror of the Nazi genocide is emphasized by an image of the Jews as normal Europeans, 'just like us.' In fact, we can only empathize with, feel ourselves into, those we can imagine as ourselves."[21] It is for this reason, Boyarin contends, that a recourse to generalized conceptions of humanity to embrace the stranger—"we're all human underneath"—often accentuates the plight of the migrant through an insistence on sameness at the expense of difference.

Having registered this caveat, Boyarin goes on to warn against the illusion of constructing otherness entirely along spatial or geographical lines, as if it has no temporal or historical dimensions: "We are so accustomed to speaking of time and space as contrasting axes that this emphasis on spatiality tends to marginalize discourses of temporal Othering. We speak of distant times, but not of places long ago. Different places exist simultaneously, but different times do not exist in the same place."[22] The implication here is that while strangers can become neighbors by virtue of spatial proximity, it does not follow that they are thereby part of a community imagined through time. Such bonds can be recreated through an ethics of memory, but the point of Boyarin's emphasis on "the past as other" is to underline that, during periods of profound social upheaval, a community may be as estranged from its own past as it is from other cultures.[23] Unlike geographical others, ancestors "are dead, rather than elsewhere," but "those who are not in a position to be interlocutors," or to answer back, should not thereby be deprived of their voices, their "critical discursive power," in the present. For Kelly and Morton, the discontinuity between the new and the old Ireland is such that there is no possibility of communication. Boyarin answers, by contrast, that "an underground tradition says our lives depend on hearing them"; the desire "to explore new ways of relating to the Other through time" may also open up new ways of negotiating the Other through space.[24]

In the mid-1960s, Jean Amery, a Holocaust survivor, drew attention to a new phenomenon in Western culture that signaled the end of time as we had known it.[25] For centuries, if not millennia, societies had looked to time as the healer of all wounds, the poultice of custom and tradition, as it were, drawing out the toxic residues of the past. The Holocaust, for Amery, brought this to an end, for memory in its aftermath is no longer a comfort zone but ineluctably a moral agency, a matter of doing justice to the past. Remembrance is one of the few consolations left for those deleted from history, while forgetfulness, whether willful or not, can become part of the original crime—indeed, as studies of trauma show, a symptom of it. The recasting of memory as a moral force in its own right derived from the primal injunction "Never Again": this was remembrance for not only the sake of the past but the sake of the future.[26]

The moral force of the injunction "Never Again" derives from the fact that though inspired by the enormity of the Holocaust, it is not confined to it. The post–World War II era witnessed the aftermath of Hiroshima and Nagasaki, and protracted global wars of decolonization, before the end of the Cold War and the War on Terror added further to the instability of the planet. As Corey Robin has thoughtfully written of the plight of exodus, emigration, and asylum seekers: "Even those of us who for reasons of personal background, religion or politics should be most sensitive to the suffering of refugees can be astonishingly indifferent to their plight." Citing the sentence in Leviticus on which, according to Cynthia Ozick, every idea of civilization is built—"The stranger that sojourneth with you shall be unto you as the home-born among you, and you shall love him as yourself; because you were strangers in the land of Egypt"—Robin argues that it rings hollow in the light of recent mass displacements and uprootings, particularly in the Middle East:

> Fine, even beautiful, words, both the original and the gloss. But where are we to find them in Israel's treatment of the Palestinians, from the exile it thrust upon them in 1948 to the ongoing hostility to their return—or, for that matter, in Ozick's anti-Arab fulminations? From one vantage, the story of Israel and Palestine can seem the most idiosyncratic of ironies: A people forced to wander thousands of years forces another people to wander for who knows how many years. From another vantage, the story is sadly universal: the refusal to see or imagine oneself in the pain of another, even—or particularly—when one has suffered a similar ordeal. If exile has any larger import, then, it is not that we all share in its status. It is that it occasions the most sacred and sublime of obligations—"love him as yourself"—and the most wretched of betrayals.[27]

It is as if to trample on the rights of others is to desecrate one's own past. It is perhaps in this dark light that Walter Benjamin compared racists to grave diggers, warning that under Nazism even the dead are no longer safe.

THE PLAYBOY OF THE WIDER WORLD

In her acute analysis of the "cultural software" of Irish racism, Ronit Lentin suggests that it may, in fact, be the disconnect from the past, the anxiety to disavow a history of emigration and—one might add—colonial subjugation, that instills a fear of reminders of this repressed past in the present: "In the Irish case, I would suggest this national repressed past is the pain of emigration, returning to haunt the Irish, through the presence of the immigrant 'other' and in its wake invoking the unseemly presence of the 'less than fully Irish' indigenous and non-indigenous racialized Irish groups, such as the Traveller, the Asian, the Black, the Jew."[28]

Lentin's sentiments acquire a new urgency in conditions where emigration and mass unemployment are no longer memories but inescapable realities, as in contemporary post–Celtic Tiger Ireland. The way the immigrant is treated at home is no more than what one expects for oneself abroad. Under the commodified delusions of the Irish boom, it was easy to mothball the Irish past, or consign it to the commemoration industry. For this reason, it is clear that it is not a sense of history but a sundering of the past that promotes the racialization of culture in contemporary Ireland. In Daniel O'Hara's witty short 2003 film, *Yu Ming Is Ainm Dom* (My Name Is Yu Ming), a young Chinese man learns Irish before emigrating to Dublin under the illusion that because it is the official language, it is also the everyday spoken language. His discomfort on arrival arises not from the fact that he encounters narrow Irish nationalists or Gaelic revivalists, but from the fact that the people he encounters don't speak Irish at all or even recognize it. At the end of the film, he is depicted as feeling more at home in the Irish-speaking Gaeltacht districts of the West of Ireland: a conceit, to be sure, but one not totally at odds with contemporary reality. Reporting the mixed welcome given to the new primary school in Balbriggan, Bracken Educate Together, opened for immigrant (mainly African) children in September 2007, Henry McDonald noted in the *Guardian*: "Outside Bracken Educate Together there was a warmer welcome from the school's neighbours—an almost exclusively white, native Irish, Gaelic-speaking primary that shares the same building. Each child held up a piece of paper with a capital letter that spelt out: Fáilte Romhaibh, Irish for Welcome to You All."[29]

In J. M. Synge's famous *The Playboy of the Western World,* premiered over one hundred years ago at the Abbey Theatre, an inarticulate, stammering outsider comes in from the cold in the West of Ireland and finds both his voice and popular acceptance in a new community.

One of the biggest hits at the Dublin Theatre Festival in 2007 was a rewriting of Synge's play by Bisi Adigun and Roddy Doyle in which the playboy is recast as a Nigerian refugee in contemporary Dublin. At the end of the play, the local community is brought to its senses through an encounter with the outsider, but the immigrant's relationship with his own Nigerian background is also restored with a sense of purpose and independence. Whereas the original drama turned on the relationship between the individual and community, the new version turns on the interaction of two communities. It would be fitting if this staging of *Playboy* provided a dress rehearsal of a future multiethnic society, a Western world renewed through its contact with other, wider worlds, but as the subsequent legal disputes over authorship and performance rights of the new *Playboy* show,[30] theatre itself offers no utopian spaces from the realities of conflict and division in contemporary Ireland.

NOTES

1. Una Crowley, Mary Gilmartin, and Rob Kitchin, "Vote Yes for Common Sense Citizenship: Immigration and the Paradoxes at the Heart of Ireland's 'Cead Mile Failte,'" NIRSA Working Papers Series 30, 2006, 20.

2. Both bodies were abolished following the Irish government budget, October 2008. Some of the ironies with regard to Ireland's own history are brought out in another short film, *Unaccompanied,* by Emer Martin, the script writer of *Nuts*. In this film, a young black boy from Nigeria goes missing in Ireland, having fallen through the loopholes and deficiencies of the child care system, and is shown wandering by the official Famine memorial on Customs House quay.

3. Ronit Lentin and Robbie McVeigh, *After Optimism?: Ireland, Racism and Globalisation* (Dublin: Metro Éireann, 2006), 174. Such criticism might also be directed at a one-size-fits-all antiracism that ignores cultural differences: "There is no 'anti-racism in one country': what does this actually mean? Essentially there is no such thing as a national anti-racist struggle" (179). It is true that there is no "stand alone" or nationally self-contained antiracism, but it does not follow that all oppositional strategies are coming from the same place. The antiracism of cultures or groups on the receiving end of racial oppression draws on different historical experiences than the often more universalist cri-

tiques that emanate from within the dominant cultures (imperial or otherwise) that have institutionalized racism.

4. *Building a Diverse Mayo: A Report on Immigration, Integration and Service Provision,* ed. Neil Middleton and Geraldine Mitchell, research by Margaret Brehony and Nóirín Clancy (Castlebar, Ireland: Mayo Intercultural Action, 2006), 8, 12. The Mayo Intercultural Action committee is a voluntary initiative established in 1999 to facilitate integration in County Mayo and is akin to other regional groups.

5. Ibid.

6. Piaras Mac Éinrí, "The Implications for Ireland and the UK Arising from the Development of Recent European Union Policy on Migration," in *Migration Policy: Reform and Harmonization: Ireland in the Broader European Context and Issues Arising from the Common Travel Area with Britain* (Dublin: National Consultative Committee on Racism and Interculturalism, 2002), 38–51.

7. Emma O'Kelly, "Musgrave's Disputes Claims of Discrimination against Foreign Workers," *Morning Ireland,* RTE, May 11, 2007.

8. *Building a Diverse Mayo,* 107.

9. Derek Scally, "Magazine Article on Poles in Ireland Criticized," *Irish Times,* September 30, 2005. As *Building a Diverse Mayo* reports the words of one Irish medical respondent: "You do not know where people are coming from, do not know their issue[s], do not have their history. It's not just about language, so many more problems—low self-esteem, depression and isolation" (109).

10. Liam Reid, "Poles Play Down 'Living Hell' for Migrant Workers," *Irish Times,* September 30, 2005.

11. Fiona Gartland, "Polls Back Migrant Worker's Rights," *Irish Times,* October 10, 2007.

12. Ali Bracken, "Asylum Families Kept Apart," *Irish Times,* June 24, 2005. This trend was given a general application through the 2004 Citizenship Referendum, which withdrew, for the first time, automatic citizenship from all children born in Ireland.

13. President Mary McAleese, "The Changing Faces of Ireland: Migration and Multiculturalism," Address to the British Council, March 14, 2007.

14. President Mary Robinson, Address to the Joint Sitting of the Houses of the Oireachtas, February 2, 1995.

15. McAleese, "Changing Faces of Ireland."

16. President Mary Robinson, Address at Grosse Île, Quebec, August 1994, www.ballinagree.freeservers.com/grosse.html.

17. Avishai Margalit, *The Ethics of Memory* (Cambridge, MA: Harvard University Press, 2002).

18. Nancy Wood, *Vectors of Memory: Legacies of Trauma in Postwar Europe* (Oxford: Berg, 1999), 62.

19. Susan Kelly and Stephen Morton, "Calling Up Annie Moore," *Public Culture* 16, no. 1 (Winter 2004): 127–28.

20. Ibid., 128.

21. Jonathan Boyarin, *Storm from Paradise: The Politics of Jewish Memory* (Minneapolis: University of Minnesota Press, 1992), 86.

22. Ibid, 81–82.

23. It is in this sense that genetic fallacies of "blood and belonging" disavow material culture and the social production of memory, which are no more rooted in biology than are attachments to place or locality.

24. Boyarin, *Storm from Paradise,* 82.

25. For this aspect of Jean Amery, see Wood, "The Victim's Resentment," in *Vectors of Memory,* 61–79.

26. This would deprive ethics of any notion of choice or alternative modes of action. Such responses are normative and, as in the kind of rules or principles that govern language, no less binding for being freely chosen. Norms woven into the texture of everyday life are more like narratives that have a certain logic and cohesion but do not close off other responses to the world. The issue here is not what is automatic but what is appropriate — what responses can truly be said to do justice to the past by ensuring injustices are not repeated in the present.

27. Corey Robin, "Strangers in the Land," *Nation,* April 10, 2006, 28.

28. Ronit Lentin, "Anti-Racist Responses to the Racialisation of Irishness: Disavowed Multiculturalism and Its Discontents," in *Racism and Anti-Racism in Ireland,*, ed. Ronit Lentin and Robbie McVeigh (Belfast: Beyond the Pale, 2002).

29. Henry McDonald, "Ireland Forced to Open Immigrant School," *Guardian* (London), September 22, 2007.

30. Martin Frawley, "Nigerian Playwright Loses Discrimination Claim Against Abbey," *Sunday Tribune* (Belfast), January 16, 2011.

CONTRIBUTORS

Pablo Rojas Coppari is a strategic advocacy officer at Migrant Rights Centre Ireland, with emphasis on irregular migration and trafficking for forced labor. He has a BA in applied languages and an MA in international development and intercultural studies from the University of Lille III, France. Prior to joining the MRCI, Pablo undertook research and casework for former unaccompanied minors seeking asylum with the Dutch Refugee Council, and worked on research projects on language and cultural issues of ethnic minorities across Europe with the European Centre for Minority Issues in Flensburg, Germany.

Mike Cronin is currently academic director of the Boston College Centre for Irish Programmes in Dublin. He has written widely on different aspects of modern Irish history, including (with Daryl Adair) *Wearing the Green: A History of St. Patrick's Day* (1999). An acknowledged expert on the role of sport in Irish life, Cronin appears regularly on television and radio to discuss the social importance of sport in Ireland. Cronin authored *Sport and Nationalism in Ireland* (1999) and edited (with John Bale) *Sport and Postcolonialism* (2003) and (with David Mayall) *Sporting Nationalisms* (1998). Cronin has also edited special issues of the *Journal of Contemporary History* and *Sport in History* on sports-related topics.

Heather Edwards is a visiting assistant professor at Ohio University. She received her PhD from the University of Notre Dame, where she specialized in British and Irish Literature of the long nineteenth century. Her article, "The Irish New Woman and Emily Lawless's *Grania: The Story of an Island*: A Congenial Geography," was published in *English Literature in Translation* in 2008. She is currently working on a project that explores how examining the colonial and rural dimensions of representations of New Women figures located in geographies outside the British metropole complicate current critical conversations about the New Woman and women's experiences of modernity at the turn of the twentieth century.

Steve Garner is senior lecturer in sociology at Aston University (Birmingham, UK). He has published on racism, immigration, and social class in a variety of contexts: Ireland, the United Kingdom, the European Union, and the Caribbean. His publications include *Racism in the Irish Experience* (2004), *Whiteness: An Introduction* (2007), and *Racisms* (2010).

Luke Gibbons is professor of Irish literary and cultural studies at the School of English, Drama and Media Studies, National University of Ireland, Maynooth. He has published widely on Irish culture, film, literature, and the visual arts, as well as on aesthetics and politics. His publications include *Gaelic Gothic: Race, Colonialism and Irish Culture* (2004), *Edmund Burke and Ireland: Aesthetics, Politics and the Colonial Sublime* (2003), *The Quiet Man* (2002), *Transformations in Irish Culture* (1996), and *Cinema and Ireland* (1988), co-written with Kevin Rockett and John Hill. He was a contributing editor to *The Field Day Anthology of Irish Writing* (1991) and has coedited two recent collections, *Re-Inventing Ireland: Culture, Society and the Global Economy* (2002) and a special issue of *The Yale Journal of Criticism* (2002).

Ronit Lentin is head of Sociology and the director of the MPhil in Race, Ethnicity, Conflict at Trinity College Dublin. She was an active member of the Trinity Immigration Initiative. Lentin has published numerous articles on racism in Ireland, gender, and Israel-Palestine.

Her books include (with Robbie McVeigh) *Racism and Anti-Racism in Ireland* (2002), (with Nahla Abdo) *Women and the Politics of Military Confrontation: Palestinian and Israeli Gendered Narratives of Dislocation* (2002), (with Robbie McVeigh) *After Optimism? Ireland, Globalisation and Racism* (2006), (with Alana Lentin) *Race and State* (2008), *Thinking Palestine* (2008), and *Co-Memory and Melancholia: Israelis Memorialising the Palestinian Nakba* (2010). She recently edited (with Elena Moreo) *Migrant Activism and Integration from Below in Ireland* (2012). She contributes regularly to *Metro Éireann*.

Robbie McVeigh has written and researched extensively on racism and sectarianism in Ireland, North and South, including his groundbreaking 1992 article "The Specificity of Irish Racism" (*Race and Class,* 1992). His research publications include *Travellers, Refugees and Racism in Tallaght* (1998), *A Place of Welcome? Refugees and Asylum Seekers in Northern Ireland* (2002), and *The Next Stephen Lawrence? Racist Violence and Criminal Justice in Northern Ireland* (2006). He has coauthored two books on racism in Ireland with Ronit Lentin: *Racism and Anti-Racism in Ireland* (2002) and *After Optimism? Ireland, Racism and Globalisation* (2006). He has coauthored with Bill Rolston critiques of the post-GFA state and its responses to racism and sectarianism: "From Good Friday to Good Relations: Sectarianism, Racism and the Northern Ireland State" (*Race and Class,* 2007) and "Civilising the Irish" (*Race and Class,* 2009).

Verona Ní Dhrisceoil graduated from National University of Ireland, Cork, in 2004 with a degree in law and Irish and in 2005 with a master's degree in criminal justice (LLM). Since then, she has combined her interests in law and language through teaching and research. In 2007–08, she worked for the Law Reform Commission of Ireland and is the principal researcher for the commission's report *Defences in Criminal Law,* published in 2009. In 2008 she was awarded a Higher Education Authority Scholarship to carry out research in the area of law and Irish language rights. Verona has also conducted research for the Irish Penal Reform Trust in the area of juvenile detention. She is coauthor of *Detention of Children: International Standards and Best Practice* (2009). In 2010, Verona was awarded a Fulbright Scholarship to attend the University of Notre Dame. She is currently pursuing a PhD in the area of law and language rights at University College Cork, Ireland.

Sean O'Brien is assistant professor of English at SUNY Canton and former assistant director of the Keough-Naughton Institute for Irish Studies. He received his BAU from Xavier University and his PhD from the University of Notre Dame. Along with his interest in contemporary Ireland, his scholarship deals with Irish prison writing. His present project examines nineteenth-century critiques of the Victorian penitentiary by Irish writer-inmates such as Michael Davitt and Oscar Wilde. For information on his research projects in Irish studies and the digital humanities, visit www.seantobrienphd.com.

Pádraig Ó Riagáin is associate professor (emeritus) of sociology of language at Trinity College, Dublin. Prior to his appointment at Trinity College, he was research professor (sociology of language) at the Institiúid Teangeolaíochta Éireann for twenty-six years. He has been a consultant to the European Commission, the Council of Europe, and the Organization for Security and Cooperation in Europe, and has also served on a number of scientific committees, projects and missions relating to language policy and minority rights issues in Europe. Recent publications include *Language Policy and Social Reproduction: Ireland 1893–1993* (1997), "Social Class, Religion, Identity and Language Attitudes: The Republic of Ireland and Northern Ireland Compared" (*International Journal of Bilingual Education and Bilingualism,* 2007) and "Irish-Language Policy 1922–2007: Balancing Maintenance and Revival," in *A New View of the Irish Language* (2008).

Mary Robinson served as president of Ireland from 1990 to 1997 and as UN high commissioner for human rights from 1997 to 2002. She is president of Realizing Rights: The Ethical Globalization Initiative and professor of practice in international affairs at Columbia University. She is the current Chancellor of Dublin University and author of *Everbody Matters: A Memoir* (2012).

Julieann Veronica Ulin is assistant professor of British and American modernism at Florida Atlantic University. She received her PhD from the University of Notre Dame in 2007; she was a graduate student at the Keough-Naughton Institute for Irish Studies before receiving the Edward Sorin Postdoctoral Fellowship in the Humanities (2007–2009). She holds an MA in English from Fordham University and a BA from Washington and Lee University. Her Irish studies scholarship has appeared in *Hungry Words: Images of Famine in the Irish Canon* (2006), *James Joyce Quarterly, Women's Studies Quarterly,* and *Joyce Studies Annual.*

INDEX

Adebari, Rotimi, xii (2007), 10, 27, 35–36
AkiDwA (African Women's Network), 62–67, 69

bailout. *See* recession
Balbriggan, 26, 191–93, 217
Belfast/Good Friday Agreement, viii (1998), 12, 46, 58–59, 75–99, 133
  and changes to GAA, 160
  and the Irish language, 140, 143–44, 150–51

Catholicism, 76–79, 83, 91, 93, 96–99, 159–60, 169–70, 178–80, 182, 194, 196, 208. *See also* education
Celtic Tiger, viii (1994), 3, 6, 31, 40, 42, 132, 134, 161, 184, 188–95, 205–6, 208
Census 2006, xii (2006), 4, 67, 109, 145, 146, 158, 183, 185, 191, 193
Census 2011, xiv (2011), 7, 14, 77, 109
Chen case (*Chen v. Secretary of State for the Home Department*), x (2004), 57, 95

citizenship, vii (1922), vii (1937), viii (1998), x (2003), xi (2004), 47, 52, 54–62, 67–69
Citizenship Referendum, xi (2004), 11, 35–36, 53–54, 56–62, 63, 67, 94–95, 187–88, 210
Coalition Against Deportations of Irish Children (CADIC), 63, 67

Devlin, Thomas, 89–90
direct provision, system of, viii (2000), xv (2011), 24, 55
Domestic Workers Action Group, 41, 43, 66

education, xiv (2010), 4, 9, 12, 24, 26
  bilingual education and language policy, 117–19, 124
  Catholic Church, 26, 77, 191–93
  conversational vs. academic proficiency in second language, 116–18
  European Commission against Racism and Intolerance (ECRI), 121